The
DEER CAMP

The
DEER CAMP

A MEMOIR OF A FATHER, A FAMILY, AND THE LAND THAT HEALED THEM

DEAN KUIPERS

BLOOMSBURY PUBLISHING
NEW YORK · LONDON · OXFORD · NEW DELHI · SYDNEY

BLOOMSBURY PUBLISHING
Bloomsbury Publishing Inc.
1385 Broadway, New York, NY 10018, USA

BLOOMSBURY, BLOOMSBURY PUBLISHING, and the Diana logo are
trademarks of Bloomsbury Publishing Plc

First published in the United States 2019

ISBN: HB: 978-1-63557-348-0; eBook: 978-1-63557-349-7

Library of Congress Cataloging-in-Publication Data

Names: Kuipers, Dean, author.
Title: The deer camp : a memoir of a father, a family, and the land
that healed them / Dean Kuipers.
Description: New York : Bloomsbury Publishing, 2019.
Identifiers: LCCN 2018059379 (print) | LCCN 2019002700 (ebook) |
ISBN 9781635573497 (ebook) | ISBN 9781635573480 (hardcover)
Subjects: LCSH: Kuipers, Dean. | Kuipers, Dean—Family. | Fathers and sons—
Michigan—Oceana County—Biography. | Deer hunting—Michigan—Oceana
County. | Country life—Michigan—Oceana County. | Farms—Conservation and
restoration—Michigan—Oceana County. | Oceana County (Mich.)—Biography.
Classification: LCC F572.O3 (ebook) | LCC F572.O3 K85 2019 (print) |
DDC 977.4/59—dc23
LC record available at https://lccn.loc.gov/2018059379

2 4 6 8 10 9 7 5 3

Typeset by Westchester Publishing Services
Printed and bound in the U.S.A. by Berryville Graphics Inc., Berryville, Virginia

To find out more about our authors and books visit www.bloomsbury.com
and sign up for our newsletters.

Bloomsbury books may be purchased for business or promotional use.
For information on bulk purchases please contact Macmillan Corporate and
Premium Sales Department at specialmarkets@macmillan.com.

To Nancy, Joe, Brett and Ayron, and especially to Bruce, who dug in

I can only seek you if I take the sand into my mouth
So I can taste resurrection

Contents

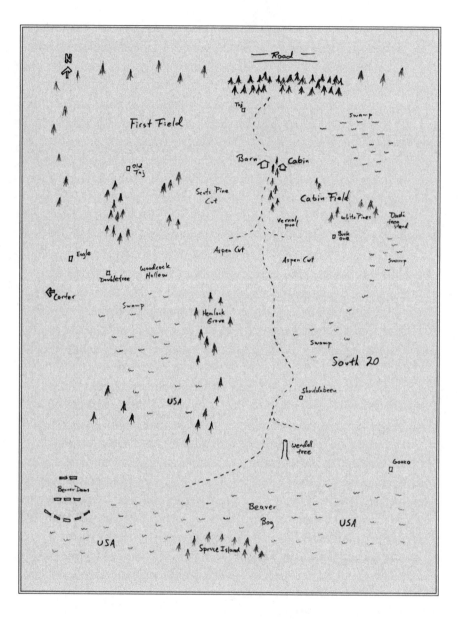

Prologue

A relative who once stayed with us at the cabin complained: "Did you hear all those people talking in the woods last night?" Our cabin sits among vast federal swamps in a depopulated corner of Michigan, with farms on either side, and other than a few barking dogs we don't hear much of the neighbors. Pretty much never. When that was pointed out to her, her eyes got wider and wider as she decided, if those weren't live people murmuring in the trees, then they must be dead ones. "Spirits," she said.

The talking out there is real enough. It wakes me up, too. A whitetail deer has been snorting outside the open window of my tiny cabin bedroom for half an hour—*CHUUU*—like a horse blowing or a person winded by hauling in a load of wood. It's the middle of a warm June night throbbing with cricket song and katydid shrill and bullfrog whomp; there are creatures moving.

But those aren't the spirits she was talking about. I woke, like I have a hundred times here, to the impression of whispering at the window screen. In the gaps between snort and whomp they're there, too low to grasp, exactly, but voices. The forest itself, I guess. I squeeze my eyes shut and focus, and when I do they seem to come from a particular direction, hard to nail down. They are softly urgent, wanting things. Like the presence of people standing stone-still in the woods.

There's no sleeping through that. I get out of bed and put on water for tea by the weak glow of a nightlight, then slip by the dogs without letting them out the sliding door and sneak onto the porch to find out what all the murmuring is about.

My youngest brother, Joe, is already out on the porch taking notes. I'm not surprised to find him out there, but it is four A.M. He's been out there pretty much all night. The universe breathes a night wind and Joe is counting the breaths, scratching on a notepad while he sits with a hoodie tied around his face and a lit cigarette to keep away the mosquitoes. He gives me a big toothy smile but doesn't say anything, turning immediately back to the field of orchard grass that stretches away into the night. He doesn't want to miss anything.

"What's that deer huffing at?" I say, low.

"You, now," he says.

Joe only sleeps one night out of every four or so, a circadian scar: a constant reminder of troubles that started long before we got this deer camp a quarter century ago. He's a big man, six foot one and running about 220, barrel-chested and banged up. One knee doesn't work and his back was broke once, and when he's not obsessively changing toilets in the apartments he owns, he's likely to be fly-fishing or sitting out here on the porch. He chews ice out of a big dirty Slurpee cup held together with duct tape. He has turned the fridge into an ice farm and superintends five trays of ice there in various states of ripeness and is constantly getting expensive dental work done.

He picks up a pair of field glasses, peers into the darkness, puts them back down.

I look at his notepad, where he's scribbled about barred owls in the south twenty. Coyote pack running through Mr. Carter's, the farmer to the west. Kept a tally of deer on the corn feeder. Raccoon fight in the red pines. Sandhill cranes. A loon.

We write down what we hear talking in the fields at night like other people write down dreams. Because they mean something.

A huge stonefly makes for the hot cherry of Joe's cigarette and bats him in the face and he snatches it; on his forearm he has a six-inch tattoo of a mayfly known to all fly fishermen as a Hendrickson, the *Ephemerella subvaria*. He studies the stonefly closely, then releases it into the darkness.

Our middle brother, Brett, emerges onto the porch with a cup of coffee and his longtime partner, Ayron, the sister we never had. She shuffles past in slippers and a jacket and says to me, low, "You going out?"

~

I go out. The night wind blows off Lake Michigan twenty miles to the west, smelling of algal water and sand and pines. Our camp is a worn-out farm halfway up Michigan's Lower Peninsula, near the knee-deep meander of the North Fork of the White River, a spit of blow-sand left between the swamps when the Laurentide ice sheet retreated from this spot a little more than fourteen thousand years ago, the receding blade of the last ice age. All around us are swamp and other hunting properties, mostly former farms like ours that were beaned to death a century earlier and left in yellow, medium-coarse sand. Some are plantations of USDA red pine, some are third-growth mixed hardwood forest. Most are empty this time of year.

This night-sitting is a tactic that turned into a practice. When I was twelve years old, my father, Bruce, and I started hunting at a camp owned by a steel contractor named Bernard Card—heavy emphasis on the first syllable, *BURN-erd*—and Mr. Card built deer blinds out of sheet metal and wood that were five-foot-by-five-foot boxes with a roof and an eighteen-inch gap in the walls all the way around, just right for sitting in a chair and watching deer.

Dad was a legendary still-hunter, and we'd always settle in at least an hour before dawn and sit in total silence, a couple of times in cold so fierce I got frostbite on my jaw and earlobes waiting for sunrise. After the sun was up, we could use the propane heater without throwing light that would spook the wildlife. But that wasn't the relief I needed. I stopped wanting the sun to come up.

Sunup meant the hunt was on, and we'd sit wordlessly for ten or eleven hours until the air in front of my face went dark again. I got to sit with my dad, but what I really needed was to talk to him. There weren't many other opportunities. I wanted to talk to him about Mom, about my role in a house where he didn't live anymore, who I should be as the oldest son. We'd sit all day, my ass aching, and after it was too dark to shoot we'd scuff down the frozen two-track toward dinner and talk in low voices about the deer and turkeys and owls we'd seen, how many, the patterns in their movements. But that's all we'd talk about. Dad was so exhausted from the intensity of his watching, practically conjuring whitetails by sheer force of will, that he'd skip all the after-dinner whiskey and dirty jokes that were standard at Bernard's and go straight to bed.

One night we lay in our beds listening to the party, and I asked Dad why he didn't have a beer and talk to the other men and women hunters. He said, "That's not why we're here."

Dad got good at killing deer. I don't know what else he was good at. He was good at building buildings. Brett had a little better idea of who Dad was, probably, because Brett worked for him for six or seven years, and little brother Joe had almost none. Even a decade after our own Kuipers family deer camp became one of the few places they actually saw each other, Joe had hardly ever had a real conversation with Dad in his life.

~

In the early morning dark, before the birds start in, it's easier to forget the names and shapes of things, to let go of working like an amateur naturalist. With no sun, one can get beyond words, to other kinds of talking. I sit in a blind and watch like Saint-Exupéry watched the fear-some Sahara, where the illusion of sameness mile upon mile so stilled the physical world that the sublime language of the spirit could be heard against it like whispers in the undulating dunes, revealing what he called the "invisible solicitations." Everything out there calls in its own voice. Sitting in my box, just like the boxes we had on Card's place, I am poked and prodded with offers, entreaties, lascivious invites.

I make notes in the dark, pages spotted with blood from where I squish mosquitoes off the veins on the backs of my hands. From the black outlines of trees and star movement I'm trying to describe a wholeness and its language, but am getting mostly parts. A chickadee lands on my shoulder—the least shy of birds—but it says nothing. Just sits, without any weight at all. It, too, is listening silently until sunrise.

Darkness starts in a place and expands in all directions at once, like space. It moves simultaneously toward you and away from you. Dark-ness is a living tissue, and ideas and signs move through it, and from those things our minds are born. Figures emerge from the darkness without warning—some memories I wasn't trying to remember, some shame because of words I said—and if I accept those figures with humility, they don't take up too much of the night. I want these things from inside my own head to hustle past so we can encourage the figures from outside to come closer. They come like nothing I've ever felt before, and yet familiar. I don't know them, yet we are related.

I didn't think I knew the new trees on our camp, for instance, but it turned out I did. They knew me. They brought me a new father. Only a dozen years ago, they shot out of the bare sand like making a new father was a job they'd been waiting a hundred years to do. When Dad looked upon them, tiny saplings leaping up out of ground he believed was barren, he gave up his long career as shadow and destroyer. He started to love all three of us boys like never before. This really happened. Love was a figure that came out of this ground, out of the darkness.

So I watch these fields, these trees, this sand. Joe and Brett and Ayron and I all watch. We are watching and listening for the figure of a family. What else out there is holding a piece of it, waiting for us to notice?

One
The Deer Camp

In the summer of 1989, Bruce called to tell me he had a new deer hunting camp in Michigan.

"Hey, Kemosabe!" my dad chirped. He could barely contain himself.

I was in my apartment on Manhattan's Lower East Side, and I hadn't talked to him in maybe half a year. I had left Kalamazoo in 1987; my mother, Nancy, had divorced Bruce in 1988; and in the intervening year he and I had fallen mostly silent. In fact, I had been telling anyone who asked that my dad was dead. I lied about him being dead, and yet there he was on the phone: the hopeful singsong of his voice and the smell of decaying leaf litter and river water that it hauled into my memory made me want to tear my teeth out in shame. I suddenly realized I was weak; I had let rage make me a liar. Out the open window, New York City rumbled and foamed.

"Is Joe okay?" I said to my dead dad. I wanted him to regret calling me. I was twenty-five years old at the time, Brett was twenty, and Joe was eighteen for a few more weeks—and I was worried about Joe. My brother was a drunk and just out of high school, and our last call together had filled me with dread that a ringing phone would summon me home for a funeral. I thought he might crash the car, or drink too much and die of alcohol poisoning. Almost all the calls from Michigan, however, were from Mom, who remained cheerful in the face of cataclysm but was worried about Joe's drinking and drug habits. Because she was worried, I worried. I just figured someone would phone me if anything happened to Joe, and I wanted to subtly but firmly remind my dad that this was one possible reason for his call.

"Ha ha!" Dad laughed. "I'm calling to tell you about our new camp. I knew you'd want to hear about it."

"Why is that funny?" I asked.

"I didn't say it was funny," Dad said.

He laughed inappropriately when he was confronted by news he didn't like or didn't know what to do with. For instance, that his own behavior contributed to Joe's suicidal alcoholism. Or that any minute I'd hang up on him. When I was seventeen and Science Student of the Year at my high school, I told him that the University of Michigan was recruiting me for an experimental six-year medical school, and he laughed in my face. On that occasion, when I asked him why he was laughing, he said, "Oh, that kind of thing's not for us."

I only realized after I bombed the interviews for the medical thing that we were a family of total hayseeds and that's what he was really afraid of.

Now the words *deer camp* hung there in the eight hundred miles between us and made my blood boil. He was dangling it like bait. Dad had raised us as hunters and fishermen, and sitting in a tree stand or wading in a tea-colored river were two places we still had respect for him, and I did miss my life in the woods. But these words signaled that he was going to try to rise from the dead and lurch back into my life.

I had left Kalamazoo to get away from being a hayseed and from being tripped up by my father's fear and defensiveness. I had moved to New York City immediately after Kalamazoo College to be a journalist because it was a way I could investigate the structure and character of power and the arts; I was in love with anarchism and punk rock and literature and deep ecology, and I had to find these ideas where they were embodied by real people. A resistance. I owned nothing but questions. On the very first night I had arrived in New York City, I lucked straight into a party for the composer John Cage and a conversation with the artist Laurie Anderson, whose work I adored. Together we looked at my car parked out front full of books and a drum kit, and I told her I knew only one person in the city, who didn't even know yet I'd arrived. "Well, now you know two," Anderson said, and assured me I'd be fine. It was a different world than the green open fields and vineyards and trout waters of Michigan, and I was freaked by how I was going to survive, but I needed to get inside the built environment of urban America. I wanted to write about politics and music, and in New York they were both blood sports. Nights, I ran into Iggy Pop at the Pyramid Club and Sonic Youth, Live Skull, and Vernon Reid at the Knitting Factory. I had moved from one experience of wildness to another.

I had left Kalamazoo because Bruce's version of how to be a man had nearly killed my mother. I was pretty sure somebody in New York could show me another way.

I had never considered whether that other way would involve having a deer hunting camp. I had lived in the city for two years at the time of his call, and I didn't know anyone I could even talk to about that. Upstate New York is thick with deer hunters and there are even fancy hunting shops in the city, but a deer camp still sounded like a redneck fantasia, like a broken toilet in the yard with flowers growing out of the bowl. I didn't expect anyone to understand that hunting was part of an ecological consciousness.

Because I am a hunter, I have always been a liberal and an environmental radical. My brothers, too, and loads of other people we know. Growing up in Michigan made the politics deadly obvious: if you wanted any wildlife at all, you wrestled it away from heavy industry. The Rouge River, like the mouth of the Cuyahoga on Lake Erie, and the Buffalo, and the Chicago, was so choked with industrial pollution when I was little it used to catch fire. In the early 1970s, you didn't dare eat a trout if you found one because Michigan rivers were clotted with PBBs, PCBs, mercury, dioxin, and other poisons; deer and turkeys were scarce; the state mascot, the wolverine, had been extirpated for more than a century; seeing an actual wild mink, the great indicator of livable habitat, was like seeing a holy apparition. Three federal laws radically altered the conditions on the ground in ways that can hardly be appreciated today: the 1970 Clean Air Act, the 1972 Clean Water Act, and the 1973 Endangered Species Act. Without them, there would be no hunting or fishing in Michigan. But nearly a century before these kicked in, Michigan hunters and anglers were already at the statehouse demanding action. In 1887 Detroit sportsmen fomented the hiring of the nation's first state game warden, regulating themselves in order to rein in market hunters who were killing every living thing to feed Michigan's logging camps.

What I saw in the 1970s was hunters and anglers shoulder to shoulder with government and activists in a cleanup that was hugely successful. That environmental action made my whole life possible. By the time I graduated from high school in the early 1980s, the state deer herd was in the millions, the ponds were full of ducks, and every little culvert under the highway shimmered with trout again.

Bruce hated politics when we were young and so presented both hunting and guns as largely apolitical, and neither were they gendered: my aunts and female cousins shot a lot more deer than we did. There was no prescribed set of beliefs or tribal allegiances one had to adopt in order to hunt or fish. My brothers and I owned no guidebooks, and we had never joined the National Rifle Association or conservation clubs. We subscribed to none of the popular magazines like *Field & Stream*. We regarded every stereotype of hunters and fishermen as false because they weren't like us. Hunting wasn't like other cultures I adopted, such as skateboarding or rock music, that blew into town on the pages of a magazine. Every scrap of hunting technique and knowledge we had was strictly local, gleaned from farmers and hunters we knew.

As a kid, I sat on the steps of Boogie Records in Kalamazoo eagerly awaiting the delivery of the first Clash import single, "White Riot," and Joe Strummer may have urged me to rise up against corporate polluters, but he never told me not to eat venison stew. As far as I could tell, neither did the Who nor Patti Smith nor any of the prog or jazz outfits I loved like Camel or the Mahavishnu Orchestra, either. Exceptions arose as I learned more (the Smiths' second album is titled *Meat Is Murder*), but if you were going to eat meat, then hunting and fishing became your politics, because that's how you ate. My dad and his five brothers grew up as farmers, and they treated hunting no differently than farming: hunting was a function of a piece of land, and fishing was a function of a stretch of water, and the more intimately you knew that dirt and that water, the more likely you were to eat.

Hunting required that we recognize deer and pheasants as thinking and feeling and making choices, that they had lives worth understanding. It was about recognizing the sentience of the other, from individual to entire habitat. You can't fish if you don't recognize that fish exhibit mindlike behavior. You can't hunt where I grew up if you don't understand that the life cycle of aspen trees determines how many grouse or woodcock you're going to see. Thinking about animals in their habitat means thinking of the whole community, including blow-sand and swamp water and vegetation and weather—and the people who touch all those things—an ecology of being.

We grew up absolutely obsessed with assessing habitat—how many berries were on the gray dogwoods, how much water was in the swamp, watching the Hendrickson hatch on the river, minding when the corn was picked. In his masterpiece, *Arctic Dreams*, Barry Lopez rightly depicts the hunt as a "wordless dialogue" not with prey or weapons or one's ego but with the land itself. "To hunt means to have the land around you like clothing," he wrote. Like a good farmer, the hunter was responsible for protecting the whole web of relationships that make up a place. To us, that meant you don't shoot predators like coyotes or wolves, and you don't shoot trophies you're not going to eat. The habitat set itself up in your imagination, and the inhabitants, from whitetails to ring-neckeds to snow to dogwoods to mothers and fathers, moved through it.

A habitat of our own was what we had always wanted. A place where we could do the real work: grow wild deer and birds with all their companion creatures, celebrate the lives of the whole forest, hunt in the fall, and eat venison stew. Our old host Bernard Card and his family didn't just throw open the gates on Opening Day and start shooting; they were there all year, planting corn and putting it up in a corn crib, gathering hay and stacking it in a small metal barn, doing whatever forestry work was required to align with state efforts to improve the deer and grouse and turkey numbers, studying game trails, working on the log cabin, digging a pond, and teaching the grandkids how to handle a gun and how to watch the woods. Hunting only happened a couple of days a year, but the management of all those relationships was the real work of the imagination. We wanted a worky place like that.

～

In New York City, I discovered I hadn't really left all that behind. I craved contact with the living terrain itself, and I found a version of it in Tompkins Square Park, three city blocks of big trees that formed the heart of the East Village. The nights there were weirdly spectacular. During the operatically hot and chaotic summers of 1988 and '89, I spent a lot of time there. It was the only park on the island that was open twenty-four hours, and I liked to sit there at night. It was a break from the heat, and I watched the massive trees and the bright New York sky for whatever might emerge. The figures that came forth felt as though they came from both my own head and somewhere outside it, like the world was manifesting my thoughts. Like turning the mind inside out.

The park was populated by spreading American elms, including the Hare Krishna tree where Swami Prabhupada first started teaching the chants of Krishna Consciousness in the United States in the 1960s. The rest were big red oaks and plane trees. The sky was so thick with heat and trapped city light that the trees threw shade at night. The leaves overhead twisted with breathy sounds against a purple-black city sky, describing in a kind of semaphore how the trees felt about the barely cooling night breeze. Just before sunup the dew would sometimes spatter out of the leaves onto the cardboard and tarps of Dinkinsville, the sprawling homeless encampment named after the mayor, and I went home with my notes full of blooming locust and starling and tropical nightcloud as reportage on a parallel world.

I had been looking for the sentient *other* to emerge from the darkness, and one of the things that turned up, at least on the day of his phone call, was Bruce.

Dad didn't know that I had killed him. He was only forty-five years old and newly divorced from my mother; the second half of his life had suddenly unfurled before him as vast prairies of undefined space, a landscape going light and dark with each passing cloud. Mom had dumped him, and she took Joe with her when she left. Brett and I had already been out of the house for years. Dad could not tolerate neediness, even the ordinary neediness of children, and I'd learned long ago not to need him for anything. I wasn't sure what other connection we had.

When I first got to New York, I was at a job interview at the Ear Inn on Spring Street, negotiating my first writing gig at the music magazine that shared a name with the bar, *Ear Magazine*. The editor of the magazine asked me about my family, and I answered with a sort of put-on sorrow, "Oh, my dad passed away." That's how I did it then. I was satisfied with the look of pity that passed over her face. It was a lie I needed in order to give myself space to live, as both loving and hating my father had so dominated my life to this point. The editor could discover the truth with one phone call, and in the next sentence I reversed myself, adding, "I don't know why I said that."

My new boss was a much better person than I was and told me I was a good and loving son and that I couldn't stand to kill my father even if we were pretty much estranged. Anyway, I got the job.

I hadn't thought of Joe, Brett, and me as good and loving sons. I had thought of us as savages leaning together over a haunch of stag in our own separate wilderness—all three of us shoulder to shoulder, muzzle-deep in blood, bristling and jostling each other and raising up to bare fang at interlopers, famished, gulping at the days, each destined to go our separate way after murdering the alpha.

"Hey, you gotta come home this fall," Dad continued. "You have to come see this place. I got it with Uncle Vern and Uncle Jack, it's incredible. *It's ninety-five acres.* A big chunk like what we always wanted. Do you think you can get out here?"

I heard my own voice say, "The three of you *bought* a camp?" Growing up, we had never had the money to buy any kind of hunting property. I paid my own way through college. This same year in New York I made a whopping nine thousand dollars. I was starving some of the time. I was insulted by the idea that he now had private hunting, and that he thought that's all it would take to have me winging home. I tried to reestablish my resistance to this idea by adding, "Mom never mentioned it."

"Why would your mother know anything about it?" he said quietly.

I talked to Mom all the time. I was in the habit of calling her about every other day, although there had been months-long gaps while she and Dad were busy divorcing. I had been home to Kalamazoo once since then, but Dad had never mentioned the divorce to me, which I thought merited some discussion after twenty-four years. He talked about how Mom was crazy, or how she was dating guys with motorcycles, none of which was true. His reticence to say the word *divorce* made him dangerous. He only wanted to talk about the benefits of scent-free underwear when stalking big bucks or the steelhead flies he'd just bought that were three Pantone shades different from the other dozen he already owned, which is part of the reason we stopped talking. He was alone and shopping in his giant house in the woods southwest of Kalamazoo, out in the agricultural lands where farmers grew Concord grapes and asparagus. When it's just you and the mountains of shit you buy off Cabela's, you're in some spiritual trouble. Still, I gave him an opening.

"Where is it?" I asked.

"Oh, it's glorious," Dad said immediately. "We put a trailer on Ike Huizenga's place, not too far from where we used to go at Silver Lake. You know Ike."

Ike was a friend of the family from Zeeland, Michigan, where Dad and his five brothers had grown up, a big-time farmer with multiple operations across the west side of the state. The farm Dad described to me hung on the southern edge of the vast green expanse of the Manistee National Forest just north of Muskegon. Huizenga had a thousand acres there bordering the Tanner Swamp, where he ran fifteen thousand hogs. Across the street, he had picked up a little seventy-five-acre sand farm that was too small for hogs and too swampy and choked with blow-sand to grow anything other than asparagus and pine trees. Ike was a childhood buddy of Dad's older brother Vern, and he said Vern, Dad, and their younger brother Jack could set up on that seventy-five and there was an adjacent twenty-acre piece they could hunt, too, owned by a guy named Pflug in Fremont. They hadn't bought it yet, though they planned to. That gave them access to a bunch of federal land in the interior of the block, including a bog a half mile long.

I knew where it was. It was south of the Pere Marquette River, where the PM—as we called it—tangled with the watershed of the White. The Pere Marquette was one of the sacred rivers. It was blue-ribbon trout water, so whole stretches lived in our imaginations. It drained a sprawling watershed of sloshy spruce and hemlock swamps and kettle lakes with low uplands of forested sand in between, glacial medium-coarse yellow-orange sand laid out in moraines and eskers snaking through the national forest. Any tall hill would have a sour cherry orchard on it, and other well-drained acreage was charged with corn or asparagus or a U.S. Forest Service pine plantation. The boggy, nonplantation stretches were soft red maple and massive yellow birch and hemlock and aspen, which Dad called "popple"; the upland stretches were heavy with oak and beech and sugar maple. Here and there were remnants of the towering white pines that had once dominated the whole area. Like the whole northwest corner of the Lower Peninsula, the last ice age had drifted the place four hundred to six hundred feet deep in duney sand.

It was a place even Ike thought was junk, a mosquito swamp, and I knew right away it was paradise. Whitetail deer love some amount of disturbance and ruin, especially if they have farms nearby where they could eat. As Dad talked, I set myself against it. I decided right then I would never go there. That made it easier to talk about.

"How did all this happen?" I asked, cringing because he might say something embarrassing, like *I got this place for you and Brett and Joe because I love you*, which would have showed I was even more of an asshole, but luckily he didn't take it in that direction.

"Your uncle Vern has hunted up there at Ike's place for years and he takes Aunt Sally and the girls, too," Dad said. "He shoots deer out of there like it's Africa."

Vern hunted everywhere like it's Africa, including Africa. He wouldn't waste his time on a place that had no deer, and if Dad said Vern liked it, then that was all the assurance any of us would need that it was teeming with food for the table.

"Are Brett or Joe going?" I asked Dad.

"Oh, I bet they'll go."

"Well, have you talked to them?"

"No, I haven't been able to get hold of them in the last few days."

"When's the last time you talked to them?"

"Oh, I talk to those guys all the time."

"Really? I've talked to Joe about once in the last six months, probably. And I can't remember the last time I talked to Brett on the phone," I said.

"Well, Brett works for me so I see him all the time. He's trying to focus on school. He's so hardheaded, you know. Sets his mind on one thing and then he only does that one thing," Dad said.

Brett was going to Western Michigan University in Kalamazoo, which was Dad's alma mater.

"I don't even know where he lives," I said. "Or his number."

"I can give you that. He shares an apartment with some guys up on West Main, up by Western's campus."

"And what about Joe?"

"Well, he lives with your mom."

"Barely."

"Ha ha! Well, sure. I think I would know," said Dad.

"He hasn't really lived there in forever. He has his own apartment, or at least he did."

"What? *No.*"

"Yes, he has a lease on a place," I explained. "And before that he lived with friends a lot of the time, or with Cassie's family, at the trailer. He was hardly home his whole senior year of high school." Cassie had been his girlfriend, and that is not her real name. I've changed it for reasons that will become obvious.

"He stayed there once in a while."

"He stayed everywhere once in a while."

"Ha ha! Listen, your brother has a drinking problem."

"No shit!"

"But he and I have a good relationship."

"Okay, Dad, I'm gonna get off the phone now."

"When are we going to see you?"

"I'm not coming out there."

Dad moped on the phone in silence, and then said, "More deer for me."

"They're all for you. You guys have fun."

～

After I hung up, I stared out the window for a while and decided I needed to get outside. I took off on a run up Avenue A and past the green painted fence around Tompkins Square Park, and then over to East River Park. I had been on a couple of good sprint relay teams in high school, and I loved to run, and even though running the steaming streets of New York City was like sucking on an exhaust pipe, moving fast on foot around the city appealed to my sense of geography.

Ours was a childhood of paper maps—Rand McNally road atlases, state maps, county maps, National Forest maps, piles and piles of misfolded USGS quadrangle topos, river system maps, hand-drawn maps—marked up with pen and highlighter and flagged with sticky notes indicating put-ins, gates, glacial eskers that formed high ridges and trails through the wet. Places we wanted to go were usually near the green spots on the map, the public lands, "the good places," Dad called them. Joe, Brett, and I would pore over Michigan maps as boys and hound Dad to take us out to fish the great rivers of the Lower Peninsula—the PM, the Au Sable, the Manistee, the Baldwin—to float the lakes, to follow our English setter bird dog through the heavy morning dew on a hayfield looking for a cackling rooster pheasant. These were the places we really loved, and, more important, these were the places where Dad really loved us. One of the few acceptable expressions of love among all the men in the Kuipers clan was to say you loved the muscular, purling tug of the Manistee River or that you loved the peat-stinking spruce island in the deep swamp where the whitetails bedded down during the day. These were the good places where love stayed put, radiating. Calling.

I realized as I ran that Dad had telephoned me so we could obsess, like we used to, over a green spot on the map.

But Mom had divorced him, and good riddance. It had become obvious to me by the time I was twelve or thirteen that Dad cheated constantly on Mom, that he'd torture her by leaving her home with three young boys while he went away for weekends with other women. We were constantly moving from one apartment and house to another, maybe chased by this lady or that, or someone's father or husband, but there was always a new place. Where he'd be a new man.

Mom divorced him at last, and a year later there was the deer camp. I didn't want to entertain another of Bruce's fake reinventions. We'd been tricked too many times.

There had been a pattern to it all. To patch things up with Mom, he'd come home without an apology but offering dirt, big dirt, fresh dirt, sometimes with a house atop it and other times not, and we'd either have to move or we'd have a new river or good spot on the map to camp. Now With New Dad! The biggest scam came in 1978, after fifteen years of truly stupendous infidelity, when he built Mom a massive custom home. It was the biggest pile of dirt he'd offered up until that time, seventeen acres of remote shagbark hickory forest southwest of Kalamazoo, high up on a ridge overlooking a spring-fed lake. He not only built a giant architectural home in order to remake the family, but he capped it all off by recommitting himself to the church, which seemed like the most false gesture of them all, since he never acknowledged his affairs. But we were good kids. We pitched in. Even as we predicted the imminent collapse of this plan.

In the end, we abandoned Dad to that house. Mom spent several of the years she lived there just sleeping on the couch night and day and hardly ever getting up. She stayed in touch with some of the moms from our earlier lives, but hardly any of them ever came out to see her. Our beautiful mom, who kind of looked like Olivia Newton-John, had slipped to less than one hundred pounds and was wasting away in what Dad called the Great Room of his modern chateau, with its immaculate white carpet and its skylights far above. She lay there dappled by the green of the hickory forest outside and the gray-white of the snow. Dad never came home. Brett and I had left the house for good, and Joe was a ghost because he was secretly drinking every day. Those other moms went on hosting Cub Scouts and going to ball games the way she used to, but she wasn't part of it. She slept in a deadly silence, a reenactment of a Grimms' fairy tale.

Kalamazoo College was only about a half hour from the house, and one time I drove out there unannounced, and she rose from the couch in her housecoat and patted at her disheveled hair in a flutter of surprise, a pale and fading member of the species, and said, "Oh, hello, Jeffrey Dean. Do you want something to eat?"

That was the first time I realized she could die of simple neglect. My sweet mom, the nicest woman you'd ever want to meet. Depression had driven her eyes back into her head. "You can't stay out here anymore, Mom," I said.

"Joe has to finish high school," she said, fussing in the kitchen. It was the first time I'd heard that she had any kind of plan. She held out that statement like it was Dumbo's feather.

"What's the point of that?" I asked.

"Joe has enough trouble," she said. And that was that. But she didn't even make it to the end of high school. She got a job in 1987 and then they walked out in 1988, in the spring of Joe's junior year.

~

I didn't have time to go out to Michigan and heap fresh dirt on Dad's grave: I was in my second year as a journalist and in the middle of a lawsuit related to a big riot in Tompkins Square Park. The riot broke out in 1988 when the city and the community board moved to oust the homeless encampment and the drug dealers and the night-sitters like me; when the cops rolled in to close the park, the whole neighborhood fought back. The cops beat the hell out of me as I was reporting and beat a girl-friend who was with me, too, and we were suing. I still had a hematoma in my chest from a police nightstick, a clot under the skin that had shrunk in size from a silver dollar to a dime but was lingering, recalcitrant.

I could feel it when I ran, and when I ran I always ran past the park. I was constantly checking on the park. Our blood was mixed into that dirt.

Dad's phone call made it grossly clear just how much of myself I'd been pouring into this drama. I had spent almost two years reporting on the struggle over this park, and I was so focused on the characters and their power relationships with one another I had forgotten that part of everyone's motivation was to maintain their relationship to the park itself. Every night I saw the same people there—moms pushing strollers, drug dealers, basketball players, punks, poets, homeless people—some of them people who had gotten their heads bashed like me fighting to keep this park open at night and maintain the slimmest connection to their big-*S* Selves, the Selves that formed part of the overall neighborhood of dirt and trees and gulls. *Of course* I had been mauled trying to defend the park: it was both land under threat and the kind of political action Dad hated. That was a fight I could not resist.

When I got to New York City in 1987, Alphabet City seemed to tremble with rage. There were loads of empty and bent buildings east of Avenue A, leaning and wobbling and shucking bricks like so many towers of Pisa. Blocks of the bombed-out neighborhood were occupied as squats, festooned with power cords and garden hoses strung building to building and punctuated by the occasional subsistence garden. I lived for a while in a sweat-equity building on East Tenth between B and C that had been homesteaded by the proto-punk hippie band the Fugs, and was formerly the poet Ed Sanders's Peace Eye Bookstore. I worked for the Fugs photographer Lanny Kenfield at his studio there; he had a giant twenty-foot-long German Velox camera that took up half a floor. My roommate, Brian, and I lived downstairs and could see right into Lanny's studio through the heavy, ancient planking in the ceiling.

Many of the artists I knew were on a war footing. Lydia Lunch came over one day and urged me to read a typewritten manuscript of what became David Wojnarowicz's book *Close to the Knives: A Memoir of Disintegration,* and for me that book revealed a truth about what lay under all the rotting buildings in Manhattan. I had come to New York because my ideas about nature and the church and the function of art made me a problem to my rural family back home. Wojnarowicz, like Lunch and so many others, had fled for his life. Wojnarowicz tore open this alienation and inhabited it at a cellular level. He claimed it. New York was full of outcasts looking for a place to be free, but he was also queer, and sick, and he exposed a savagery at the heart of the country. As more and more of my neighbors and friends grew intensely ill and died of HIV/AIDS, we all watched the government and mainstream culture sanction their deaths, blaming them for their own illness. The rivers that bathe the island of Manhattan drew out the heat and kept it from descending into open street fighting, but that could only go on for so long. Sitting in the Odessa diner, I read from Wojnarowicz's pages: "I wake up every morning in this killing machine called america and I'm carrying this rage like a blood filled egg and there's a thin line between the inside and the outside a thin line between thought and action and that line is simply made up of blood and muscle and bone."

Wojnarowicz wrote about flying his motorcycle into that place in the sky where the air itself would receive him and he could disappear. In his writing, all the boundaries became as thin as eggshell. Under enough pressure, dirt and sky could become blood as easy as anything.

I spent my evenings covering meetings with strident housing advocates at war with real estate developers eager to convert the 'hood into pricey condos. The park was the symbol of the resistance. At least once a week I'd have to wake up a homeless person who had stolen my motorcycle cover to use as a tent. I saw it there in the middle of Dinkinsville, spraypainted with "D-E-A-N" in giant block letters, and I waded in among the tents saying, "Hello? I'm back to get my motorcycle cover." None of the campers ever gave me any grief.

A writer named Bill Weinberg introduced me to the *Earth First! Journal*, where I first read about the FBI infiltration of the radical Earth First! movement in Arizona, and I immediately flew out there to talk to the target of that investigation, the Earth First! co-founder Dave Foreman, for *Spin* magazine. These were people putting their bodies in the way of logging and mining and development and dams, people who dismantled machinery in order to protect the last remaining wild places; those places were so deeply a part of the fabric of who I was that I had to know more about who was doing it. The same year as the park riot, 1988, agents of the Sea Shepherd Conservation Society had sunk Iceland's whaling fleet in Reykjavik Harbor, and I had begun to dedicate myself to reporting on this radical cohort. I started following a huge mobilization to save the coastal redwoods of California that would really kick off in 1990 with the car bombing of the activists Judi Bari and Darryl Cherney. I sat in the park under the elms reading Bill Devall and George Sessions's primer,

Deep Ecology, and I saw the basic conflict of the streets being the lost contact with the living earth that lay beneath.

The park was never a dangerous place, to me, until the police moved in during July and August 1988 to impose a one A.M. curfew. On August 6, the neighborhood erupted in bloody street fighting in which bony punks in painted leather jackets and old babushkas teamed up against over four hundred berserk cops. It was the English enclosure movement all over again: cops who had removed their badges or covered them with black tape were taking away access to the only bit of public dirt left open to the night, and, for that and a million other reasons good and bad, residents exploded with fury. I watched a Ukrainian grandma smacking wild-eyed policemen on the head with her handbag, screaming, "Shame on you!" The *New York Times* ran an editorial titled "Yes, a Police Riot."

While I was out reporting for *Downtown*, a girlfriend from Kalamazoo and I were overrun by a cordon of police. As they shoved us in the back with sticks and told us to move on down St. Mark's Place, pushing us away from the park, a couple of them said some racist and nasty things to my girlfriend, who was black. When I turned to explain I was a reporter, the police surged forward and pinned me down on my back in the middle of the street and pounded me, while the sharp hooves of police horses danced within inches of my head. One of them punched or kicked me in the balls. It's hard to pull out your reporter's notebook when the constables are smashing you in the face. While my girlfriend looked on with her hands over her mouth, a cop stepped up behind her and clubbed her on the back of the head, dropping her to the concrete. She got up with an oozy head gash, and I was left with a spreading purple horror in my chest that looked like death. They didn't arrest me. I guess we were lucky to get up and hobble away, but we were even luckier that Clayton Patterson—the legendary Lower East Side video artist who famously makes his own hats—happened to be on the same street and got most of it on tape.

The whole thing gave me a crazy sense of belonging. The thin line had been crossed, the inside had become the outside, and I was exactly where I needed to be: beaten bloody, filthy, impoverished, a jean jacket for a winter coat, one pair of leaky running shoes, finding love in the trenches, defending a patch of dirt. A lot of nights I was in some squatter's pad talking housing strategy while their kids did homework, or I was meeting with other reporters at *Downtown*'s tiny offices or at one of the poet Allen Ginsberg's three apartments on Twelfth Street as he tried to transform the rage in the streets into meaningful and peaceful action. The struggle was embodied. It was the Paris Commune of 1968, but with shittier wine.

I sent copies of the stories I wrote to Dad and also a letter, in which I explained I was trying to be "part of the solution" to these issues, but he didn't reply. Years later, I would find that he had saved them, carefully filing them away.

It was easy to see that the Ukrainian and Puerto Rican families and the poets and punks who lived in the tenements would get pushed off Manhattan by dreaded yuppies (my *Spin* editor and mentor, Legs McNeil, was then writing a very funny satirical book called *Yuppie Like Me*). I was one of the people fighting back. I saw the park as habitat. But what was I doing to take care of my own family? Nothing. I had abandoned my family back in Michigan. I was shoulder to shoulder with strangers getting billy clubbed and trampled by horses and bombed with beer bottles and M-80s over a piece of land no one in my Michigan life had ever even seen. To this day, none of them except my mom have been to New York City. But here was Bruce, my actual father, who was making a bid for renewed life by proffering a chunk of feral Michigan swamp, and I was turning my back on him.

~

Maybe Dad and I were the same: we could relate to people only through a piece of land. If he wanted to renew a relationship to me, I needed him to drive out to New York and talk to me, to take an interest in my life. Not laugh at it. But he couldn't do that. He didn't see love naturally residing in himself or in us as a family; he saw it waiting *out there*, always separated from the things that threatened him, in a remote piece of dirt. And I wasn't about to go see him, either. I'd rather pitch in on this fight over Tompkins Square Park.

During the summer of Dad's phone call, the quasi-permanent homeless encampment had been routed out of the park, evidence that bigger changes were imminent in the neighborhood, and the land felt haunted. The ungrassed dirt shone through, soil packed by about three hundred years of immigrant boots. For the community that had been camped there for the previous several years, relatedness was certainly a function of the land; without it, the community was forcibly unraveled.

This idea of *relatedness* had become part of my obsession with assessing habitat. When I sat in the park at night, I thought of everything I saw as an ecology of relations. The people who hung out there. Pigeons. Buildings. How were love and families made out of that? It seemed more and more clear to me that love happened in a place. It might even be a function of place. It didn't just involve person meeting person but also the night sky and trees and crows and taxis. Did that mean Dad was right to trust place above all else? How were nonhuman elements involved? If love needed place-ful-ness in which to happen, did the rest of our emotions and our minds themselves also need place-ful-ness?

Was the structure of our minds and our fragile sanity actually a product of the material world, an amalgam of parks and dreams and graffiti and a plenary of consciousness?

I was an avid reader on ecology since my middle teens, caught up in the excitement of the environmental movement that I'd witnessed changing Michigan. When I was about six or seven, my mother took a photo of me holding a cardboard sign I'd made that said STOP POLLUTION, and ecology was a hot topic in school. I'd come across a 1961 essay titled "The Role of the Nonhuman Environment," by the psychoanalyst Harold Searles. In it, Searles opined that good mental health required a "mature relatedness" with both people and the environment around us. The psyche, he said, wasn't just in our heads: it was a product of the land and the buildings and streets. This interested me intensely. I found his essay in a 1971 book I treasured titled *Environ/mental*, edited by the well-known ecologists Paul Shepard and Daniel McKinley. In this essay and other writings, Searles laid out his hypothesis that the human being has a psychic relationship to the nonhuman world that he ignores "at peril to his psychological well-being." The maturity Searles described is not understood simply as an ability to get along in adult human society but involves a *"readiness to face the question* of what is one's position about this great portion of one's total environment."

The context of the essay, and the book, was that a global ecological crisis, in which wild creatures died and humans lived mired in pollution, might be driving us all mad. I understood from it that one's surroundings actively co-created one's psyche.

Searles argued that psychology itself was unable to face that question and did a disservice to patients by treating them as though their minds resided only in their skulls, when the roots of illness may be in the environment. The total environment had to be considered in psychological treatment. To be mature, then, meant understanding that your relationship to other people happened in a place, and your responsibility to the relationship also involved that place and its well-being. A good relationship between a parent and a child or two lovers required finding the right balance between being individuals and being together, neither merging nor holding too much autonomy; the same was true for the relationship between you and the dirt under your feet. Maintaining a forced dualism with the earth was a path to loneliness. To let the earth go mad was to let yourself go mad.

I read this as a kid trying to make sense of Dad. He was miserably conflicted. He loved wild places, the "good places," but he saw them as proving grounds. He pitted himself against wildness in order to extract a fish or deer, but he'd never done any habitat work like plant a berry bush for the birds. He had a somewhat similar attitude toward people and family: he loved them in theory, but he constantly stiff-armed everyone so that no one got too close. He very carefully built critic-proof space around himself. He needed to be separate. He sought relatedness, but his distrust of people and nature generated loneliness.

Crowded into a house with us, Dad was a stranger.

Dad made it clear he thought there was something wrong with Mom, and that's why he slept elsewhere. Something wrong with Joe and Brett and me, too. We weren't good enough. He wasn't *like* us. I read Searles because he raised the prospect that it was the whole culture that worked against us, and not just some failure on our part.

The great American anarchist Edward Abbey is probably not a terrific role model for mature relatedness—by all reports, he had prickly relationships with other people and, like Henry David Thoreau, needed the solitude he so extolled. But in *Desert Solitaire*, Abbey addressed that need to confront our position vis-à-vis the nonhuman world. He understood that accepting the agency of the material world means risking everything we've been taught about our own minds:

I am here not only to evade for a while the clamor and filth and confusion of the cultural apparatus but also to confront, immediately and directly if it's possible, the bare bones of existence, the elemental and fundamental, the bedrock which sustains us. I want to be able to look at and into a juniper tree, a piece of quartz, a vulture, a spider, and see it as it is in itself, devoid of all humanly ascribed qualities, anti-Katan, even the categories of scientific description. To meet God or Medusa face-to-face, even if it means risking everything human in myself. I dream of a hard and brutal mysticism in which the naked self merges with a non-human world and yet somehow survives still intact, individual, separate. Paradox and bedrock.

Dad's deer camp was in my head. If he was offering us the chance to actually work those ninety-five acres like Mr. Card did, growing crops, managing trees, confronting the bedrock that sustains us, it would be the kind of habitat project that Joe, Brett, and I would jump at. It would still be a confrontation, but it might be one we needed to have with our father.

$$\sim$$

On the day of Dad's call, I ran up and down the East River, and ended up back at Tompkins Square Park, heaving, drenched in filthy city sweat. I noticed a girl sitting on the sidewalk underneath a pay phone with her head down between her knees. She had been there the night before and seemed like she hadn't moved in about fifteen hours. I walked over to one of the plainclothes cops who worked the park after the riot and asked if he'd go take a look at her.

"What makes you tink ima cop?" he said in a cartoonish Archie Bunker accent. He had on a green polo shirt with a nightstick shoved up the back.

"C'mon, man, can you go check? She hasn't moved in like a day."

"Why, you tink she's dead?"

"Don't you think it's worth finding out?"

He looked hard at me. "What's wrong wich you?" he said.

"What?" I reached up to touch my face and my hand came away full of blood. Blood was pouring out of my nose like a spigot. When I looked down, it spattered my shirt. I went into a bodega to get a handful of napkins, and when I came out the girl was in the exact same fetal position but now tipped over on her side, not looking any more alive, and the cop was crouching next to her, so I tilted my head up to the sooty sky and walked home.

I'd had some nosebleeds after the police beating, but they ended after a week or so. This one didn't. It bled on and off for months, and I knew it was about this hunting camp. It's the only psychosomatic illness I can honestly say I've ever had, and it was a doozy. It just wouldn't quit. Maybe the beating broke something inside my head, but it's important to note that I am ordinarily pretty robust—a reliable chainsawyer of trees, a skier of steeps, a football captain. The commie doctor who had been treating my hematoma—who had introduced himself to me by saying, "First off, I'm a commie doctor, is that going to be okay?"—finally told me I had two choices regarding the nosebleed: leave New York or leave New York. He knew I was a country boy and figured the city was getting to me.

But I knew different. It was Bruce's sand farm. I'd breached that thin line by starting to care, and everything I'd held away from him threatened to come out in great bouts of soured affection and rage. There was no way I was going to ignore this new dirt he was offering.

∼

I wouldn't see the deer camp until the following year, in the summer of 1990, when I left New York City for good. That visit would be inspired by Joe's hard landing at rock bottom, a fraught and maddening introduction, but it would also be the start of a slow and agonizing turn for our family. It wouldn't be until 1997 that we'd all be there again, after a boycott of seven years, during which I would move to California to cover the radical environmental movement and I'd see Dad only once or twice a year and never see the camp at all. But when we all finally got to the property again, and dug in, we found the fragments of our family already scattered there. And traces in the weather-blasted sand for how they would go back together.

Two
Hello, Winter Maker

I called Mom the day after I talked with Dad. Joe had already mentioned the deer camp to her. I told her I didn't want to go to this hunting camp because I didn't want to endorse one of Dad's fake reinventions.

"Well, it's the only thing he can think of that you boys will care about," she said. "If he just showed up in New York you'd be mad at him."

"Right, and that would be appropriate. But he doesn't want to face that. He wants to hide in the woods and have us come to him."

"But it's also how he signals that he feels bad," said Mom. "He wants to give you something that he knows you're going to love. He just assumes that everything you love is outside somewhere. Bruce taught me that there are a lot of beautiful places in the mountains and on the ocean out West that I never would have seen. I didn't leave home looking for those places—I probably never would have left Holland if it weren't for him—but you boys were looking to get into the outdoors from the minute you were born.

"You remember when your father and I split up the first time, it was the fall of 1975 and we were in the house by Crooked Lake: What was the first thing Bruce did? He sent you out into the swamp to start a trap line."

We lived in the country and there were farm fields and wetlands everywhere, places people would drive by without even noticing. We were trapping for muskrats; a trap "line" meant that we set the steel-jawed traps in a kind of line or sequence across the marsh so that we could easily check them all in about an hour every morning.

"It was the dead of winter," Mom continued. "He knew he couldn't be at the house with you and thought it would be fun for the two of you. You were *eleven years old*, a mile away in the swamp, in your waders, in the dark. You loved that. I hated it, but you loved it."

"Right. He helped me set it up, but then he left me out there."

"Well, okay, this is the problem."

"I did it all by myself most of the time, in the freezing cold dark, because I didn't want him to be mad."

"And I didn't like that. But the original *idea* of it was good."

∼

In 1975 they had split up for what would turn out to be three years. A couple of weeks in, Dad bopped over and announced in a rush of excitement that he and I would set up a trap line to catch muskrats. Deep emotional trouble meant swamp time. This was the Kuipers Way. I didn't know any other kid in my school who trapped, but they all knew what it was: there were swamps and culverts in every direction and trapping was not uncommon. We lived in rural Michigan, whose history had been shaped by the fur trade. There were brokers in town who'd buy pelts. In my dad's family, lots of people trapped. Dad had a plastic milk crate full of steel long-spring traps he had used in Crooked Lake by our house, but I had never had my own line. The fierce Michigan winter was coming on, and I thought it was a beautiful idea.

I imagined we'd get rich off furs. Trappers in our area who were serious about it could make money. Muskrat pelts were worth about five dollars each that winter. Winter was fur trapping season, when the muskrat kits were mostly grown and the 'rats maintained open runs of water around their domed stick houses and were easier to find. Our friend Pat DeBoer gave us access to her family's property on a shallow wetland called Pine Island, maybe a mile west of our house on the other side of Crooked Lake. The place was dotted with muskrat houses, and when we waded into the canary grass, there were plenty of signs that the houses were being used. After it iced over that November, Dad and I went out and hung a few number-one-size traps on stakes knocked in among the cattails and snow-bent reeds, and baited them with field corn.

Dad was in great form that day, singing funny songs and laughing. At eleven years old, I didn't have enough forearm power to squeeze the stiff springs of the trap and set them—it's hard to do even as an adult—so I had to slosh around looking for a log or a piece of dry ground to put the trap on so I could stand on the spring. I'd slip off and the trap would jump up and the finger-crushing jaws would snap at the air like a wolf, with Dad shouting gleefully, "Ach du lieber!"—a shortened version of the Dutch expression "Ach du lieber himmel" ("Oh, for the love of heaven"). But even though I was having some trouble setting the traps, he didn't step in and do it for me; he just let me figure it out myself.

Dad gave no sign that day that he didn't live with us anymore. Maybe he didn't believe it himself. He let his silly side run wild. He was quoting from *The Cat in the Hat* and other Dr. Seuss books he loved to read to us as kids, and singing Loudon Wainwright's song about the dead skunk in the middle of the road, yelling out the end of the chorus, "*Stinkin' to HIGH heaven!*" When he was in good spirits, he took on a kind of antic persona I associated with the Beatles movies, like *A Hard Day's Night*, and he would make a madcap dash across the ice at any moment just to be funny. When we carefully lowered a set trap into the icy water he hissed like a comic villain, "Yassss. Oh yassss!" With his longish 1970s hair and his bright onyx mustache, he looked like a Beatle, maybe George because he was long and lanky, though Bruce had fierce eyebrows forming a V at the top of his face that made even his resting expression look like fury. Dad's skin was also dark in a way none of ours would ever be; some of our relatives said there must be some Spanish in our Dutch blood, for he was olive-skinned like his dad, my grandpa Henry. When Bruce was a kid, he would tan so dark that he was sometimes mistaken for one of the Mexican migrants he worked with in the onion fields by his house. Dad was six foot three and a regular in a game of pickup basketball down at the Texas Corners Volunteer Fire Department, a man hardened by swinging a hammer and shockingly strong for his thin build. All that fall he had been tiptoeing around Mom, but I was glad to be out in the frozen swamp with him on a day when he could be goofy and happy again.

And then our line was set, and we had to wait. I was religious about checking my traps. I'd get outside on winter mornings at about five thirty A.M., in full darkness, and put on Dad's size twelve hip waders and thunk-a-chunk my yellow Cheater Slick bicycle around Crooked Lake wearing a ski jacket and gloves. We had to be on the school bus by seven. When there wasn't snow clotting the air, there was the constellation Orion sinking into the southwest, the figure the Ojibwa (Chippewa) in

Michigan call the Winter Maker. I must have learned that name when I was very young because all my life, when it was hunting season or ski season, I'd look up in the sky and see Orion's drawn bow and say, "Hello, Winter Maker." I waded into the marsh and plowed through the thin ice to check my sets, and if I had to change a bait or reset a sprung trap, I shucked my coat and rolled my sleeves way up because otherwise my clothes would freeze solid while I rode home.

Mom didn't like it. "Bruce, he's just little and he's out there in the freezing cold water in the middle of the night! He might go in over his head! You should go with him," she said.

"He's fine. He has to learn how to do it himself," Dad replied quietly.

Trapping season was already over in March before I figured out that Dad's idea of running the trap line "together" meant that I did it alone. He couldn't get out to our trap line in the mornings from his new apartment on the edge of Kalamazoo and didn't want to anyway. He thought I'd rather do it alone because that's how *he'd* rather do it; he was sure his kid wouldn't want his dad looking over his shoulder.

I finally caught one sweet muskrat, which I admired greatly, with its beautiful chocolate-milk fur and soft little mitts, and even though I'd been around dead deer hanging in garages in our neighborhood and ate piles of pheasants and stringers of fish, I went through paroxysms of guilt that I'd drowned it. I decided it was wrong to kill something we weren't going to eat. Dad didn't seem that happy it was dead, either, like he'd kind of gone off the whole project, but he was proud of me for getting it. I sold it to a fur buyer for five dollars, which was a bag of groceries or a tank of gas for Mom. At that time, she worked as a bookkeeper and night manager at Osco Drug, and without Dad in the house money was tight.

That one muskrat was like an offering on the family altar. I was still too young to hunt, but like every fish I'd ever caught, this trap-line catch instantly reactivated the dialogue among the Kuipers clan. My uncles, aunts, and cousins on the Kuipers side were almost uniformly fanatical about the outdoors. Dad and his brothers, in order from oldest to youngest, were Dale, Ron, Vern, Bruce, Jack, and Mike. Even though Dale lived in Manitoba and Ron lived outside Washington, D.C., when they called on the phone they'd ask to be passed to me, and the grilling would start: "How many 'rats you got now?" they'd query. "Where in the run are you putting your sets? How often are you checking 'em? Are you changing the bait? How thick is the ice?"

Vern and Jack lived nearby, in the farmlands west of Kalamazoo, and they'd run by now and then to see where I was trapping. They'd just drive by to look at the swamp. If their nephew was trapping there, it took on a new significance. I found it hard to judge Dad's interest in trapping—he was only out in the swamp with me a handful of days—but Dad's youngest brother, Mike, is a legendary trapper, and he assured me Bruce knew what he was doing.

"Mink are my life, and what your dad taught me about mink, when I was a little kid, is that they lived in the water like a pike," said Mike. "The lake by your house would be frozen like a brick, and there'd be muskrat houses and he would have traps in the runs between houses and catch mink. Once I got to know trappers and I could buy books, I was told they were like a raccoon: they lived along the shore right where the water meets the land. Anyhow, after thirty years and really learning about mink, I agree with your dad now. I treat them as though they are a pike. The deeper the water, the better, and they live on the bottom like an otter. And I always think of your dad."

Dad never told me these things. But I guess I didn't ask. I was wary of him being around too much, because of what was going on between him and Mom. But Dad had information that I desperately needed.

∾

"You have *got* to come home and see Joe now," said Mom, after our discussion of the trap line. Her voice on the phone turned clipped and serious. She is a small person, five foot three, blonde and blue-eyed with anxious hands, but she could summon a fair amount of maternal authority. "You have to. I am saying this as your mother. He needs you."

"Where is he? I can't ever get him on the phone. He doesn't still live with you, does he?"

"Well, he still comes here," she said, exasperated. "I mean, I keep his *room* for him."

I'd left home when Joe and Brett were twelve and fourteen; I had no picture in my head of their lives at ages eighteen and twenty. I knew that Brett worked part-time with Dad's steel building contracting company,

Delta Design, in order to pay for college, driving materials around on the company stake-bed truck and doing some construction work, and that Mom called him anytime around the clock when she needed help with Joe. Brett had spent a lot of his life taking care of Joe, and the fact that Brett and I didn't talk much just indicated to me he was trying to squirrel away as much time for himself as all this allowed. I knew, at least abstractly, that Joe was on a nonstop vodka bender. I had rarely seen him drunk, but then I rarely saw either one of them. I'd see them on once-a-year fishing trips Dad organized to one of Michigan's good rivers or a ski trip to Steamboat or Killington, but I wasn't up to speed on their emotional and chemical lives. I enlisted Nancy's help in tracking them down, but she was way ahead of me. She saw this deer camp idea as a catalyst for getting some help for Joe, who was slipping far beyond her motherly abilities.

"Where does he go the other nights?" I asked.

"Well, he and Cassie broke up, so not over there anymore."

"Oh, really? They've been together, what, about five years?"

"Five years, on and off. More on than off."

"So he's living with someone else? Or he's just out crashing around?"

"Well, I think he still has that apartment where he stays sometimes. And then he could be staying at your father's place."

"Never. Dad says he's over there with you."

"Joe calls me sometimes when he's in trouble and I just go get him. Or Brett does. Usually in town somewhere. I don't ask about much because I just want him to come home," she said.

Joe himself told me he was getting into LSD. Nancy was not naive about partying, but she never knew he was on acid. She spent a lot of nights swabbing Joe's head with a cool washcloth while he lay on the floor of their apartment, begging to die. She handed out the water and aspirin or coffee, and then she had to go work: in late 1987, about a year before she divorced Bruce, she got an amazing new job as an executive secretary to one of the bigwigs at the accounting firm Plante Moran, and she loved this job. It had probably saved her life. She'd come home late and Joe would be gone. Once in a while he'd work for Dad, too, cleaning up a jobsite or delivering lumber, but when he went out at night it wasn't to work. He drove a brown VW Rabbit with an added toggle switch on the dash that read WARP DRIVE.

"I don't know where he is most of the time, I guess," Mom said. "But I really wish you'd come out here and see him. He needs his big brother."

"He needs something more than me."

"He needs you guys."

~

After a lot of ringing at Mom's house, I got Joe on the phone and asked him if he was going to Dad's deer camp. He didn't even hesitate. "Oh, hell yeah. I'll go," he said.

"Really? What, just to make him feel good?" I said.

"No, I want to go hunting again."

It had been a few years: like all of us, Joe had gone up to Mr. Card's place with Dad every fall, but then he was caught getting naked with the daughter of one of the other guests in the cabin. They were both sixteen, and Joe decided it would be too embarrassing to Dad if he ever went back to Bernie's place.

"But doesn't it make you feel bad when you sit there for days and Dad never talks to you?"

"Well, he never talks to me anywhere. At least I get to sit in the woods," Joe said.

"But do you think he really cares about having us with him out there?" I asked. "Or is it some kind of ego thing, like not wanting to look bad in front of Vern and Jack?"

"It could be that, but you don't know how it's been around here."

"What do you mean?"

"For a while, Dad would call the apartment every night, sobbing," Joe said. "I mean, he was bawling his eyes out."

"What'd he say?"

" 'You gotta come back. You gotta come back to the house. Tell your mom to call me.' "

"Shit," I said.

"Yeah, shit."

"What'd you say to him?"

"I'd say I'll tell Mom and then try to hang up. But I wouldn't tell her most of the time."

"Dude!"

"Well, fuck *that*. Big fuckin' baby."

~

Mom insisted I come out, so I did. It was late summer 1989, only a few weeks after Dad had originally called me about the camp. Mom was happy I was there. I saw her nice little two-bedroom apartment in Texas Corners, part of a series of fourplexes standing in what used to be a corn-field behind the Texas Take Out liquor store. It was less than a mile from where we'd lived by Crooked Lake. There wasn't much in Joe's room but a single bed, sheets thrown on the carpet, and a few clothes wadded up on the floor of the closet. Nothing on the walls.

Mom looked good. She wore her hair in a short, highlighted new 'do that was smart and unfussy for the offices of Plante Moran, and she'd lost the pallor she'd taken on while living on the couch. The skin around her eyes had filled out, and she looked healthy. But she had always been anxious, and she was a little fidgety when she talked about Joe.

"I think it would be a good idea if you took Joe to the big lake," she said to me. "Someplace you both feel good." I ran that by Joe, and he said he didn't have anything else to do.

Joe and I drove out to South Haven and sat on the sand on the shore of Lake Michigan in the middle of the night. The bright curl of the waves lit by streetlamps leaped up out of the black-green expanse of the big lake as it sighed and whispered its troubled decay. The water smelled faintly of rot, as if the millions of sardine-like alewives that used to wash up on the shore when we were kids were still detectably putrefying under the sand. The state Department of Natural Resources (DNR) had planted so many Chinook salmon in the lake they'd about eliminated the alewife, and Joe and I were fine with that; now there were more big salmon to catch. The night was perfumed with the thrill of death, and we were laughing our faces off.

Because he didn't die, Joe's stories about life as an alcoholic were funny, and he used these tales to stave off his own imminent toodle-oo as he talked, tears running down his sunburned face. There he was, after all, alive on the sand, not in a car wreck, not bludgeoned by some lady's husband, apparently not brain-damaged by drink. Joe had started drinking casually at fourteen, after I was already away at college, filching a couple of beers here and there like kids did at our rural Class C school, Mattawan. But it fed a profound loneliness in him and turned him into a lover and a clown, and his drunken antics made him popular. He was handsome and dimpled and a big-time baseball star, a left-handed pitcher and a switch-hitter with power going both ways—that is, before he decided sports were stupid and he got too drunk to turn up for games. He was voted "Best Smile," and by the time he was sixteen, in his sophomore year, he was grinning in the face of full-blown alcoholism. He told me later he was drinking "a fifth of vodka a day" and keeping it "in my locker." He got busted only once, when he and Steve Lee drank a fifth of Jack Daniels on the bus on the way to school in the morning and arrived shit-faced, for which they were hauled straight to the principal's office. He had to serve a three-day suspension in the office, and showed up freshly dressed every day and easily dispatched with his homework and made such a good impression that someone on the office staff wrote a note to Mom remarking that Joe was a great kid. It was already apparent that he was the brightest of the three of us kids. What he needed was someone to notice. But no one did, so he went straight back to guzzling.

During his senior year, Joe had three or four places he could crash, sometimes as long as a week at a time. But he never wanted to wear out his welcome. For the last few months before he graduated from high school, Joe was the lessee of an apartment that Dad never knew about in a Kalamazoo party complex called Knollwood, where he crashed on the floor with five other guys and was eating loads of acid, even while he was commuting twenty miles one-way to high school. The more Joe told me, the more furious I became: How was Dad so dissociated from his own kid that he didn't know where he went after school every day? That he didn't know Joe was flapping back into school every morning still tripping balls? Mom knew, but she didn't do anything about it. She had evidently visited this unfurnished crash pad on various occasions and dropped off McDonald's, a lasagna big enough for all the guys, bags of groceries. She knew enough to know Joe was in deep trouble, but she couldn't call Dad: he blamed her for Joe's alcoholism and ripped her off during their divorce, paying almost nothing. He even convinced the church to take his side and tried to force her to move out of state. Calling Dad was an invitation for more abuse. So Joe got no help from either one of them. Every sentence Joe uttered was like a punch to the heart.

He did his best to soften the blows. He wanted to laugh about it all. On the night we sat on the beach, he had just turned nineteen and wore his light brown hair in an unironic Billy Ray Cyrus mullet that curled around his neck. In his T-shirt with the sleeves cut off, he looked like a big, acid-eating, baby-faced redneck.

"I was out with Tate—you remember him," he started, "and we were partying and it was like two A.M. and Tate wanted to go home, so we were headed out West Main and I was loaded on acid and I was like, *I'm not going home.* So I just got out of the car at a traffic light and started walking downtown. Tate didn't even say anything. The light turned green and he just split."

He told me this story as an example of what his nights were like in Kalamazoo. He walked to Brett's apartment about a half mile away but no one would open the door, and he left in a hail of insults from the other residents. Eventually, the road tipped downward into the broad Kalamazoo River Valley, past the graveyard shrouded in sugar maples that held the remains of the Arctic explorer Edward Israel, and past Kalamazoo College, where I'd gone to school. He skirted Kalamazoo's black neighborhoods on the north side where the cars bumped N.W.A.'s *Straight Outta Compton*, which had just come out and was the advent of a more confrontational soundtrack to the hours between dark and dawn. But nobody bothered him. Folks there knew better than to accost an angry-looking redneck talking to himself and possibly sobbing, especially downtown, home to the Kalamazoo Psychiatric Hospital—a giant facility with a medieval Castle Dracula water tower that dominated the city skyline and was formerly known as the Michigan Asylum for the Insane. On the street, Joe looked like just another lunatic.

"Somehow, after a really long time, I got to the Flamingo Lounge, and I was waling on the door there," Joe said, sniffing back tears.

The Pink Flamingo Lounge was a house in the Vine Street Neighborhood, where our old neighbor Dan Paulsen lived with four other guys, friends of both Brett and Joe. The Flamingo threw famous parties at the Knights of Columbus Hall, and many weekends they'd bring the magic home by having keggers in the house itself, and Brett and the guys rode mopeds up and down the inside stairs like D-Day from *Animal House.*

"Dan opened the door and said, 'Oh, man, you look like shit! What the hell are you doing here?' I was like, 'Jus' lookin' for someone to party with.' So Dan said, 'You can crash on the couch if you want.'"

I started adding up the miles, but Joe wasn't done.

"I couldn't sleep on all that acid, so I decided to walk back to Mom's."

Which, if you're not taking the shortcut down I-94, is a good seventeen miles. On top of the four he'd already walked. That's when I started laughing. The sun came up by the time he reached Portage and his feet were hot and wet in his sneakers and developing blisters—Joe's one of those guys who has big legs and a big body but dainty little sprinter's ankles, which had both been broken multiple times—and pure dread herded him down the road. He didn't feel better; he knew he would never feel *better*.

"I was looking for that place that I was going to feel okay. 'Oh, Mom's house will be good, I'll go there and feel great.' Then I'd get there and I didn't feel any better."

Every passing truck blasted the leaves of new corn in the fields. The sun was hot and burned his fair skin and cooked his scalp and his mouth felt full of dirt from the shoulder of the road.

"I got there and I was just stuck on the couch, still tripping. Mom was there. I knew she had to go to work. She was like, 'Oh, Joe, honey, are you okay? Do you want a cup of coffee?'"

Our dear, poor mom.

"So that's what been happening," Joe said, winding it up. "A lot of nights, anyway."

~

The halyards of sailboats clanged against the masts where the river disgorged into Lake Michigan, and stray dogs fought behind the ice-cream shops, and girls and boys chased each other across the sand in the dark. Someone in the marina was playing Journey, and Joe sang along to it, easily reaching the high notes in "Who's Crying Now." It was comforting to stare at the lake because its life was bigger than ours. The lake was what the lake had always been: a bottomless, algae-stinking pool of reality. Nightjars swooped over the beach catching insects and crying their ghastly cries. Gulls stood one-legged on the sand and faced west with their eyes closed.

"Going to the lake always makes me feel more sane," I said.

"It'll get sick of me. Everybody's sick of me. *I'm* sick of me," said Joe.

"I just think that everybody feels that way some of the time."

"Nope," said Joe. "If people felt like I do, they'd be driving straight into bridge abutments and blowing their brains out all over the place. It'd be like a horror movie out here."

"But you felt okay when you were at Cassie's?"

"Our whole relationship was based on getting me through the night. We'd get loaded in the trailer at night and laugh and fuck about five times, then I'd be despondent again right after, like, 'Oh, I'm a big piece of shit,' but it was enough to get me through. The next day I'd start drinking as soon as I could and just hang on until I could get back to Cassie. At least there was sex, that one thing I could *do* to make life bearable."

Cassie and Joe had met in the clean, orderly hallways of the Mattawan Consolidated Schools when he was thirteen and she was twelve. Her family lived in a mobile home trailer west of Mattawan, over by Paw Paw, and when high school started Joe was hanging out over there and Cassie's family just sort of adopted him. He didn't actually live there, because Dad wanted him home at night, but he found ways to stay there a lot. Dad didn't approve of her because, as he said, she was "from the wrong side of the tracks," but Joe and Cassie loved each other like crazy. By the time they were sixteen and fifteen they couldn't function without each other. "Those two are totally codependent," Dad told me. He read that term in a magazine. "They break up and then they just talk on the phone for hours until they can get back together. She leaves these messages on the home answering machine: 'Joe, you were supposed to come over and fuck me.' She has to know that that's the house phone used by your mother and I."

They broke up every couple of weeks but only for a day or two, and then they had a few sips and were back in the sack and it was on again. They were so happy. Cassie's dad was a bantam little dude with a reputation for violence and pranking, but he liked Joe because they could talk about hunting and fishing together and Joe didn't judge him despite being half again his size. He never gave the boy any grief. Cassie's mom once caught Joe and her daughter getting it on in the bathtub and smoking weed, and barked at them to get in the living room "Right NOW!" And when they appeared, hastily dressed and sober with fear, she burned them with a face of parental scorn as long as she could hold it and then burst out laughing. "I'm just messing with you guys," she said. There's no place to hide what goes on in a trailer home. The walls are nothing. Anyway, Cassie's dad was wound so tight he had a fatal stroke sometime in his forties, but Joe thought he was an all right guy.

Joe was surprised when school ended and Cassie dumped him.

"I know I sound like a total fuckin' pussy, like this girl is God or something, but I can't figure out how to live without her," Joe said. "The lack of self, for a better word, or ego or whatever you want to call it—as soon as my significant other disappears, I always get so despondent because I don't know how to feel okay without that. I have nothing left of myself. I'm just, like, hollowed out."

"There's no sliver of light? You seem good right now," I said on the beach.

"That's 'cause we're at the lake. I mean, the only time I actually feel *good* good is when I'm standing in a river."

I seized on this. "Then you should stand in a river every day. Why the hell not, if that's what it takes to live?"

"Because it's just running away."

"So what? If the alternative is dying."

"Right, you say that, but then eventually you'll be like everyone else and asking why I don't have a job."

Have you ever tried to talk someone out of killing themselves, or at least not driving their pickup out onto the spring ice? The more you talk, the more you realize the whole mess at the end is going to be your fault. My words sounded ridiculous and puny. They splished against that final silence with no more power than a wad of spit hocked at a tornado. Joe was very matter-of-fact about trying to find out how far was too far, and he dared me to refute the logic: like tripping or getting drunk, dying was pain relief that would actually work. I didn't have anything like that in my bag. I felt helpless, like I could see him fading from the surface of the earth but there was nothing I could do to stop him from going.

~

Our family friend Scott, who'd grown up near us on Eagle Lake, told me he and Joe had been given several sheets of free blotter acid from a kid who thought the government was after him. Joe went on dosing even after the other guys left the Knollwood apartment.

"Joe is scary," Scott said. "One night he said, 'I bet I can just beer-bong this entire bottle of vodka.' It was like a fifth of Smirnoff's or something. I said, 'Joe, that's how you get alcohol poisoning and die.' He called me a chickenshit and he drank most of it. He drank about a half gallon of orange juice so that would dilute it.

"Another night he decides that he's going to go, to get in shape," Scott added. "So he takes off running around the apartment complex. He's doing laps around the complex. Well, everyone goes, 'Oh shit, where's Joe? Where did Joey go?' and panicking. It's always about taking care of fuckin' Joe. 'Cause if anybody's going to die it's going to be him. So the whole fuckin' party takes off out the door and they're all running. There's like twenty people running laps in the middle of the night, yelling, 'Joe! Joe!' And then pretty soon he's sitting on the steps like fuckin' Road Runner in the cartoons waiting for Wile E. to zoom past. Unbelievable."

∼

Joe talked about dying even while he was trying hard to stay alive. The talk about dying was both a desperate attempt to externalize feeling like shit and an equally desperate plea for some project that would make feeling like shit worthwhile. He needed a way to get the inside and the outside in sync. I had all kinds of ideas, most of them dangerous in retrospect. Earlier that same summer, I had left New York for a week or two to write a story about those Arizona Earth First!ers who were infiltrated by the FBI, and I thought their story might light a fire in Joe. It had lit a fire in me.

They called themselves the Evan Mecham Eco Terrorist International Conspiracy, or EMETIC. No matter how you felt about Mecham, the car dealer turned Republican governor of Arizona who got himself impeached for being at once racist and corrupt, the group's joke name was funny. They were nonviolent and cheery like the characters in Edward Abbey's *The Monkey Wrench Gang*, and had made a name for themselves when they sabotaged a ski area and some power lines to a nuke plant. They were from the ornery northern mountain towns of Flagstaff and Prescott, and believed that more than enough desert had been paved and turned into Phoenix.

Mark Davis, one of the guys in EMETIC, assured me that "unless humans begin to show some of the beauty they were born with, our little biological experiment here is ended." Meaning *Homo sapiens*. I looked at him in his prison blues in the Maricopa County Jail and at the unbelonging sprawl outside frying in the 112-degree-Fahrenheit heat, and I didn't see any reason to disagree with him. Davis was a kickboxer and a student of ecology, very intelligent if over-the-top intense, and I needed to know more about where he got all this juice. So the next morning, one of Davis's fellow activists took me on a hike up a mountain trail near his home in Prescott.

"He runs this trail all the time," she told me, as we scuffed through sand washes and up sections of razor rock and cholla cactus that seem to glow with a special sunny menace. "A lot of the time he runs it barefoot."

Barefoot. This I understood. Most of my ideas about skiing and running consisted of subtle and powerful feelings in the bottoms of my feet. I memorized mountains and streets through my feet. Feet understand place differently than eyes do. The feet are rarely dazzled. The feet are rarely lost. When Davis ran that mountain, it sent its own ideas up through his feet. I wanted to try it, but I knew I'd be bloody before I could decipher the language of raw rock.

When I told Joe this story, he said, "Oh, I could get into that. I like when I walk in a river in my wading shoes, because you feel the whole river through the bottoms of your feet."

"I think the mountain told him he needed to defend that desert," I said.

"Rivers tell me that all the time," Joe said. "Sometimes I fish up to a bridge somewhere and find a tire in the river, or a refrigerator someone chucked there, and I have to try to fix it. Who thought that throwing a refrigerator in the river is a good idea?"

Joe knew what I was driving at. Wildness needed defending in Michigan just like it did in Arizona, and there were worse offenders than hillbillies chucking the old Frigidaire. Wouldn't it be life-affirming to protect those waters? I mean, as opposed to killing himself? There were few limits on what kinds of actions you could take when the alternative was suicide. Like I said, my ideas were more desperate than good.

"God, that would feel so good to just *do* those things," Joe said. "Find a problem, take it out."

He laid back on the sand. "Ah, I'd probably get killed immediately."

"What do you mean?"

"I'd take it too far. The secret to getting away with that stuff is knowing when to stop."

~

We had dinner at Dad's house while I was in town, and Brett came, too. I hadn't seen him in a year, I guess. He was about the same height as Joe but fifty pounds lighter, and he was rocking the mullet, too, a slightly darker shade of brown. My ponytail went halfway down my back. There was a lot of hair.

"Christ, it's like Molly Hatchet came for dinner," I said.

We were all half-committed to some kind of goatee or Fu Manchu or lack of shaving and looked like hell. All three of us were living in genuine poverty and wearing worn-out shoes and thrift-store flannels that were moth-eaten compared with Dad's togs, which were conservative but always bespoke or at least expensive. Even when Bruce was young and broke, he always spent money on clothes. Joe was big like the Molly Hatchet singer Danny Joe Brown and started snarling out, "Ah'm travlin' down the road 'n' Ah'm flertin' with diz-ASS-ter!" When we got together we would sing. Brett was a guitar player and I had been a drummer in a couple of bands. We all joined in: "Got the pedal to the floor 'n' my lahf is runnin' faster!"

Dad laughed at our singing. He was mortified by how we looked and called us "hillwilliams," but he was so excited to have all his boys there for the first time since the divorce; it was heartbreaking. He saw Brett all the time, but having the three of us in the house only emphasized how much time he spent alone. Dad kept talking about how much he liked living there by himself—"The ladies who come out from Molly Maids are so *interesting*," he said. Which meant they were the only people in the world he ever talked to. He dashed around the house, fussing over a slab of lake trout sizzling on the grill and some boiled red potatoes and salads he'd bought, still in their containers from the grocery. It was basically camp cooking, but I was starved and happy for a meal.

The big house was immaculate and soggy as a dishrag with summer humidity. It felt like the place would suck up a million pounds of water every summer and sink a few inches deeper into the hillside. I couldn't help but feel proud of the house because I had helped build it, a luxurious rustic contemporary with four bedrooms and three baths spread over three floors and organized around a central spiral staircase in black metal. The whole thing was sided in stained cedar that withdrew into the dark of the hickory forest.

Brett, who claimed he loved this house so much, was nervous as a finch. Only a few years earlier, Dad had beat his ass in it, and in front of all his friends.

On that occasion, Mom and Dad and Joe had gone to Silver Lake for a few days with Mom's siblings and their kids, but Brett was seventeen and he stayed home and decided to have a small party. Brett had never caused one lick of trouble and was not one of the popular crowd, but he kinda hoped, in a seventeen-year-old way, that some of the cool kids would turn up to his one and only illicit high school party. He had one or two cases of beer. Dad suspected something was afoot, and he couldn't stand going to Silver Lake anyway because it was a resort lake and he couldn't do any real fishing because all his young nieces and nephews wanted to bang away on his aluminum boat with their Fanta bottles and stuff, so they came home a day early. Joe stopped getting drunk in the woods with our cousin just long enough to borrow a bike and ride like hell to a store to call Brett, but when he got there the pay phone was broken.

When Dad came roaring through the door of the house, Mattawan High School's finest were leaping off the deck and running into the woods to get away from The Terror, and our father waded into the Yngwie Malmsteen or whatever was on the turntable and tore the shirt clean off Brett's back and slammed him into the wall. He was completely unhinged. "NONE OF YOU WILL EVER SET FOOT IN THIS HOUSE AGAIN!" he bellowed. Mom and Joe stood by the car and waited it out. Dan Paulsen, whose own giant of a father had left him fearing no man, walked calmly past Dad as he thrashed Brett and down the driveway, and Dad hurled after him, "I'm so disappointed, Daniel! I thought we were friends!" To which Dan turned and replied, "We are friends, Bruce. We're just drinking a beer." Dan later ended up working for Dad at Delta Design, so I guess that's some kind of lesson about life.

The worst part was that Dad saw this as an opportunity to apply some of his freshly discovered church discipline, since he'd rejoined the Christian Reformed Church only a few years before. So he dragged Brett around to see the parents of kids who were at the party and to explain that Dishonoring Thy Father and Mother was a breach of God's covenant. Some of those people took pity on Brett, but some didn't. One of them yelled at Dad, "What the hell's going on over there? My daughter came back *missing her bra*!"

Despite Dad's mad bid for control, Brett still stayed as close to him as he did to Mom and Joe. He didn't have much patience for just hanging out, but it was because he wanted time to play his guitar and fish and read sci-fi and be his own person.

While all of us waited for dinner in our hair and discomfort, Brett stood out on the deck, chain-smoking and looking through binoculars at something in the woods. None of us really knew what to do with Dad if we weren't outdoors; I seriously considered chopping some wood or raking. Brett called me over and handed me the glasses and indicated an old mulch heap. There were seven-foot-tall cannabis plants growing there. "Dad thinks they're ragweed," he said.

We wandered around like strangers. We still had rusty pellet guns and moldy shoes in the closets, but we didn't live there anymore.

When Dad went out to his truck, we checked out the cabinet above the fridge where he kept the liquor: the same dozen dusty bottles of crème de menthe and Martini & Rossi and Kahlúa were in there that I'd moved into the house ten years earlier, but they were all half-empty.

"I used to get in there in the middle of the night and I'd pour a little bit of each one into a two-liter of something and make a nasty Kamikaze and just down it," said Joe. "I was desperate. That's why I tried to never stay here once I started drinking. I refilled them with water so that's mostly just water in those bottles."

"But why doesn't he throw this stuff out?" I said.

"To tempt me," Joe growled. "Just to make me fucking miserable."

I flipped through Dad's CDs and put on a new Bonnie Raitt album I liked, *Nick of Time*. The rest were mostly gospel and Reba. Dad had always been an audiophile and had fitted the house with giant Polk tower speakers, but I couldn't find his vinyl LPs.

"Dad, where's all your *good* records?" I shouted to him.

"Those ones there are all good. Put on the Oak Ridge Boys CD. I like that 'Elvira.'"

"No, I mean the *good* ones. You had Isaac Hayes and Lou Rawls, Roberta Flack, all them."

"Oh, I got rid of those a long time ago. They're just not what I like to listen to now."

Bruce's collection had been mostly Motown, soul, and jazz, plus a few Crystal Gayle or Melissa Manchester albums that he clearly bought because he thought they were sexy babes. He'd had George Benson's *Good King Bad*, Marvin Gaye and Tammi Terrell, Aretha, Earl Klugh, a bunch by Ray Charles—a stack totaling about fifty albums. When I was twelve years old, I spent hours fantasizing about the hot girl on the cover of the R&B organist Earl Grant's *Gently Swingin'*.

"He got rid of those records because them were for *doin' the deed*," Brett said matter-of-factly.

"What? No, uh, I just didn't listen to them anymore, that's all."

The house sat at the far western edge of the time zone, so the sun figured to stay up half the night, with a breeze blowing shards of reflected lake light up into the undersides of the trees on the ridge. We ate in the screened porch, my favorite room in the house, which hung about twelve feet high in the trees. The screens puffed in and out with the breathing of the forest. Brett zeroed in on his food and started humming; he hummed when he was eating something he liked. Joe evidently hadn't had a drink yet and looked bloated and wretched. He and I talked about how nice it was at South Haven, but Dad cut in and started talking about the deer camp. I immediately deflected this toward Brett, mostly as a way to stop that insane humming.

"Brett, you gonna go in November?" I said.

"What? Oh, to the hunting camp? Yeah, I'm gonna go," he said, diving back into his plate and humming louder, signaling that he didn't want to talk about it.

"We're full the first weekend, so Brett's gonna go the second weekend," said Dad. "With Jack and Jane, I think."

"I'm going to find my own little place to sit out there by that bog you talked about, Dad," said Brett.

"People drive around the edge of that federal swamp sometimes, so you'll have to stake out a place and make sure no one sits on our spot," said Bruce.

"I'll probably just sit on a bucket or something. As long as I've got some smokes and a thermos of coffee I can sit out there all day."

"Ha ha! You know, those deer can smell the smoke," Dad said, tearing off a series of paper towels to put under each item on the table.

"Nobody better bug me about smoking," Brett bristled.

"Oooh, shit, I am gonna smoke out there like a *chimney*," said Joe.

"Ha ha! Oh God!" choked Dad.

"That's the whole reason I'm going there: there's nothing more satisfying than smoking in the woods," said Joe.

Dad piled on the paper towels. "It can't be total anarchy," he said.

"It's just the opposite," said Brett. "Cigarettes are how I organize my world."

Bruce knew they were winding him up, and he was doing his best just to take it and be some facsimile of what he thought "good-natured" was supposed to look like, but his jaw got tight and he was suddenly deadly interested in those paper towels. He fought the unrelenting urge to hold us down and shave our heads and jam the cigarettes and books by the ecophilosopher Arne Naess into the toilet.

"That big buck will know you're there," said Dad. "You'll wreck it for everybody."

"Oh, the deer don't give a shit," Brett retorted. "Remember Jim Card?" That was Bernard's son who was Dad's age. "That guy would sit in a La-Z-Boy in his blind and smoke cigarettes and he'd still get a deer about every other year."

I remembered Jim's cigarette smoke drifting through the woods, and his bone-rattling snoring.

"He'd be watching football on his little battery-powered TV, too," added Joe.

"Well, you'll get a deer but you won't get the bull of the woods, because the big ones get too smart," said Dad. "And I think we've got some big ones around Ike's place."

"I'm shooting anything that comes by," said Brett, trying to keep a straight face.

"If it's brown it's down," said Joe, nodding sagely.

The sun refused to go away. We finished dinner and it was like noon, and Dad grabbed thick packets of photographs and a couple of maps he had staged on the kitchen table, so he could talk about the exact details of how they were going to run the deer camp out of the trailer they had put there, and that was Brett's signal it was time to go. Doing construction with Dad was fine, but sitting around while our father fretted over camp details like exactly where we could sit and on what, how we would scout the place without scaring the deer, what clothes to bring, who was bringing the powdered milk, and all the rest just ruined it for Brett. Dad was distressed to see him go and leaped into the kitchen and started filling Brett's arms with food to take with him.

"I know it seems ridiculous, but we can't just show up there and not have this stuff organized, because we're staying there with Vern and he'll want to know exactly what we're doing," Dad said, following him out the door. I signaled Dad to stay inside because I never got to see Brett.

Standing at the door of Brett's truck, I said to him, "I thought going up north to Dad's deer camp would be about the last thing in the world you'd want to do."

"No, see, that's the *only* thing I want to do with him," he replied. "It's being here that sucks. Where we never get to talk about what's going on in our lives. But being out in the woods is fine."

"I guess I see it all as the same, now," I said.

"I want to sit in that swamp. Don't you?"

He hugged me good-bye.

"You're so lucky you live in New York." He got in his little truck, cranked up Ritchie Blackmore's Rainbow, lit a cigarette, and split.

∼

The closets in my room were stacked with mildewed boxes, and Dad asked me to go through them while I was home to see if there was anything I could get rid of. In one of them I found notes on the ecologist and cyberneticist Gregory Bateson and a quote that I had taped to my wall in college: "You decide that you want to get rid of the byproducts of human life and that Lake Erie will be a good place to put them. You forget that the eco-mental system of Lake Erie is part of *your* wider eco-mental system—and that if Lake Erie is driven insane, its insanity is incorporated into the larger system of *your* thought and experience."

I understood the Lake Erie reference because of the fires on the Cuyahoga and the Buffalo. The lake had been driven insane.

Bateson had given me the first real understanding that my mind wasn't separate from nature, that in fact most of what I called "my" mind was really a subset of the gargantuan, messy, mind-like entanglement of thinking out there, in the world. The material world and the natural processes going on outside my body were probably generating most of the awareness that I called my "self." Descartes's declaration really should have been "I think, therefore we are," or "It thinks, therefore I am," or something like that. I read Bateson at an age when I didn't understand some of it, but the epistemology he laid out in *Steps to an Ecology of Mind* changed everything:

> Now, let us consider for a moment the question of whether a computer thinks. I would state that it does not. What "thinks" and engages in "trial and error" is the man *plus* the computer *plus* the environment. And the lines between computer, man, and environment are purely artificial, fictitious lines. They are lines *across* the pathways along which difference or information is transmitted. They are not boundaries of the thinking system. What thinks is the total system which engages in trial and error, which is man plus environment.

The takeaway, for me, was the phrase *What thinks is the total system.* By extension, I figured that the total system is different for every being, human or other-than-human. The environment and I were a total system. A single white pine and its environment were a total system. If thinking meant to engage in trial and error, then surely that included pine martens and goldenrod and Lake Erie itself—the lake makes a bid to digest a plastic diaper, fails, tries a fire, partly succeeds; the lake grows a reed marsh to protect its banks from infill, the reed marsh is burned, it tries again; the lake occupies a glacial hole, is sucked back into the ice sheet during the ice age, comes pouring out again when it's done to fill a differently shaped hole. Trial and error. Thinking.

Our family and Dad's big house on the hickory hill were a total system. But the forest here had clearly gone mad. It looked gorgeous, yet it was defiled. Mom had nearly died and I'd killed Dad, and Joe was still dragging one hand through the void between life and death trying to get a handhold and yank himself through to the other side, and Brett was doing his limited best to hold all of us together. Why weren't we able to help one another? Which part of the total system was shattered or polluted or simply gone? Why had we driven one another insane?

≈

Back in New York, I got Joe on the phone and we started talking fishing.

"Oh, I was thinking about this after we went to South Haven," he said. "There was one time in my life that Dad treated me like an honest-to-God human being, and it explains everything about why I feel good standing in a river."

Dad had started taking Joe and Brett to the primeval North Branch of the Manistee when they were seven and nine. They had fished in the warm-water lakes around our house and had learned how to catch bass and pike on spin-casting rigs on their own, just the two of them figuring it out together, but they had rarely fished for trout. Dad considered trout the real prize, elusive, cherished, a mystery worth pursuing with mindfulness. It was 1978 when they first waded out in their jeans and Keds into the forty-five-degree-Fahrenheit water of the Manistee for the April trout opener, and there was still snow on the banks. They didn't have waders, but froze their little balls off because they wanted to prove they could fish with Dad.

Just like when I ran the trap line with Dad, however, it wasn't long before he disappeared. As soon as the boys started getting snagged in the alders and red osier willows, or broke a hook off, Dad started fuming, and the fuming turned to shouting and cursing—and then he announced, in his waders and his vest dangling with gear, that he was going upstream without them. He told them to fish upstream until they came to a deep hole that had boulders in it "as big as Volkswagen Beetles," and he would wait for them there. And then he was gone.

Because Brett and Joe were born seventeen months apart, Dad and Mom always treated them as though they were twins and had to do everything together. For most of their lives at home they had the same clothes, the same shoes, the same lunch, the same sporting gear. Everyone assumed they were looking after each other, but that often meant Brett had to care for Joe. The age gap between them was just enough that Brett acquired every skill first, so when Joe had a bad tangle or a fish swallowed his hook, Brett had to help. Joe learned fast, because he didn't want to burden his brother, but the skills flowed from older to younger, from swimming to riding minibikes to hunting. Still, they both agreed they better not bother Dad. They had to prove they were self-reliant as fishermen.

They didn't get in the way or get hypothermia or get lost, so they won themselves some more trips to the river. Eventually, Dad bought them some green rubber waders, but Joe didn't wear them half the time because if you fell down they could fill with water and stuff you under a log and drown you and even Brett might not be able to save him.

"Dad took us fishing, but we basically taught each other how to fish," Joe said.

On the particular year of Joe's story, he was thirteen, and it was just him and Dad on the river. Joe already had some renown as a fisherman. By that time, there were famous stories of him catching a monster crappie in Silver Lake, a miracle steelhead off the pier at Pentwater, trout after trout on a family trip out West. When he caught up with Dad at the hallowed pool with boulders as big as Volkswagens, the deep water was almost black in the failing light. I knew from fishing on the Manistee how it would look: the midsummer boreal sunset turned the sandy needle duff pink and ignited the jack pines and cedars and set them flaring against the sky as he made a few last, careful casts.

Brett had landed a decent fish there two years earlier, and Dad had unleashed such a shit-storm of anxiety on him, hurling instructions down the bank, that Brett had informed Dad on the spot that he'd never fish with him again, and he hadn't. It was the end of their father-and-son fishing for years. Joe's experience went the other way. He made a last cast and something huge, something soft and big-shouldered, sucked in his crawler, and then the steady pressure and the drag on his reel began to sing. In the riffles above the hole they clearly saw the big fish scattering gravel as it dug northward.

"My God, son! That's the biggest river fish I've ever seen!" Dad shouted from the bank. "It's a tuna!"

"Let him have line! Oooohhhh, son! You'll probably never land that fish, we just don't know how to catch fish like that, but it sure is great to see him!"

By then, we'd all spent so much time hunting and fishing with Dad that his responses were as predictable as a diner jukebox: you dropped in a slug of hope or surprise and strange abuse dressed up as self-loathing came warbling out. He vomited his mad instructions down the bank about setting the drag and how to reel, but Joe stopped listening. All he heard was fish. Joe knew in that moment that he adored fishing. "I realized I *loved* this fish," he said. "I didn't feel lost or inadequate or split; I just felt at home." He and this fish were the same: more than anything else, they wanted to live, and they needed the river to do it.

The fish took pretty much the whole spool, maybe one hundred yards of line strung along the river, stretched from rock to tag alder to cedar through islands of blackberry and lady slipper orchid and along all manner of deadfall strainers laced across the creek. Line was strung all through the woods. There was little chance of untangling a fish from that web, but Joe stood there above the hole and patiently started reeling and then reeling in earnest, and after a while the line came in freely.

"I think he spit the hook," he said after a while, reeling in unweighted line.

"You just can't land a fish like that," Dad continued, and then, "OH MY GOD, SON, THERE HE IS!"

And there it was, the heavy back splitting the creek, a big-bellied rainbow trout barreling downstream like an exposed submarine racing for deep water, right past Joe's boots and then farther across the hole and around the next bend, line still firmly attached.

Not only attached but mostly untangled. It's about as likely as having a fish handed to you by a bear. The line came in with sticks and algae winding onto the reel, but it came in and about half of it went right back out again, disappearing downstream. A fish heading downstream, however, is like a wounded deer heading down-mountain: if the deer thinks it will recover, it climbs up to higher ground where its eyesight and hearing give it an advantage over predators who will smell the injury; if the hurt is grievous, it gives up its advantage and heads down to water and sweet grass and the deeper cover of thickets. This fish was waving the white flag, and soon it was played out and Joe began the long reel-in. The whole fight lasted about fifteen life-changing minutes, and then the fish came dragging slowly to the shallows at Joe's feet.

"We didn't even bring a net," Dad lamented, splashing into the dark river.

Joe grabbed the monster by the gills and hoisted him up, a beautiful, solid, twenty-five-and-a-half-inch rainbow (Dad had a tape measure). It was the essence of fish. It was the dream that fish themselves dream. Night had fallen.

Dad was nearly in tears. "I can't believe it, Joe! I can't believe it! Don't drop him, son."

Joe inhaled Dad's excitement like a drug and just about pissed his pants; he shook in little quivers. Dad was normally so angry about every-thing that just to see him excited about a fish—*his* fish—was the pinnacle of Joe's life at that point. Dad was standing in the river smiling and he rarely smiled in the river. The fish was hardly even the most important thing; the important thing was: *my dad is smiling at me.*

"I'm keeping it," Joe quavered, struggling up onto the shore trying to manage the pole and clutching the fish as though Dad might take it from him and throw it back or somehow screw up this moment.

"Of course we're keeping it," Dad said, splashing after him. "We're gonna eat it!"

"It's a big fish, man!"

"Oh, it's glorious."

Father and son clambered up the bank with Joe holding the fish tight and spilled out onto a darkened meadow there with all their gear and relief. They laid the fish in the grass and admired it.

"The fish of a lifetime, Joe!"

Those were words that would never fade. Six years later, as we talked, he was living off them.

"That was the first time in my life I felt like a whole person," Joe said. "That Dad accepted me for who I was. He didn't attribute the fish to God or fate, it was just me. The river made that happen."

Neither Brett nor I had ever had a moment like that. I couldn't believe no one had told me this story before; they probably had, and in my own self-involvement I'd forgotten it. Joe had obviously come closer than any of us did to having a father-son moment with our dad, and I think it made Joe half-crazy with craving. Dad tried to teach Brett and me lessons all the time by hacking off our relatedness somewhere short of mature, but Joe had received a full charge. It changed everything to know that at least one of us had done something that earned unqualified praise.

"After that, standing in a river is all I want to do," Joe said to me. "And I want to do it *with Dad.* That's why I want to go to the deer camp. That's how I feel good. I always want to feel the way I feel when we're up at the North Branch."

≈

In November 1989, Joe went up to Dad's new deer camp for Opening Day of rifle season. I didn't think it would actually happen. When aunts and uncles asked him what he'd been up to, was he supposed to regale them with stories of the cool stuff he saw on acid? I asked him to call me afterward if he did go, because I was dead curious to know what it looked and felt like. Joe did call. Maybe he'd had a drink or two and then called me. November marks the beginning of the hardest time for depressives in Michigan, when the sun disappears until late April. He gave me just enough detail about what he saw of the land and the birds and clouds so that I could tell that the hunt had mattered to him.

Vern and Jack had put a trailer on the property, a pull-behind travel trailer that Vern had bought from a widow he knew. Jack told me they'd hauled it out there behind her short-block Dodge pickup, swerving and bucking like crazy. They didn't have water or electric hookup, but it was a private camp. The 95 acres butted up to 120 acres of public land in the middle of the block, and there was no access except through private land, so they felt pretty sure they wouldn't have yahoos walking through their hunting spots all day.

Card's place had been like that, too, but we didn't take it for granted. Most of the seven hundred thousand or so hunters who flooded into the Michigan woods for deer hunting that fall staked out a spot on public land and were almost certain to be disturbed by other people.

It took Joe three hours to drive up from Kalamazoo, and it was already dark before he left town. Dad and Vern were unhappy that Joe would arrive late, stirring up the woods when they'd rather it mellow, but he had to work, and among Calvinists work is sacred. He had just landed a job selling gold chains at a kiosk in the mall called the Golden Chain Gang; it was only for minimum wage and would end up lasting less than a month, but work was work.

He went up and down the remote road a few times trying to find the unmarked two-track that ran onto Ike's little piece of sand. You didn't want to go hammering into the woods on the day before gun season and test someone's tolerance for trespassers. Finally he snapped his lights off and plunged the Rabbit down a trail. The two-track was frozen sand and the night air smelled of cold swamp and snow. Dad greeted him at the trailer door.

"Kemosabe!" he whispered. "You made it!"

The trailer slept four and the other hunters were Vern and his daughter Jennifer, who was Joe's age and in his class at Mattawan. We have sixteen cousins on that side, so you never knew who might turn up. She was a serious hunter and a partier, too, probably the only other one in the whole Kuipers clan besides Joe, but even though she was a featherweight compared with him, the judgment she endured was worse because she was a woman. She fought back against the whole family with a kind of chipper resistance and love that made space for kids like Joe and her. She had bigger balls than the rest of us.

Joe lay awake for a few hours. It felt good to be hunting. It had been three years since the quiet debacle at Card's, and it was important to him to be back on the land with Dad. At about four forty-five A.M. everyone got up to paint their faces and Dad filled a thermos with hot tea, and by five thirty they pulled coats over their coats and hoods over their hats and there was the sober sound of rifle cartridges snapped-to and one racked into the chamber, and they were standing outdoors in the smell of coming snow with clouds of breath ringing their heads. They smiled at one another and walked away in silence, each one to a separate piece of dawn.

"I went to the south . . . east, I guess, through a kind of swampy drain area and then up on a low ridge along the property line with the people on the east side. It wasn't up high, really, but you can see up there off into that south twenty and back into the swamp and over onto the neighbor's piece. Dad and them don't have any blinds set up yet, so I just sat against a tree. It started to snow. There were cardinals and chickadees and pileateds."

He smoked cigarettes and snow piled up on his hood. To the east, Joe could see through the trees to bits of a weedy pond of about eighty acres that was part of the neighbor's camp, a shallow pan of ice stuck through with cattails and rushes and little islands where geese would nest in the spring. The wind blew out of the west and toward the pond, and only the neighbor's cows would smell Joe's smoke. Joe had a left-handed .30-06 and thoughts in full stampede. He'd tapered off the LSD as the supply ran down, and started going to a day clinic run by Bronson Hospital in the town of Oshtemo. It was a group-therapy affair where mostly they'd sit around and talk about boozing, but he kept going back. He liked riding his bike into Oshtemo to get there, a ride of about five or six miles from Mom's place past the horsefly swamps of Eighth Street, past the Boy Scout's Camp Rota-Kiwan and the city water wells in the Al Sabo Preserve. He was getting in shape.

It was easy to commit to the rehab because everyone agreed he should go. But it wasn't easy to figure out what to do other than that. By the end of the summer season, the guys he'd partied with had stumbled off to colleges and vocational schools and jobs—even Scott left to take a course in aircraft repair in Oklahoma. Nervous girls walked up to Joe all day in the mall and let him put gold chains around their necks and look down their shirts.

Dad sat in the darkness out to the west, watching the edge of Mr. Carter's corn.

Dad was happy Joe was there, and Joe felt good about that. Out here, on the hunt, Vern and Jen and Dad all trusted Joe; his reputation as a sportsman was already well established: he was the catcher of giant fish. It was just everywhere else that they considered him messy. That was good enough for one morning.

"There was a lot of shooting all around us, but none of us saw anything," Joe said. "But that was fine. It felt good. Very peaceful. Dad was so relieved I was there. We all came in around noon and talked about what birds we saw and stuff like that, where we thought the deer were. Dad was super disappointed we didn't see anything. Especially when we used to see about thirty or forty every day at Card's. But I didn't care. I had to go straight back to work."

"Would you go back up there?" I asked.

"Sure. Why not."

When I called Dad about it later, he called that feeling "grace." Joe had experienced grace, he said.

Brett went up the following weekend with Uncle Jack and Aunt Jane, and he found his redoubt in the blueberry bushes along the bog and listened to beavers slapping at the water. He smoked and drank coffee, and he told me he liked the place, too. No one shot anything that first year, and Dad was giving out about the smoking and so on, but Brett and Joe weren't disappointed at all because they were allowed to sit in the woods. The place raised all kinds of possibilities. Maybe the next summer they'd be allowed to do some habitat work out there, or hunt a grouse. Like me, they were looking for a place that made them feel sane.

Three

The Big Chair

Love is made in a place and love is destroyed in a place. Maybe every conflict, human and otherwise, is about habitat.

I felt a little bit sick about missing the 1989 deer season. I was still living in New York, and I traveled to Scandinavia to write a *Spin* cover story on Mötley Crüe and to Amsterdam for another on Jane's Addiction. Places still mattered. At one point, Tommy Lee leaned over to the guys in Mötley Crüe as we ate at the Strand Hotel in Stockholm and whispered, "I'm surprised the manager of this hotel has been so cool. Last time we were here, we *destroyed* this place." I loved writing these stories, but for every music or pop culture story I did, I made a deal with myself that I'd write a big outdoors story. The authorities finally closed Tompkins Square Park at night. I started to look elsewhere.

Over the winter of 1989–90, the timber wars were ramping up in the West. Years earlier, when I was in college, I had lived in Philo, a tiny village with a weathered old store and a post office just north of Booneville in Mendocino County, so I knew California's coastal mountains a little. I started to dig in. The big timber companies in Northern California, notably Pacific Lumber (Maxxam), Louisiana-Pacific, and Georgia-Pacific, were racing to cut the last of the state's old-growth redwood and Douglas fir before a slew of November 1990 ballot initiatives could stop them. These were some of the last old-growth stands in the country. The logging was resisted by small mobs of local hippies and union members dressed as bears and endangered marbled murrelets and spotted owls stopping logging trucks on Highway 101 and protesting at timber company offices.

The people in costumes were greeted by their neighbors with death threats and attempted murders.

In February 1990, three lead activists named Judi Bari, Darryl Cherney, and Greg King, with whom I'd do a number of stories in the future, put out an alert for a summer of action they called Mississippi Summer in the Redwoods, or Redwood Summer for short. It was modeled after the call for Freedom Riders to come to Mississippi to register African Americans to vote in 1964. Their press release read: "It's going to be a long hard summer in Northern California . . . We are putting out a call for Freedom Riders for the Forest to come to Northern California this summer and defend the last of the redwoods with nonviolent civil disobedience."

That's what Joe and Brett and I needed, I thought. To get dirty saving some trees. I made plans to spend the summer of 1990 reporting in the redwoods. Joe was drifting along, not getting better, not getting worse. Brett was in school. I was obsessed with the idea we should all get to Northern California.

~

Joe and Scott went up to the main branch of Michigan's Manistee River for the trout opener in April 1990. They drove up in Scott's old three-on-the-tree Ford F100 pickup and found a quiet bluff on the Deward Tract near the sacred headwaters of both the Manistee and the Au Sable, where one of the last stands of virgin white pine was cut to end Michigan's timber boom. The man who had owned that timber, David Ward, stipulated in his will that the land could only be logged for ten years after his death, and so in 1910 the mill was dismantled and the town of Deward, which once had as many as eight hundred residents, blew off with the icy winter wind. Only a few chunks of cement buried deep in the grass remained. The big white pines had not returned.

It was cold so they sat in the truck and drank a twelve-pack of beer. Joe was still in and out of the Bronson Hospital talk-therapy program in Oshtemo and wasn't drinking heavily. Scotty wasn't supposed to drink, either, as he'd just finished a round of chemotherapy a few days before.

In the fall after high school, when Joe found short-term employment at the Golden Chain Gang in the mall, Scott started airplane mechanic school in Oklahoma, but it wasn't long before he started feeling sick. Soon he was so sick with a pain in his stomach that he couldn't stand himself, and finally he quit school and moved back to his folks' house on Eagle Lake. He went in for a few tests—a CAT scan, an upper GI X-ray series, a lower GI X-ray series—but nothing turned up. Then one day he was so eaten up with it that he had his folks paged where they were shopping at the massive Meijer Thrifty Acres grocery in Kalamazoo, and they rushed him to the hospital.

Where, once again, their machines found nothing. But even at nineteen years old Scott was a tough old cob. He told the doctor, "Either you open me up right now and do exploratory surgery or I'm going to go home and kill myself. I'm done with this pain."

The doctor said he had to do more tests.

"How long does it take to line that up?" asked Scott.

"Could be tomorrow," the doctor said.

"I'll most likely be dead by then," Scott said, stone-faced. "Last chance." They admitted him and did tests and then opened him up.

Turns out he might have been dead anyway, with a tumor the size of a grapefruit on his lower intestine, which was finally identified as a rare non-Hodgkin lymphoma called Burkitt's lymphoma.

The chemo made the beer taste funny, but Scott figured the cancer would probably kill him in the long run, and it was the trout opener, so they sat in the truck and drank and told funny stories. They fell asleep in the truck and about froze to death, and when they woke up, there was a foot of new snow on the ground.

The water was high but they got out in it in their waders, and it kept coming up as the day got warmer. Pretty soon the air was about seventy degrees Fahrenheit and the snow was gone, but the high water had blown out the fishing.

It was bound to get cold again that night: they were camped right in the heart of that outlandish temperature sink south of Gaylord where it's always ten to twenty degrees colder than anywhere else in the Lower Peninsula, so they decided to move.

"Let's go down to your deer camp," Scott said.

"I'm not allowed," said Joe. "We're not allowed to go there unless Dad or one of my uncles is there. Those are the rules."

By that time, Dad, Vern, and Jack had bought the place from Ike, plus the other twenty acres to the south, too, and they put their rules on it. Joe, Brett, me, and Vern's daughter Jennifer were only allowed when Dad or other elders were there, because we couldn't be trusted, because we listened to rotten music like Judas Priest and Gang of Four. And for nondualistic thinking. But the other kids of these uncles and aunts, who were more pious and went to Christian schools, could go to the cabin unescorted and play hymns on guitars and that kind of thing.

"The uncles would freak out if they found us there," continued Joe.

"Dude, I'm probably dying," said Scott.

"I agree that it makes no fuckin' sense."

"Your dad is cool. He likes me."

"Good old Laughin' Bruce! Be that as it may, you are also banished. For your iniquity."

"What do they think is going to happen?"

"That we're going to go there with a bunch of assholes and drink and wreck the place like we did at Knollwood. Catch the woods on fire."

"But we would never do that. We go up north to get *away* from all those guys."

"I know it!"

"I don't care what we do, but let's go," said Scott. "This river's too high. We have to find another place to fish."

They drove south. The truck drove itself right to the property. It's about a two-hour drive south from the Manistee, and they could camp there for free and fish the PM or the Baldwin. Scott wanted to see it because it was Joe's place, and that made it worse for Joe because it obviously wasn't his place. It was supposed to be his family place, but he was exiled.

They rolled onto the camp in the middle of the day. The travel trailer had been dragged out of there, but the sandy knob where it had sat had been flagged for excavation, the site where Dad was putting the new cabin for the Kuipers Hunt Club, which is what they'd taken to calling it. Since Dad was a contractor, building the cabin was his job. It was obvious from the truck tracks and the stuff lying around that the local builder who was subcontracting the job was there quite a bit, and Joe was nervous someone would drive in any second. He and Scott didn't set up a tent, but laid out their bags on moss-covered sand under the new pole the power company had set up to run a line in from the street. They had a dozen fresh cans of beer.

"We gotta build a fire later," said Scott.

"No fire. Drink this beer," said Joe.

The day was warm and they wanted to explore, but Joe told Scott to stay away from the new cabin site.

"Don't even go over there. We can't get boot prints around it."

"What?"

"If they see boot prints I swear they will take pictures and make me show them my boots. They'll call the sheriff and launch a whole thing."

"Joe, I gotta say: Fuck this. We're grown men. With lymphoma. All we're trying to do is camp and fish and be in the woods. That's what hunting camps are supposed to be for."

They walked over the pine litter so they wouldn't leave footprints and climbed up in a maple tree that looked down on the yellow sand of the cabin site and drank their beer.

"I can't believe you put up with this bullshit," said Scott, throwing a can down.

They stayed up almost all night with their eyes turned upward to the star-spackled black. They walked out into a five-acre field that was the first opening you encountered coming in from the road so we came to call it First Field. It was pure sand covered with a crust of reindeer moss and ant lions and one or two dried-up sticks of grass. The men lay down there and looked at the sky. The place called to both of them, and they wished they could cut wood or shovel sand or do something to earn their keep. Being there made you want to do something.

To the northeast, the Big Dipper hung in the sky because summer was coming.

"The big, fuckin' . . . chair. It looks like a chair," said Scott.

"The Big Chair."

⁓

On May 24, 1990, the Redwood Summer organizers Judi Bari and Darryl Cherney were car bombed in Oakland, California. I was still living in New York but had been talking to a group in Berkeley called Seeds of Peace, whose members were gearing up to provide the support camp for the summer of resistance. Bari and Cherney had just left the Seeds house that morning on their way to Santa Cruz to play a concert to recruit activists when a motion-activated pipe bomb wrapped in nails exploded under the driver's seat of Bari's Subaru wagon. The bomb shattered her pelvis and shot nails through her body and left her hovering near death, and blew out Cherney's eardrums. The first authorities to reach the car, before Oakland PD or an ambulance, were the FBI. That was odd. Bari said later, "As though they were waiting around the corner with their fingers in their ears." She didn't die, but the environmental movement all over America took notice: singing funny songs about habitat would now get you killed.

That story became my priority, but I had a few assignments to finish first. I was working down in the coastal Louisiana town of Morgan City, a depressing place where they built and manned the oil-drilling platforms that dotted the Gulf. I was doing a story for *Spin* about oil-field workers who had become pirates, dismantling and selling oil equipment on the black market. I had ridden my beat old BMW R100 motorcycle down there from New York City, and I drove out into the Atchafalaya at night to listen to the roar of insects, frogs, and birds. For about a week, I lived in a disused van in the yard of a crawfisherman I had befriended until his neighbor got stabbed to death by his wife while they were on a drunk about fifty yards from where I was sleeping, and everyone decided having the press around was just too freaky, so they asked me to clear out.

I called Joe from a pay phone but didn't get him, then got Mom at work. She said Joe was punching holes in the walls in the apartment and was doing his best to disappear into them. He'd dropped into a new, swirling depression, she said, and I had to get up there. So I turned away from California and headed toward Michigan.

I drove into New Orleans. I stayed one night with some friends, planning to head north in the morning, and we all went out to a place on Bourbon Street where one of them was tending bar. We ordered one pitcher of beer between five or six people and then it was about twelve hours later. I woke up feeling great and had no idea what had happened. "You are a total asshole," said my former friend, who evidently had stopped being my friend during the night. I had blacked out, which had never happened to me before, and then gone mobile, trying to jump from one convertible to another while we were driving, making enemies, puking on one bar or another, breaking off the key in the elevator and waking the whole building by ringing the alarm.

I was asked to clear out again and walked down Magazine Street looking for my motorcycle. I was scared my brother would die, but I guess no one would know that because no one was talking to me anymore. I threw up next to a fire hydrant, and as I was bent over at the curb a car went off the road and smashed into the hydrant, and all I did was pull my hand off the top of the hydrant as the car's bumper crumpled on it and kept on puking.

I found my bike in an alley in the French Quarter and my helmet bowled down to the end against a house. Evidently I had driven it there. I packed a few things into the hardbags and then got on I-55 and lay down on the gas tank, sick as anything, and didn't really look up again for fifteen hours and a thousand miles.

My then girlfriend, Anne, had been with me on part of this trip and flew home to work, and my vomit-flavored hangover cracked open my general feelings of morbid guilt. I had thought of myself as more successful than Joe, more together, but I was probably worse. I was cheating on Anne with one of the editors at *Spin*. I had been trying not to think about why. What the hell was wrong with me? Anne was fierce and soulful and real as a mountain and I was honestly in love with her, so the idea that I'd sneak into this other woman's bed filled me with self-loathing. Endless fields of calf-high corn ripped past like a roaring belt sander of righteousness and tore away what remained of my self-respect. I understood more about Dad in those hours than I ever had before. I didn't want to be like him. He had abused and degraded my mother, and driven her almost to the end of her sanity. I *wasn't* like him—I didn't have any kids; I wasn't married. But did that matter? I couldn't be like him because I fell deeply in love with my girlfriends. But then I thought: *Maybe he did, too.* I had never thought of that idea before, and it sickened me. Maybe he was not only using women to cloak himself in a reality he didn't have or couldn't feel, but he simply fell hard for anyone who paid him any attention. That was desperate and weak. I was like that. People in New Orleans didn't like me anymore. I looked down at the pavement drifting by at ninety miles per hour inches beneath my feet and saw the easy way out. I thought I should just pick up Joe and head north, into Canada, see how far we could get before we were both dead in a ditch and covered in flies. I stopped sniveling about this after a couple of hours, and when I pulled into Mom's apartment in Texas Corners I had nothing but tape hiss in my head.

"Well, you look like dogshit," Joe said when I got there. My long hair was dirty and wind-whipped and still had puke in it. My leather jacket, helmet, shirt, and neck were plastered with bug splatter. The pipes on my bike plinked and tinked as they cooled, the smoking-hot metal warping through rainbows of decalescent color. The fields beyond the new little fourplexes smelled of hot briars and crabgrass the way summery old corn-sand will.

"Yep," I said, sitting down on the outside steps. "How you doing?"

"Oh, you know." He sat down next to me and lit a cigarette.

"Me, too," I said. How was I supposed to help him get his life together? I was a total fraud. We were quiet. Huge grasshoppers snapped and scissored over the field of briars. I'd been home all of a minute and we'd already said most of what we were going to say.

~

Mom called me in New York a month or so later, in July, and started in crisply, "*Well.* I just wanted to let you know," and I knew Joe was dead. I had never seen or heard my mother cry, ever, and there had been lots to cry about, so I knew when that call came she'd be crisp about it instead of blubbering. It was just her way. So the crispness folded my legs up and I slunk down against the wall in my apartment and sat on the floor.

"Joe's in a hospital . . ." she continued.

So he wasn't dead. I had my hand in my armpit and started shivering like I was freezing cold.

". . . a psychiatric hospital . . ."

She talked for a while and said stuff I couldn't hear, and then I tried to stop my stomach from shaking and said, "So, physically, he's okay?"

"Well, that part will be okay, I think. But he is not okay."

A few nights before, Mom had come home late. Her new beau, Tom, was sometimes around, but he had his own apartment and wasn't with her. Mom walked in and found a framed picture of Joe shattered on the floor and glass everywhere. Joe was out on the porch outside his room raking a big glass shard down his forearm as rivulets of blood ran out on the floor. He wasn't saying anything, but Mom said she could see he had regressed, like a child.

"So I talked to him like a mother to a small child," she said. "I said, 'Joey, Mom's going to help you, okay? Put this wet towel on your arm. Come inside. Come inside, now.'"

Joe crawled into the apartment and lay on the hallway floor in the fetal position, like he had done many times before.

"'I'm going to call Daddy now, okay? Daddy's going to come.'"

Dad rushed over there and on the way he called a psych hospital that some church people had told him about. He was the first guy we knew to have a car phone and had had one for years. He scooped up Joe and Nancy and drove them all at one hundred miles per hour, which was how he always drove anyway, straight to Grand Rapids. Where Joe was committed and the door was locked. Nancy didn't know much more.

A few days later, Joe called me from a pay phone inside the place after they'd moved him into residential care.

"I really love you, brother," I said.

"I don't deserve it."

"That's not how it works."

"I know, but that kinda makes it worse. It would be easier if you were faking it. Because how can you love me when I don't? That means something's wrong with me. I look at myself, I see a piece of shit. I don't have what it takes to *not* see that. I'm missing a gene or something."

"When did you last actually feel good?"

"On the river with Scott."

"How's Scotty?"

"I don't know. He doesn't want to die."

"How is it in there?"

"This place? Oh, it's all right now. I'm pretty happy to just hole up in my room and sleep."

"Anybody come see you?"

"No. I don't care. I don't care who knows I'm here or not."

"You remember I was up at Holland Hospital when I was going to Hope College?"

"I know something happened. As usual with our family, Dad was so ashamed of it he pretended it never happened. He never told us a goddamn thing."

"Well, I had to take a little break."

"What happened?"

"I wanted to quit that school, and I couldn't figure out how to do it."

If you were in the Christian Reformed Church, you attended either Calvin College or Hope, and quitting that school, for me, meant quitting the religion. I needed to do both. In my freshman year, I bought an old Kawasaki KH400 and drove it to Chicago, then climbed the fire escape on a high-rise along the Gold Coast and sat near the top, swinging my legs and looking down at the dark, cold lake. It would have been a lot easier to die than to face leaving the church, but I climbed down and went back to school. The break was already in me, though.

I never had to leave the church; they threw me out. I did leave Hope in my sophomore year, and a few months later I got a letter from the consistory saying, "Your membership has been terminated." The letter was signed by the nice dad of a nice kid I played football against. The CRC doesn't have excommunication, per se; they called it "disfellowship." Not a single church member contacted me to ask what was going on. I figured Bruce simply told them to kick me out.

The only way to leave Hope was to decide I didn't care. I spent a week or so in the psych wing at Holland Hospital not caring.

I was in a locked ward with about a dozen other people, and we had all these group therapies. It was torture because one or two of the people were actually nuts, and when you heard them talk you just knew they would kill themselves the minute they got back on the street. I felt like I was in there to keep those people alive. There was a woman in there from my biology class at school. The campus was only a couple of blocks away, so when people bugged out this is where they came. She asked me what was going on, and I said, "I think it would be called a 'crisis of faith.'" Since it was a religious school, she understood. "You can't take that stuff so seriously," she said. She was totally sane.

Mom and Dad were in Maui on a business trip, but someone got hold of them. I was going to leave the school and a couple of administrators came to see me, and the iffy looks on their faces made it seem like they were happy to get rid of me. Finally my folks showed up, and they brought me a whole beautiful pineapple from Hawaii. The staff said I could have it, so the woman from biology and I went in the little kitchenette and carved it up. They gave us some kind of plastic knife and we hacked away at it, just talking and sawing until we had eaten the whole thing. Pineapple is crazy acidic and we just chomped it down, carried away by how exotic it was—"Wow! Yum! So good!"—without noticing that our mouths had started to bleed. We never felt it until both of us had paper towels jammed on our faces to stop the blood from pouring off our dissolved lips.

It was good to feel that stinging and smell the iron-and-ozone of blood. When I felt that, I knew I wasn't crazy. I just couldn't explain to anyone in the church or its school that human minds were partly made by rivers and fields and that rivers and fields could be driven insane. I figured I better keep that to myself.

"Send me a pineapple," Joe said from the lockup. "I want to try that."

"Naw, see, I already ruined it by telling you it makes your mouth bleed."

"But it's real. Bleeding is real."

There was a long silence from somewhere in Grand Rapids.

"They put me in a Christian rehab, man," said Joe.

"Oh shit. Really? Is that going to be okay?"

"I can't tell yet. I just want to be a real person. Somebody has to agree that *I am here*, that I am flesh and blood and I don't feel good and that it's not because God thinks I'm a bad person or some lies like that. I drink because I don't feel good. If they start telling me Jesus wants me to do this or that, they're going to have a corpse on their hands. I want what's *real*."

That day I mailed him some things I had in the apartment in New York. My dog-eared copy of *The Nick Adams Stories*. Some promo cassette tapes of music that hadn't come out yet in stores, by Jane's Addiction and some other bands. He didn't tell me this until years later, but up until that point in his life Joe had never actually read a whole book. He was almost twenty years old. But he read that one.

This was late July 1990, and I just couldn't be anywhere except with Joe. So Anne and I packed up our apartment at Third and A in the space of a week and we were gone. We were headed to Michigan for however long, and then on to San Francisco for new lives.

We rented a big truck and put the motorcycle and all our stuff in it. Somewhere in the back of my mind, I did think of this as a way to remake my relationship to Anne. I knew that Dad always did this and that it never worked, but there had to be some good to come out of all this insane stress. Straight out of high school, Anne had been managing bands and running punk and dance music labels, working at Factory, Rough Trade, and Blast First, but she'd decided to move on and she had already enrolled for the fall term at UC Berkeley, where her father was a world-renowned mathematician. So we just moved up our departure date. *Spin* very quickly made a position for me as their West Coast editor, and my first assignment there was to look into the car bombing and Redwood Summer. As we rolled West, I prayed that Joe would be all right, that Anne and I would be all right, that all of us would survive the summer.

The day we left New York City, my nose stopped bleeding.

~

Brett and our family friend Mike, whose folks had owned the Texas Take Out, were on their way to see a rock concert in Grand Rapids and decided to stop at the rehab. Joe had been tangled in a life-or-death struggle for so long that Brett was ready for anything that might bring some positive change, but the locked doors did make it clear that there was some chance our little brother might cark it. For that reason, Brett wasn't planning on staying long. Too much exposure would just wreck him.

On some level with which he was not really in touch, Brett was angry at Joe for making a fuss about his life and causing everyone to be in a panic about him cutting himself and beer-bonging vodka and eating fistfuls of acid and being a selfish turd. Brett was twenty-one years old and deadly practical, and his obvious solution was that Joe should just move away from Dad and live his life in the wilderness somewhere. Brett wanted Joe to be okay, but he'd done a lot of two A.M. rescues and he needed an end to all this acting out. Like me, he'd been dreading Joe's death for so long that he was worn out. He hoped this rehab place would work. Joe couldn't just go on demanding everybody's attention forever.

But then there they were, he and Mike, in the visiting room with Joe. He looked pale and had fresh scars on his arm but was otherwise the same as ever.

"What's up, dude?" Brett asked, sitting down as he fished out a pack of Camel Lights.

"Nothing much, just hanging out," Joe said, already smoking.

All three of them were serious smokers and they had smokes, so they focused on really, really smoking. They smoked indoors because Michigan was one of those indoor-smoking places, like Murmansk. There were other people in the room, including a woman they all noticed who was Joe's age and who was in the back talking to someone else.

"You guys ever seen that new show, *Northern Exposure?*" Joe asked. He had begun watching that show during his free time, to give some focus to the obsessive, circular thoughts that otherwise ran round and round his head. The staff had already established that Joe had a high IQ and an outrageous memory: a clinician kept giving him longer and longer sequences of ordered numbers, saying them out loud, and even when they got very long Joe could repeat them back no sweat. He discovered in this task that he used music as his mnemonic strategy. Music happens in a temporal line; it unrolls sequentially, and Joe found he associated numbers with notes in a song. And then when he wasn't talking with a therapist or being tested or probed, he watched TV, and this show *Northern Exposure* was about a doctor from New York City practicing in a small town in Alaska. Neither Brett nor Mike had seen it.

"Anyway, you should check it out," said Joe. "I've watched a couple episodes now, and I was sitting here and I thought: *I could just go there.* Alaska looks fantastic. Big flat rivers full of salmon. Eagles. Bears. People are fishing and splitting wood. Sitting in here is so depressing."

"This is what I've been saying," said Brett. "You can make that happen yourself, without any of this getting in the way. It's your life."

They only stayed about fifteen minutes and Brett and Mike asked about the program in the joint, but Joe didn't really go into it too much.

"I just do whatever they tell me to do until I can get out of here," he said.

Then he leaned in and quietly added, "You see that girl over there? We were out in the sunroom and she seduced me. We had sex in the sunroom in the middle of the day. That was awesome."

"Okay, well, cool. Hope you're okay," Brett said, getting up to go.

≈

Anne and I got to Dad's house with the moving truck at night, and he was full of nervous energy. "Captain Midnight!" he shouted as he greeted us on the cement apron in front of his garage. Sitting in the kitchen, he told us Joe was getting out for the weekend. "But when he gets here, don't ask about the hospital or any of that," Dad said.

"What? Of course I'm going to ask him about it. That's why I just drove seven hundred miles," I said.

"Nope, nope, see—we have to keep this whole thing quiet, because Joe will be so embarrassed. We don't want anybody to know about this," said Dad. He stooped his shoulders to emphasize the weight of this burden.

"Every single person in Kalamazoo already knows. Joe is like a party celebrity."

"Well, it will be harder for him if everybody starts to look at him funny," said Dad. "So let's just not talk about it."

"You can't treat Joe like he has to keep a terrible secret, or you're just going to make him worse. You'll kill him," I said.

"No, it's the stigma that will kill him," he said, shaking his head.

"Look, you sent him to a psych hospital that's run by your church and Dutch people who are all related to one another. Within the space of an hour I'm sure every one of our thirty-four first cousins already knew he was in there. A couple of them probably work there. Joe doesn't care about that."

Bruce looked at the floor and sighed. I knew the place was expensive, and he was thinking that money bought him some secrecy. He was pissed off at the idea that Joe and I might mess that up.

"We're going to give him a chance to get better," Dad said finally.

"And *talking* is what's going to do it," I said.

～

Joe was pale when he got out of Dad's truck, pale and puffy and unshaven and furtive like a guy with a world-record hangover. He stood in the driveway at Dad's house in the hickories and smoked. The scars on his arm were still white and pink.

"Hello, brother," I said.

"Hello," he replied with a show of teeth.

His mullet was long. I hugged him and his body felt powerful; it was like hugging a black bear. His face was soft but he could snap me in two.

"Are you okay?" I whispered.

"Oh, I don't know," he said.

"Is the lockup all right?"

"Nah, it's a fucking nightmare. But I'm going to get out of there pretty soon."

We sat in the screened porch, drinking iced tea to the pulsing electric howl and fiddle of cicadas and spring peepers breaking in waves across the trees. Brett came to the house for a little while. He wasn't much interested in why Anne and I were moving to San Francisco. "Well, you're just moving far away again, and all this shit is going on here and all of us have to deal with it when you're gone," he said. We sat gulping at the scintillating, overwhelming roar of the forest until deep in the night.

In the morning, Joe and I sat on the floor of Dad's pole barn working on Joe's motorcycle, a corroded old Yamaha that wasn't running. We really needed Brett and his mechanical genius, but while Joe and I tried to figure it out, Joe talked. Anne sat with us and took photos.

"Dean told me you don't like the rehab," Anne said.

"Oh, the regular staff are okay, they really try to help you. But the doctors are such arrogant cocks."

"Doesn't that defeat the whole purpose?"

"Well, I think so," he said. "Their basic assumption doesn't work for someone like me. I tell them I feel ill or depressed, and then these cocks, they don't ask me much about why I feel that way, because they already know. They tell me, right to my face, that I feel that way because I don't have a relationship to Jesus Christ, and if I did, then I would feel good.

"Pain is supposed to be the body's way of telling you something is really wrong. So I go in there thinking, 'Shit, I'm a real flesh-and-blood person with real feelings and real problems,' and they say, 'No, you're just an ungrateful dick who rejects Christ so fuck off.' They assume it's my fault I feel bad. But it's not my fault; I just feel bad. Every day in this place I'm told, 'All the feelings you have are wrong.'"

Somewhere during that explanation I realized that Dad and Mom had taken me to see a counselor once who was affiliated with the same place they had taken Joe. I had had questions born of the chaos of their shattered relationship, but the very first words out of that guy's mouth were: "Let's get on our knees and pray for forgiveness for your arrogance and your disrespect to your parents." I had left them on their knees and walked out, but I had had more ego left than Joe did.

"If I can't be a real person, they don't understand that they're leaving me no choice but to kill myself," Joe said.

I sat there on the cool concrete floor of Dad's barn with my hands caked with grease.

"Well, then we're going to get you out of there," I said to Joe.

"Oh, whatever. Dad feels good about the place."

"I'll talk to him."

"Don't. It's fine. Seriously. It's a pretty expensive place. I give them files full of stories so they feel like they really cracked me. I just talk and talk. But I know it's wasted breath because in the end they cannot care about anything except my salvation."

"What I care about is that you just said you had to kill yourself."

"But see, if I choose to live, despite all their bullshit and lies, then I win," Joe said, smiling.

"Right, but they're not helping you live. They're convincing you to go the other way."

"So what's new? Nobody helps me. Now when I get time to myself I sit there listening to that Jane's Addiction tape you sent me. That's about all I do but at least that music is real."

Ritual de lo Habitual hadn't been released yet and Joe was one of its first devoted listeners. He lay in his room with a Walkman and let his head fill with the soaring bass-driven suite of songs that constitute the second half of the recording: "Three Days," "Then She Did . . . ," "Of Course," and "Classic Girl." Lots of stuff that is pretty about this album was born in pain and awareness, like the song "Then She Did . . . ," which is about Perry Farrell's mother, who committed suicide when he was only three years old. In the song, she meets in the afterlife with Perry's girl-friend, who died of an overdose. Joe figured if someone could live through that kind of double loss and make something out of it that was not only beautiful but also reverent and even celebratory, a paean to life itself, then there was hope for him, too.

"That album saved my life," Joe said. "That's not an exaggeration."

I'll have to tell Perry that one day. We cranked over the Yamaha for a bit and it ran.

"Hey!" said Dad as Joe buzzed it up and down the driveway. "It runs!"

"We want to go to a river," I told him.

"Let's go see the new cabin," said Dad.

~

I didn't want to go to the cabin because I was afraid of the disappoint-ment. It couldn't be what we wanted, so why subject ourselves to the misery? I had come here to see Joe, not indulge Dad's happy-family fantasy. But Joe was only out of rehab for the weekend, and Dad was so excited about the cabin he had just built on the deer camp. In fact, he had stopped referring to it as "the deer camp" and started calling it "the cabin." Joe didn't really want to go there, either, but he told me, "Oh, what the fuck. At least it's outdoors," and then off we went.

Dad was forty-six and divorced and starting to make real money with Delta Design so of course he bought a Harley. We gave him no end of shit about it. He tried to hide his distress at the way it messed up his pretty black hair. We teased him: "Gonna get the outlaw gang back together and open a hair salon?"

"Screw you guys; I was riding before you were born," he replied, looking hurt. That was true; I have an old black-and-white picture of me astride his Honda 90 while I was still in diapers.

Anne rode with Dad and Joe rode with me on my BMW. His old Yamaha wasn't running well enough to take it that far. It was good to have a direction shaped only by hot August wind. Vectors and curls of air hurrying eastward rushed at us from across the bright Concord vineyards and the backs of Holsteins. Beyond every fencerow rose more sizzling hay and corn. We stopped to run our hands through the yellow water of the Rabbit River where it tumbled over the short millpond dam at Hamilton.

Joe told me not to expect too much from the deer camp. It had twenty acres of popple that had been logged for pulp and pallets about five or more years earlier, a good bit of forested swamp, and then a lot of sand up front along the road.

"Ike said he never put any hogs or anything on that seventy-five because it was all sand," Dad said. "His boy, Iran, saw a lot of deer in there, though."

I had reread Aldo Leopold's *A Sand County Almanac* during the conflict over Tompkins Square Park, and I thought there might be some parallels with Bruce's place. As far as I could tell, they seemed similar in their soil and their history, and the reasons they came into the lives of our respective families. Leopold was looking for a hunting camp in 1934 when he bought a ruined farm along the Wisconsin River for eight bucks an acre, a lot of blow-sand cut over during the big timber boom and then put to corn that had quickly exhausted the thin humus. His place in "Sand County," which was a made-up name, had a tiny old outbuilding on it that he rebuilt as a cabin and that his five kids called "the shack." The spring geese and woodcock he observed so beautifully in that book came around as he and his wife and kids all dug in to replant the native pines. But then he saw more.

Leopold was no mystic, but rather a scientist largely regarded as the father of modern wild game management, and he came to see the moral purpose and even the fate of humankind as intertwined with the land. This revelation came from observing his family's engagement with the worn-out cornfields: the more time Leopold's family spent at the shack, the more the place called to them, and they started restoring it to native plants. The more the place responded to their restoration work, the more they all loved it. It wasn't an economic transaction; it was a love relationship. It was relatedness. The love they felt for each other came partly from the land, and Leopold saw he needed to extend ethical consideration to it. His subsequent essay, "The Land Ethic," stated that the biotic community that included the land deserved more than just an economic value, but actual moral or ethical protection.

"We can be ethical only in relation to something we can see, feel, understand, love, or otherwise have faith in," he wrote in that essay.

Maybe we had that kind of sand farm, I didn't know. The only hunting cabin I had ever known was Mr. Card's, which was a square box of peeled pine logs with two small bedrooms and a bathroom behind a large room with a fieldstone fireplace and an open kitchen. He ran a generator for electricity and water. I figured Dad was building a cabin like that.

But I was afraid to expect anything from it. I wasn't about to plant a berry bush and then get criticized if it grew thorns or died. I was desperate to get my hands in that dirt, but everything I'd ever known about Dad said it was a setup for judgment and failure. He was too rigid and controlling to let this be a place of freedom. Leopold's family was probably close-knit long before they started restoring their land, and both their feelings and their place only got better as they worked. I believed, sadly, that Dad had some idea like that in his own head, but we weren't close.

Joe seemed happy to be out on the road, so I decided to simply enjoy a nice ride together. We were on our way to a green spot on the map.

After about three hours of riding, we got into a remote area near the White River, and Dad slowed down on a piece of humpy two-lane where the swamp and winter frost had heaved the road up in spots. We plowed through thick clouds of gnats and turned onto a two-track entering the camp. You could barely see the entrance in the tall grass along the road, and that's how the uncles liked it. The heavy bikes slowly bounced along the two-track with a blackwater forest of red maple and aspen to the left; on the right shimmered acre after acre of lichen-covered yellow sand. Joe wasn't kidding when he said the front seventy-five was mostly sand. South of this big field stood a five-acre plantation of orange, wind-gnarled Scots pines and then more exposed sand with the occasional tree stuck in it. The sun was intense when the wind dropped. White cumulous clouds blotted the blue sky. A long train of deerflies formed behind us as we rolled up the sandy tractor path to a thin stand of forty-foot red pines and a spanking new cabin beneath them sided in blood-brown cedar, where we stopped.

I pulled off my helmet and the place rushed at me. A stand of aspen along the swamp shimmered and hurrahed. The flies looped in comet-like trajectories. Slow-building gusts of hot west wind puffed out the cheeks of the red pines above us, blown out in long, satisfied exhalations, *shwaaaaaaahhhhhhhhhh*. The absence of human sounds was tremendous. The shade falling on the cabin smelled of pine and the root-beer odor of sassafras roots pulled from disturbed sand and reindeer lichen and black swamp muck and a long emptiness.

As green spots on the map go, it was everything that I ever wanted in this world. Dad knew us so well. I knew he honestly wanted all of us to love it. I did love it, instantly.

Dad combed his hair and moved us into the cabin, which was a small, pine-smelling house with a walkout basement. It had a good-sized living room and three teeny bedrooms upstairs for the uncles and aunts and then three bunkrooms downstairs and double doors to the outside wide enough to drive a tractor into the basement. He had begun construction in May and now it was the end of August and it was pretty much done. Brett was the only one who had seen it under construction, as he had used the wheezy old Delta Design truck to deliver the pine siding that made up the interior walls. The curtains were hung. It was full of a mish-mash of furnishings and appliances from the houses of my uncles and aunts. I pushed the curtains back and stared out the windows.

"No, hey, we keep the curtains shut so the deer don't see us," said Dad.

I looked at him. "It's the middle of summer."

"We just don't want to spook them," he said. "Let's leave them closed."

This didn't bode well. I jerked the slider open and went out on the sand where the porch would be. If I was going to spook the deer, I was going to spook them all the way. It was searing hot in the sun. Out in front of the cabin lay a two-acre field of sand with a couple of immature oaks. I needed to feel that field under my feet, so I walked out there. Dad came out and draped a white handkerchief on his coif to keep the bugs off, then pointed out the lay of the place: the 75-acre front piece ran parallel to the road, and then the 20-acre woodlot came off it to the south like the stem of a *T*. He had showed us on the plat map how, south of that stand of pulpwood, lay a 120-acre beaver bog marked "USA," which meant it was federal land.

"I need to see that bog," I said, suddenly feeling like a man set before a gigantic feast. The bog lay in the center of the mile-square section, far from the road no matter which side you came in on. "Let's go back there."

Dad said he didn't want to disturb the place by walking through it, but he could see I was excited, and after a minute he relented. The two-track leading through the south twenty was pocked everywhere with hoofprints large and small; deer were thick in there. Turkeys had kicked up the leaves and we found marks in the sand where a grouse had dusted its feathers against ticks. We spent some time by the bog examining a great old hollow yellow birch full of porcupines and ringed with an avalanche of porcupine poo. But you wouldn't say the place was pretty. It was a wreck. The openings on the front seventy-five were like the pictures of Leopold's sand farm before he started to plant, when it was just a few trees sticking out of thin grass and weeds. In contrast with the dense third-growth oak forests, cedar swamps, and lush farm fields that lay all around it, this deer camp was caught between phases: it wasn't a forest or a swamp or a farm. As we kicked through it, our bootlaces and pant legs were bejeweled with burdock and sand bur. The twenty-acre popple woodlot was thick with head-high suckers, and beyond that was the bog where loons and geese were screaming. The front acreage seemed starved for shade. It was like a beggar with her hand out on the side of a lost country road.

The horticulturalist John Evelyn wrote in his 1664 book, *Sylva*, the first great book on forestry, "The earth, especially if fresh, has a certain magnetism in it, by which it attracts the salt, power, or virtue (call it either) which gives it life, and it is the logic of all the labor and stir we keep about it, to sustain us."

Evelyn and I were both interested in the relationship between this "magnetism" and the "salt, power, or virtue" it attracts. How the call goes out for all the elements that sustain life and how the call is answered. This place was calling. Screaming. This imperfect, manhandled place had its own appeal and its own needs. It needed us. I heard it loud and clear. The land presented itself, and I could feel glimpses of the heavy forest it probably once was, dense with towering hemlock and white pine, and what it could be again with some attention. Maybe part of the salt it attracted was us. I was suddenly very aware of my feet.

Joe seemed shy when confronted by the place. He was fuzzy from the long ride and he was quiet and distracted. He looked out over the bog and seemed to listen intently. He cocked his head toward the ground and looked up into the tops of the trees and didn't say much. He swatted at mosquitoes like the rest of us. He walked in silence.

When we got back to the cabin, Joe went up a sugar maple and stood there on a low branch for a while, just three or four feet off the ground, like the earth was too hot to stand on. Joe had always had a certain soft-footedness when he was sober, a way of hanging back. Anne took a photo of him there that is one of my favorites. In it, he looks like a child caught in a game of hide-and-seek.

"You should put the open fields here to grass," I said to Dad.

"Oh, the deer have lots of stuff to eat. Plus, we don't want to go out there and booger everything up."

"How would that booger it up?" asked Joe from his tree.

"All the farming and stuff. We just want to keep it quiet here. That's what deer like. There's farms all around; this is where they can come to hide."

We had made Dad happy and that counted for something. But after Joe came down, he and I both remarked that it was odd we had come *here* when Joe only had a day or two to be out in the world. Some of Joe's troubles—and, for that matter, mine and Mom's and Brett's—were the result of Dad defining our world and determining how we could be in it, and yet, here we were, letting it go right on happening.

He and I stood in the shade of the red pines, and I knelt down and put my hands in the coarse sand. The iron-tinted sand dug out of the basement was tawny gold, probably Roselawn or Rubicon sand, and I imagined it extending down hundreds of feet.

"Dad really likes it here," I said.

"*I* really like here," said Joe.

"You do?"

"Yeah."

"Me, too. What do you like about it?" I asked.

"It's so imperfect—and yet, Dad likes it. He's proud of it, he's claimed it as his place and he barely even knows it. He's protective of it. See, that's what I want."

∿

We all ducked into the cabin for a drink of water, and I saw Dad's shoulders up around his ears with tension and I thought, *Oh no, he's going to have a talk with us.* It was such a rare event I didn't know whether to be scared or curious. But I was twenty-six years old: even if he said something outrageous, I could just walk away from it. What did he want to talk about? Drugs and drinking? About what happened between him and Mom, finally? Maybe he met someone new? He kept his girlfriends secret the whole time they were married, so if he did have a serious romance maybe it was hard to talk about. I tried to give him the benefit of the doubt. Anne took one shot of me sitting at the kitchen table laughing with Joe and putting a good face on it. Joe was singing Jane's Addiction's "Standing in the Shower . . . Thinking," and Dad didn't know why we were laughing. It was because we both knew he was about to ruin everything.

"*And the water is piping hot!*" sang Joe.

"I thought it was, '*And the water is fucking hot*,' " I said.

"That's because you have a filthy mind!" yelled Joe. "Filth!"

"Well, I just want to let you know that this isn't going to be like old Bernard Card's place," Dad started, breaking the tension.

"I like Bernie's cabin," I said. "It's great there."

"Well, he's a generous man and he really likes you, but there was a lot that went on there that I just didn't appreciate." I could see this had been bugging him for years. His jaw was tightened around a kind of half smile, probably for Anne's benefit. Bernie drank whiskey and his guests told dirty jokes, and once in a while he had a wild guest who might shoot extra deer or stay up drinking all night and bounce a car through the woods. Bernard's sons and daughters-in-law were very serious hunters, but these one or two others were what Dad called "slob hunters." Slob hunters were people who poached or drank or thought it was funny to use a military weapon for hunting, or who killed for sport or left wounded animals in the woods. The idea that someone might mess up his hunting or make it somehow unethical made Dad visibly anxious. When we stayed with Mr. Card in his log cabin, Dad would wash dishes after dinner as everyone prepared to drink and play euchre and then he'd go straight to bed as a kind of protest. I'd play cards and eventually fall asleep on the floor in front of the big fireplace.

"I shouldn't have taken you boys up there and I apologize for it. I wouldn't do that today. I don't think that was sending the right message."

"I'm not sorry," I said. "You taught me how to watch the woods at that place. That was really important to me."

"We're just not going to have that atmosphere," Dad said. "We're not going to have anybody up here except family."

I thought of a line from an old church song—and we know all of them—"Like a bird from prison bars has flown, I'll fly away." I was already halfway out the door. Bruce had created another place to separate himself from the dirty old world. Up here at the Kuipers Hunt Club, we weren't going to talk about any shitty divorce or anybody slashing their arms with broken glass. No way! If that stuff had to happen, it didn't happen here. This place was about the communion of saints.

Dad then grimly spat out the rules that he and the uncles had made to keep the place pure, so nobody would "booger it up": No going out into the woods when it wasn't hunting season. No wandering the place or camping out on it or putting in sit-spots that were unapproved, not even over on the USA. No bushwacking off the trails. No tearing around with motocross motorcycles, which Brett had, or snowshoes or skis. No hunting with dogs at all, because everybody knows dogs run deer, and no dogs in the cabin. No drinking. No smoking. No bonfires. No visits without one of the three uncles present. No guests. And, above all, no dirty boots in the cabin. Don't bring the outside in.

"That way, it can be for the whole family," Dad said. He looked at Joe.

"Sounds about right," Joe lied, then sang: "*The water is so piping ha-ah-ot!*" Joe looked out the window. Dad clearly believed this place had something to do with keeping Joe alive, but from the look on my brother's soft and puffy face I thought that was unlikely.

"How do you feel, Joe?" asked Anne, seeing his faraway eyes.

"I like all them people just fine," he said, answering a different question.

"We can fish the PM and the Baldwin from here, too," I said. "It's so close."

"Well, it's not a hotel," Dad said.

"What do you mean?"

"Pretty soon everybody would be staying here to go fishing or canoeing or whatever. We didn't build it for that. It's for hunting this property."

Dad made being in the woods sound like a cruel psychology experiment: short hours on the land while hunting and then long hours shut indoors with shitloads of people; fourteen or fifteen uncles, aunts, and cousins were expected in the fall, and our cousins hadn't even started having babies yet. Like being rolled up in a piece of carpet with just a circle of light showing at the end.

The place had the potential to be so beautiful, but there was no way we could hang here.

"We're going to fill these woods with hot lead!" Joe suddenly joked, perking up. I knew from the way he said it he'd just come to a decision; they'd be lucky if he stayed here even one night. Where would he go in the middle of the night if he couldn't sleep? Where would he walk? Where would he smoke? How could you watch the night if you got in trouble for even opening the curtains?

"The hunting is going to be awesome here," I said, backing him up.

Dad jumped on our comments, taking them for enthusiasm, "Oh, you guys should come in the fall when all your cousins are here. We really will have *so much fun.*"

Joe and I went out on the sand and stood looking up at the tall red pines alongside the cabin and Joe lit a cigarette.

Dad put his head out the slider: "Joe, we really don't want smoking up here because the deer can smell it," he said, hanging in the doorway.

"Dad, I'm gonna smoke this cigarette," Joe said without pulling his gaze out of the trees. He wasn't angry. The clouds formed question marks in the sky. The world was vast and had its own agenda. Dad withdrew and closed the slider after him.

"It's like prison with camo," I said.

"On the other hand, that's the most Dad's talked to me in at least ten years," Joe said.

In the quiet between us, my body pitched toward the fields out there. I could feel my whole organism responding to the call of the place. I knew Joe felt it, too. I wanted to slosh through every inch of those marshy woods and find every porcupine and watch every fawn being born and coax blades of grass out of the hot sand one by one. I looked at the sky and thought of a phrase that the phenomenologist Maurice Merleau-Ponty had written in his book *Phenomenology of Perception*; when describing the blue of the sky, he noted that he wasn't merely observing the sky but communicating with it. He and the sky each had their own subjectivity, and together they shared an intersubjectivity. He borrowed a line from Paul Valéry and said of the sky: "It thinks itself within me." That sky thought itself within me.

But Dad, on the contrary, had built a monument to his own separateness. There wasn't space for us in it. It was crushing, because the dirt that he was offering was the best ever.

I went from being disappointed to being pissed off as we rumbled back out to the tarred road. Joe sat behind me on the BMW in a kind of daze. Dad had built him a place to heal and then denied him half the medicine. The Hunt Club's dualistic strategy—to keep man and nature totally separate—was more of the same wrongheaded shit we'd grown up with. Deep down, Dad knew this, and we knew he knew that we knew it. But, as in many cases in American life, or at least ours, there was an absolute disconnect between the truth and what was presented in public. He was just hoping we'd accept half a deal, half a real identity, half a truth. It was another betrayal. And we were grown men. It felt like we'd never get another chance at this.

"Aren't you fucking angry?" I said over my shoulder.

"Why? It's the same as it's always been," Joe shouted. "I just can't be a real person." Dad saw me turn back to look at him and he gave a big fake smile. I gave him a big fake smile back.

I drove the moving truck out of Bruce's driveway the next morning, worried I'd next see Joe in another less luxurious rehab, in an ICU, or in a box. When I had told Joe that he should come with us, he just waved and said, "I've got my Jane's Addiction tape." I left in tears.

About a week later, Joe was set to leave the psychiatric hospital and Mom went to pick him up. As they sat in the lobby waiting to be discharged, it was revealed to Joe that he would go stay with a family as a kind of halfway house to transition him back to the world. He even walked outside and met the family, but Mom saw he couldn't do it, and they went back into the lobby. There he broke down again, shaking and crying, and told Mom he'd likely hurt somebody if he had to stay with strangers. So he was readmitted for another week or so and then finally allowed to go back to Dad's house.

About a week later, Mom and her fiancé, Tom, went to Mexico and got married. They drove into Nuevo Laredo on a sightseeing tour with my uncle Marlan, who lives in Texas, and decided to tie the knot. On Joe's birthday, of all days. That was a spot of welcome good news in a hard summer.

I didn't see the deer camp again for seven years.

Four

The Darkness

Dad hardly told me a single thing about his childhood. He just didn't want to talk about it. Once, he and I were sitting at the Marathon station in Texas Corners in our old red F100—the Jesse, we called it; it was like the one Scott had later. It had a suicide knob bolted to the steering wheel and Dad would hang on that and stare out the window like he was in a movie. I was sixteen and we were having a fight. He was in a white T-shirt and his stupid straw cowboy hat and he had been hissing at me that I should probably just get out, that sixteen was when a man should get out of his father's house, and I asked him where he thought I should go, and then he felt bad and got quiet. He hung there a minute on the knob.

"My dad was a smart guy, smarter than I knew, but all I wanted was to get away from him. That's why we started to hunt," he said.

That was the first I'd heard him talk about Grandpa Henry. He said he and his three older brothers were obsessed with getting away from him. They had to get out of that house and do things he didn't do. One thing Henry didn't do was hunt.

"What was so bad about Grandpa Henry?" I asked.

It was summer. Blades of corn across the street sawed at the watery air.

"The darkness," he said.

After a minute he added, "My dad worked like a mule. Really, like a dumb animal. And nothing we did was ever good enough. His take on life was so grim, he made farm life so miserable. So if we could get to the crick, down there we'd feel like we had a life."

I loved my grandpa for the way he purred when he talked, for the roasted coffee color of his skin and its leathery texture and his wave of silver hair, but something morbid attended him.

Dad, Mom, and I lived with Grandpa and Grandma for a few weeks in their brick house outside Zeeland, Michigan, when I was four, and one of the first times I had dinner at their house I was reaching for the dish nearest to me when Dad put his hand on my arm and told me to wait for Grandpa. "I'll read the scripture," Henry said without other comment, looking down as he took his black leather-bound Bible off the table. Then he began a remarkable performance. He opened to his place and proceeded to read in a voice that none of us could hear. He enunciated carefully in a half whisper like the sound of small creek water moving over stones. My mouth hung open as I strained to hear: his voice was mesmerizing and transporting. But it clearly wasn't for us. Grandma Gertrude told him, "Heinie, speak up. No one can hear you." His voice rose for half a verse and then submerged again. I'd been around a fair amount of prayer, as my surrogate grandparents, Roy and Vesta Sutter, prayed, too, but this was the first time I'd ever really been aware of someone talking directly to God in what seemed like a private conversation. Grandpa Henry's God was mysterious and powerful and far out of reach. He teased us with the text's mystery as though he were sprinkling us with holy water, a substance charged with meaning we could not understand, and it felt like a game, like he was hiding the words somewhere around the room.

When Dad and his three older brothers were small, Henry and Gertrude bought their first farm, a twenty-acre piece with a good house and a couple of small outbuildings just south of Zeeland on Perry Street. They weren't there long, though, and it was on their second farm that all six boys really grew up, a one-hundred-acre chunk of prime prairie loam and elm trees a few miles east of town. Everyone referred to that farm as the Kasslander Place after the former owners, one of the founding families of Zeeland. Henry grew corn, wheat, oats, and hay, and kept about twenty dairy cows on pasture. He also rented the twenty or forty acres across the road.

For most farmers, working 120 or 140 acres was a full-time job, but it was only Henry's side hustle. His real job was an hour away at Keeler Brass in Grand Rapids, where he did piecework buffing brass hardware. It was dirty and loud, polishing one item at a time in a spray of oily brass filings, and he did this five days a week and sometimes half days on Saturdays for his entire adult working life. Because he was paid by the piece, the pace was inhuman, but he was proud that he was not a union man because unions were communist and thus godless, in his estimation. The true cost of a union pension was damnation.

"So here's a guy, he has the biggest farm in the neighborhood. Nobody else works in the factory; they all work their farms. But then he's got a full-time job in the factory," said my uncle Ron, who made a career in the CIA and is a reliable reporter. "And he's got six kids. But always at least four. Who were a lot of trouble. Because we were all rambunctious. None of us were good kids. Heh heh. And your dad was one of the worst. I might have been one of the worst. Well, Dale was the worst."

Before and after school there were lengthy chores to do, and during Michigan's short, sticky summers Henry wasn't home during the day so the boys did the farming. Anyone who's done it knows there's no rest in it. And there was also cooking and doing housework with Grandma Gertrude. Henry had grown up plowing behind horses, and he was both cheap and set against the tyranny of the new, so if there was a hard way to do something, like lifting grain down from the upper barn in buckets rather than build a grain chute, that's the way he'd do it. Hard Way Productions. According to Ron, the boys hardly did any homework because they were exhausted.

Henry could speak high school Spanish to field hands and high school French, whenever that occasion arose, but he would tell you in English he was mortally afraid of hell. His goal for living was to die in the Lord. He liked going to the neighbors for pie or leaning on the fence at the cattle auction, if that's what the day brought, but he was eager to walk on the clean side of the clouds and not be tormented by the insult of this life and the failures of all his relations. He was devoted to the one church he knew could save him, the Christian Reformed Church, but guilt hung on him like a shroud. He didn't have an "attaboy" for good work, at least not for the older kids, and he didn't waste one minute of time trying to make the farm work fun.

He came by these attitudes honestly. The inscription on the tombstone of my great-great-grandpa Henry J. and his wife, Gezina, over in the Graafschap Cemetery south of Holland, is a line from Revelation: "Blessed are the dead who die in the Lord from now on. They will rest from their labor, for their deeds will follow them." I'm surprised every day that excess pride doesn't drip like syrup from the clouds above Holland. The Kuipers were puffed up by the prospect of their election to heaven. Threatening that pride risked violence and madness.

I never met Grandpa Henry's dad, Great-Grandpa John, but his pride took a beating. The first thing people say about him is that he lost two barns in separate fires, at least one from putting up wet hay. He had two years of schooling and worked like a maniac to keep his children alive through the Depression: farming, hauling gravel, selling firewood. His first wife, my great-grandma Frances, died after eight children (two of whom, the girls, died), so he took up with his housekeeper, Henrietta, and married her when she got pregnant. He left his church for a while after that, and moved farms. But maybe that wasn't pride; maybe they gave him the heave-ho like they did me. He never went to any of his seven boys' weddings. Two of them, Jason and Nelson, ran off to live with my grandpa Henry, since he was the oldest. John came to reclaim them because he needed the labor. He was a powerful man, hardened by work and living in a wilderness all his own, but Henry faced him down, and Jason and Nelson were forever grateful. From time to time Henry also took care of his little brother Stanley, who was probably autistic, but artful, and would appear in school plays; Great-Grandpa John put him on a grim county work farm where he spent most of his life, but Henry would get him home for weekends now and then.

When Grandpa once overheard me talking about a 1970s TV show with my cousins, he put a gnarled brown paw on my shoulder and said in his low and sinking thrum, "Boys, boys. Satan is at work in the world today and he works through TV and magazines and music. Eternal damnation is forever, just think about that."

"Heinie, stop being morose!" Grandma yelled from the kitchen.

∾

Bruce was no more or less badly behaved than his three older brothers, but he was more willing to throw his behavior in Henry's face. He and Henry had a bloody fistfight that effectively ended his childhood when he was sixteen. Which, I guess, is why he told me to get out at sixteen, too.

Henry wouldn't own a TV and the boys weren't allowed to see movies, but when Bruce was fourteen, Henry let him drive the car into Zeeland to get to the roller rink, which was the only place he might have a chance to hold a girl's hand or experience any of the actual culture of the 1950s. But the cops later reported to Henry that instead of parking at the roller rink, my father was flying up and down Main Street as fast as he could go. He wasn't trying to hide it. The whole point was to show off.

Dad was beautiful and vain and dressed like James Dean. He pushed back on his own darkness with cigarettes rolled in the sleeve of his white T-shirt and his hair slicked back in a perfect, jet-black DA.

"Your dad was in my sister's class at Holland Christian," said my great-aunt Frieda Kuipers. "He was kind of rowdy, hair combed back like Elvis Presley. He wore a black leather jacket with the collar turned up."

He strutted the halls of Holland Christian, bestowing his bright smile on this girl and that. That smile contrasted with his dark skin; in old farm photos, he looks like a Native American hunter with a spread of pheasants laid before him. One of my favorites shows him looking impossibly glamorous sitting bareback astride his blue roan horse in white jeans, sweater, and penny loafers. Henry had bought the horse for Bruce when he was fifteen.

But the photos give more away. Most things about Bruce were right on the surface. You could peer through his dark, nearly indigenous face and his movie-star lips and his mod wardrobe and see that his heart was full but his soul was thin and malnourished on rage and fear. He didn't know what he was meant to be.

He worked busing tables at Van Raalte's, the Zeeland restaurant named after the Secessionist Church dominie who founded the Christian colony of Holland and the Christian Reformed Church, and whatever money Bruce made he spent on clothes and gas and cigarettes. He was fastidious and jealous about his look, and would be for life. He went to Zeeland Christian schools up through ninth grade, and he wanted to go to the public school, Zeeland High, where all his friends went. That's where all the Kuipers boys wanted to go, but Henry sent them to Holland Christian High School and there was no discussing it.

"I first laid eyes on him when we were sophomores in high school," said my mom. "We had assembly and this mass of new kids were there. I sat about three rows behind him."

They were both fifteen and went on a date within weeks, to watch the Zeeland High School Chix play football, but they didn't date each other exclusively. Mom had guys lining up to ask her out, and Dad had girlfriends hidden away in Zeeland, one of whom became Nancy's crosstown rival. "He was tall, dark, and handsome. He was a hit with the girls," Mom said. Dad had a Ford that broke down a lot, and Nancy recalled a few dates at the auto shop. But when it ran, they would skip school and drive to Grand Rapids just to go to a diner, or go to Lake Michigan.

Bruce's big brothers, Dale and Vern, were both Marlon Brando–handsome and ladies' men, and had cut a trail for Bruce at Holland Christian. Bruce was dogged and enthusiastic and ecumenical in his tastes; you might say he was liberal. He was girl-crazy, and he put immense energy into getting under those poodle skirts. He broke hearts, and when he did he went back to Nancy. They never did go steady, but they liked each other's company. Bruce needed to be out on dates, because when he was home he just got deeper and deeper in trouble.

"Your dad had an incredible ability to push buttons," said Jack. "I remember sitting outside one day and I hear this hellacious commotion in the house, yelling and carrying on, and your dad comes cuttin' out of that back door. You had the old wooden screen door on a spring and WHAM! That door slaps open and he comes across the back porch, and here's this little mother right behind him about five feet tall, with a mop. And she took a swing at him and she broke that green mop handle right off across his back!"

When fall 1960 came around, Bruce told Nancy he wasn't going to Holland Christian for his junior year but was switching to the public high school in Zeeland. He never informed Henry, and it took a couple of weeks for the old man to find out. But when he did, he found Bruce doing chores out back and meant to give him a demonstration of what hell would be like. Henry hadn't had to resort much to the belt, but he came at Bruce, and much to his surprise, his sixteen-year-old son fought back and slugged his father right in his leathery face. "He punched him. If I remember right, I think he broke Henry's jaw," said Ron.

"He broke his jaw," affirmed Jack. "Out in the corncrib. Dad came in and said he fell on some machinery or something and hurt himself, but that wasn't the real story."

Mike, who was about four at the time, said, "Your dad was unruly, and Mom was trying to keep the peace and Henry was wild-eyed."

Henry threw him out, but Grandma Gertrude saved him. She convinced Henry to let him stay until he could figure out where to go. No family could fly apart with her in it. Gertrude was Heinie's one saving grace, and he adored her. She was a short bolt of energy with curly red hair, and unless we were going to church I never once saw her wear anything other than a raggedy flower-print housedress. She could match Henry's mulish work ethic step for step. As she constantly cleaned and gardened and prepared coffee and meals, she would whistle parts of hymns that she never finished. She was easy to talk to and knew more than she let on. The two of them were in love for life, and Henry truly believed that God had bestowed on him at least this one blessing, and her sanity constantly pulled him back from the edge.

Dad announced he was joining the Air Force, and he never went back to high school. He lived on the farm for another year and a half and worked as a clerk at Van's grocery. He and Nancy continued to date as she finished school.

I had never heard about his fight with Grandpa before I started working on this book. My mother had been on the Kuipers farm many times, but she'd never heard of it, either. It was another one of the things they didn't talk about.

"It was very painful to watch the adults, or the big people in your life, fight," said Jack.

"I missed some of this, because I was so determined to get the hell out," said Ron. "I never said a word to my dad from about the age of fourteen to seventeen. I refused to speak to him. So I was the most trouble, that way. I would only grunt. I moved out at eighteen, and when I say I moved out, I really closed my eyes. I didn't look back. I didn't go to visit or anything. I moved in with [his wife] Ruthie's parents, who lived two or three miles away. They were my new parents, really."

~

At every opportunity, the boys ducked out of the house and into the fields to hunt.

"I hated the isolation on the farm," said Ron. "We just weren't part of the world. On Sundays, we had to stay in the house because you had to read Christian literature and we had no interest in that. You had the *Banner*, and it was awful reading, of course. So we'd sneak out the upstairs window on Sunday afternoons."

"I figured out that if I took the stock off my .22 rifle, I could stick it down my pants," Ron added, laughing. "So you'd just have the barrel and the trigger mechanism, and we'd go out with that."

"We just didn't have a lot of other stuff to do," said Jack. "You'd get a winter day, and if you could find something to shoot, you'd shoot it."

They had to slip out from under the shadow of the afterlife and be part of the living. A quarter mile to the west ran the Black River, which they called the "swamp ditch" because it dragged sluggish and rank through a broad river valley black with rich muck planted in onions and celery. In its tannic flow thrashed and shrieked their living salvation. Sometimes they took pitchforks and gigged for carp, aiming at the little bow wave the fish made on the surface. The boys saw that the Latino migrants who worked the muck had a better method: they would use a big piece of chicken-wire fencing as a net, hauling out carp and cooking them.

"Somehow we managed not to stab ourselves in the feet, as we were barefoot in there, though sometimes we'd step on a big snapper," said Ron. "We were hillbillies."

The boys were around lots of people who hunted, including Grandma Gertrude's brothers Jay and Hank Brink, who had deer camps. Jay worked for General Motors and went to the Upper Peninsula every fall to hunt deer and play cards and tell jokes around a fire, and Great-Uncle Hank had a place near Dead Stream Swamp, a huge white cedar bog northeast of Cadillac that was lousy with deer. Their experiences were probably the germ of the great dream of cabin life that resided within my dad and all his brothers, a refuge from the tension of being constantly separate from the world, a bivouac you returned to over and over and that inspired thinking about the habitat.

"The Brinks have a better-balanced life. They like to have a beer and laugh, and go hunting and play cards. They weren't so tense," said Mike. "So Dale and them gravitated toward the Brinks. Plus, Dale worked construction and he was always around great fishermen and great poachers, or whatever. He learned well!"

Dale charged off into the fields, and Ron and Vern and Dad were right behind him. Like the farmers all around them in that era, their methods were far from discriminating. They shot hawks and bald eagles and crows and owls, mostly because those birds killed chickens. Given the fervor with which everyone killed these predators and scavengers, you would have thought chickens to be the most important economic asset in the county. On the once-a-year occasion that a red fox would make the grave mistake of entering the township, the Kuipers boys would wage an all-out campaign to snuff it, trespassing across fields and chasing it in cars. The dog would bark in the night, and they'd all pile out the door in their underwear to take turns blasting at a raccoon in the big tree in the yard. They trapped muskrats and mink along the river when they could find them, and shot pigeons out of the top of the silo and songbirds in the bushes for no reason at all. They routinely killed cats, because feral cats eat game birds, but that had consequences. "You'd throw open the doors to the barn and the walls would rattle with rats," said Great-Uncle George, Grandpa Henry's younger half brother. So they shot rats in the barn, even after Vern found a couple of boxes of dynamite up in the beams and realized they'd been shooting at them.

One year when Dale was home from his mission work, there was a big migration of snowy owls from the Arctic and every farm had a white owl or two sitting on the fence posts. Dale drove around in the car and shot them by the scores. It wasn't to eat. It was just plain ignorance and sublimated rage.

"If it moved, we killed it," said Ron. "But why? Why would we shoot a blue heron?"

They would have shot a whitetail deer, but they rarely saw one near the farm. Deer were few in the southern half of the Lower Peninsula, and the intensive deer-range management programs that created today's two-million-strong deer herd didn't start until 1971. The farmers they grew up with weren't big on self-examination; they went on extirpating every wild thing from their farms until they themselves passed away.

Even Jack and Mike, who came along seven and thirteen years after Bruce, respectively, and got along better with Henry, still managed to find trouble. "I got a new .22 rifle and I was driving with my friends and there was a rabbit and I started blazing away out the window," said Jack. "I didn't see there was a cop right behind us. Henry had to come bail me out of jail and when we got home, it was pretty much the worst night of my life."

To eat, they shot quail and rabbits out of the fencerows and the prize of all prizes, the ring-necked pheasant, a big, robust bird imported from the steppes of Asia that thrived on corn and grain fields. They treated pheasants much differently than other game. To kill a pheasant was to bag a delicious meal, and three or four could feed their large family. Grandma Gertrude pan-fried the pieced birds in butter and salt, which is the same way my mom, Nancy, would make them, and that is a gorgeous dinner.

"On the farm, we'd eat them year-round," said my great-uncle George. "You'd go out in the snowstorm, in the corn that didn't get picked, and those birds would be buried deep in the snow to keep warm, but the tail feathers would be sticking out and you'd just grab him."

When it was pheasant season, the boys kept a loaded shotgun on the tractor, in the barn, and one behind the door of the mudroom, a room they called by some kind of mangled Dutch phrase, the back "haukie" or "hawkie." If one of them had a car, there was always a disassembled twelve-gauge underneath the front seat, with a few shells easily accessible in the glove box; if a rooster flew over, you slapped that gun together and grabbed the shells and left the car in the middle of the road. Pheasants were an obsession. Pheasants were holy.

∾

The Henry I knew was morose, but soft. A couple of my cousins told me he hit them when he was angry, but to me he seemed bruised. I was eating lunch with him at his house when I was a kid, one of Grandma's noontime spreads of fried Spam, applesauce, Roman Meal bread with room-temperature butter, sliced tomatoes, radishes, and coffee. He took some tomatoes and said in his muted purr: "You know there's only two types of people in the world."

"What are they?" I said, wide-eyed.

"Those who put sugar on a tomato, and those who put salt."

He then proceeded to sprinkle sugar on his. That's when I knew: softy. Bruce ate his with sugar, too. Wounded romantics, both. I like tomatoes just like they are, with neither sugar nor salt. I'm the third type of person who likes the flavor of the world just as it is.

Dad broke Henry's jaw, and Ron wouldn't speak to him, but Dale's rebellion was the most flamboyant. He got his name in the paper for poaching a few times, and then there was this headline on the front page of the *Holland Evening Sentinel* of November 10, 1956:

Zeeland (Special)—Elvis' best fan is out $25 and won't be able to see his idol's name on the city water tower anymore. Dale Kuipers, 21, Route 3 Zeeland, admitted to Zeeland police and city superintendent L. A. Sears that he climbed the 135-foot tower east of the city on M 21 and painted "Home of Elvis" in red letters four-feet high beneath the city's name. Kuipers said he climbed the ladder alone, carrying a can of barn paint, and told Sears he was willing to pay $25 to have the lettering removed.

Dale left school and went straight to work doing construction. In the winters, he chased the bikini-clad women of Florida. He discovered his life's purpose after meeting a charismatic and influential Baptist preacher named Garland Cofield in Holland and later attended a Bible college in Tennessee.

After Dale found the Lord, he was forever trying his damnedest to convert everyone in sight, the way a formerly wild person will when they want to make up for lost time, and he horse-collared Bruce when he was seventeen. Dad had already been baptized in the Christian Reformed Church but Dale and Rev. Cofield dunked him anew as a Baptist.

"Bruce came to me one night and we were supposed to have a date or something and he said, 'I got saved last night,'" said Mom. "And I was really happy about that, but then he proceeded through that evening to try to save me.

"And I said, 'I don't need to be saved. I am saved. I know Jesus.'

"'No. Nope,' he said. 'Your church is not—' He was totally indoctrinated with the fact that my church was not the right church and Rose Park Baptist was the place. He says, 'Well, then I can't see you anymore.'

"I came home and, man, I didn't go to school the next day and Mom let me stay home 'cause she could see how upset I was," said Nancy. "I said, 'He told me I'm not good enough. I think I'm good enough. I don't need to be saved *again*.' And then he started dating a girl from that church and he was very, very thick with Uncle Dale and Aunt Sandy."

And that's the way they left it. The two young lovers didn't see each other much and then Bruce's eighteenth birthday came, and the great maw of the Vietnam War opened and took him, and down at Lackland Air Force Base in San Antonio he was remade as government issue.

~

Henry's fraught relationship with farming marked all six of his sons. The five oldest all became guys who wore suits: Dale as a minister, Ron at the State Department, Vern and Jack with an insurance company, Bruce with his construction company, where he wore suits a majority of the time. He owned about fifty of them. Years later, when working on the deer camp, Dad would curse the sand and kick at it when rye and buckwheat didn't come up. "You grew up on a farm. Don't you know how to do this?" I asked him. "No, because my dad wouldn't tell me," he said.

No one knew if Henry withheld information because he was mean, or insecure, or just didn't know. Mike asked him loads of farming questions he'd never answer. When Ron was writing an analyst's report about North Africa once for the CIA, he called Henry and asked him about an agricultural technique they had used on the farm, but Henry refused to talk about it.

I once asked Grandma Gertrude if any of my uncles were farmers, and she sang out, in her high and nasal croon, "Oh, goo'ness, I guess not. The only reason they were innerested in a farm is if they could shoot a pheasant there."

Mike was the only one of my uncles whom I really knew when he himself was still a kid, and he developed a relationship to the land that went beyond the hunt. Only seven years older than me, he grew up mostly in Grandpa and Grandma's last place, a brick ranch house on forty acres where Henry ran a few feeder calves. Mike worked a rural postal route near Hamilton, Michigan, and read history and spent more time afield than the other brothers. He mostly liked trapping, and he knew every culvert that held a muskrat and every mink that put tracks on the creekside mud for miles around Holland. He once tried to teach me in a farmer's field how you could tell where the Potawatomi people would have put their encampment, and we walked out there and found a chert arrowhead in the freshly turned earth, right where he had predicted. He had a shoebox full of these kinds of treasures and was hyperaware of the land, and he bought and sold property. When he was a teen, he had a chopper motorcycle and played electric guitar; when I was twelve, we sat in his room while he introduced me to *Frampton Comes Alive!*—but Grandpa just didn't come down on him.

"He treated me as good as you could ever hope to be treated, but I guess he really struggled with the other kids," Mike concedes.

Mike went to the Black River every day after school and skipped dinner, the reading of the Bible, the whole thing. I guess by that time Henry was more kind and mellow, or maybe broken and morose, but either way more sugar than salt. Grandma would heat up something for Mike when he got home after dark. He pretty much stayed out there in the fields his whole life. He didn't have the social ambition that the other brothers had and didn't go to all the family events; he loved the people who were close to him and grew close to the people he served on his mail route, but he was more intellectual than the other brothers and felt more comfortable with the landforms and the mink and their language. He developed the kind of relatedness to the land that Joe and Brett and I all craved, and that our father kept at arm's length. We were fascinated with him, and his brothers were, too.

∾

Mom also grew up on a farm, but her family dynamic did not have anyone bolting out the door to kill the local wildlife. She was one of six children born to Marvin and Dorothy Nienhuis—everyone called them Bub and Dot—so among the Nienhuises I had another five sets of aunts and uncles and eighteen more first cousins. They had a pickle farm in South Olive, just north of Holland about fifteen miles from the Kuipers place. Mom and her family were close and loving and fun, and she was not particularly eager to leave them or the dirt under her nails from digging potatoes. Their farmhouse was the hub of all family activity, and I knew it as a place of huge softball games in the yard and the family singing together. They never quit farming. They also belonged to the Christian Reformed Church, but where Grandpa Kuipers saw doom, Grandpa Nienhuis saw beauty and light. He had been close to his father, whose original farm was only a mile away down the dirt road, and he took comfort in the relative homogeneity of his Dutch world, comprising Holland, Zeeland, and the spread of nearby satellite towns such as

Drenthe, Overisel, Graafschap, Noordeloos, Crisp, and Bentheim. But he had room in his mind for diversity.

Inclusion and diversity were not among the church's founding principles. Rather, the explicit desire of the colonists who came over from the Old World was separateness and purity. When Rev. Albertus Van Raalte first arrived to found the city of Holland on the untamed shores of Black Lake in 1846, he wasn't looking to convert the Ottawa people or assimilate into America. He was one of a handful of ministers who split from the Netherlands' state-sponsored Reformed Church after King William I attempted to modernize the church in the early 1800s. They called themselves Secessionists and chose to stick with a strict interpretation of the Protestant leader John Calvin's teachings, such as salvation by election. Van Raalte was seeking only an unpeopled chunk of wilderness where he could create a "colony for Christians," and his flock birthed the strict Christian Reformed Church in the United States.

As Larry ten Harmsel wrote in his book *Dutch in Michigan*, "One could say that the people who led boatloads of Hollanders to Michigan were among the few American immigrants to flee a spirit of *tolerance* in their native land."

There's no way I can escape the influence of this history. Like rot in the heart of an old tree, I saw this constant bid for separateness ruin my father's life. My great-great-great-great-grandparents on my mom's side, Berend Koijers and his wife, Johanna (Woordes), and their kids were among the first arrivals to Holland in 1847, and the Kuipers from Germany's Dutch-speaking County Bentheim arrived not long after; since all the Dutch kept to themselves and intermarried, it's not unreasonable to say I'm related to just about everyone in town.

Grandpa Bub defied this history of separateness. He was a sunny, rugged, action-oriented farmer who was an enthusiastic participant in world events. He wasn't liberal, by any stretch of the imagination, but he loved humanity and he had an innate trust in the earth and in life. He read *National Geographic* as well as the Bible, and he marveled over scientific discovery and the newest technologies, such as the Apollo program. I sat with him and Grandma Dot and several of my other uncles and aunts and baby cousins in the living room of the old farmhouse in 1969, absolutely riveted by the TV spectacle of Neil Armstrong and Buzz Aldrin walking on the moon. Grandpa Bub sang in the choir and played the piano, and he was a huge booster of the Lightbearers Quartet, a gospel outfit including two of my uncles (and a third on guitar) that put out a series of vinyl albums. He regularly traveled around the world distributing Bibles to remote populations with his cousin Chet Schemper, who was president of the World Home Bible League. Together, the two of them would jump into a private jet and blaze down to some remote airstrip in the Amazon or Central America to deliver boxes of the New Testament translated into local languages, though I'm not sure which ones.

Bub's dad pulled him out of Holland Christian during the Depression to go to work, but he went back and graduated from high school at age twenty-one. He had an astonishingly inclusive and generous take on the world. He had seen suffering and starvation during the Depression—his own feet were mangled because he hadn't been able to buy new shoes during those bleak years—and he told me that President Franklin D. Roosevelt's vision for a welfare state was a Christian gesture that made him the greatest president the United States had ever had.

When he read the Bible over dinner, he would practically sing it. He would look up from the text and catch your eye and smile, like he was saying, *Here, this is for you.* I always marveled that my two grandfathers could come out of the same religion with such different takes on life. It wasn't the doctrine itself; it was how you lived it.

For my part, I grew up believing that no one gets to go to heaven unless everyone goes, a help-your-neighbor-or-else kind of thing. I knew that was not a popular idea in the Abrahamic religions, but why would God want anyone in heaven who believed they stood apart from the others? I figured God would take everything, even plants and animals. Our fates were tied together, and if there was a heaven, it was big enough for all of us, for worlds within worlds. Maybe I got some of that from Grandpa Bub.

I would bring my BB guns to his farm, and Brett brought his .22 one time to hunt for rabbits and squirrels in the five-acre woodlot in the back, but Grandpa wasn't really keen on that. He had an ancient oak-beamed barn built in 1897 that was full of pigs and a farmyard peopled with ducks and geese and goats and some exotics including golden pheasants and peacocks. He loved his farm companions and didn't like the prospect of young hunters loose on the place. He warned us not to shoot anything other than rabbits and squirrels. Bub and Dot lived on that farm together for well over sixty years, and their whole world sprang from the soil beneath their feet.

But they didn't hunt.

~

As a kid, I begged Bruce to show me the farms where he'd grown up, and he always refused. I explored the Black River with Mike, and I didn't realize until later in life that we sometimes passed by the Kasslander Place. Dad never acknowledged it. But he did show me their first farm once, by mistake. He and I went to see Grandma Gertrude one day when she lived in the Royal Atrium retirement community just south of Zeeland, and as we drove west on Perry Street, he pointed at a farm and said offhandedly, "That was our first farm." I threatened to jump out of the car, so he swung around and parked in the driveway. I got out and poked around, but Bruce stayed in the car. The farmhouse was old but someone lived there, and a car sat under the massive old maple trees spreading over the yard. I could see into the twenty-acre field behind the outbuildings and I wanted to go back there and see and smell the swamp ditch.

"Let's ask if we can walk back there," I said, pointing.

"Get in the car," Bruce said. I did and he rolled away without looking back.

He added, "I never liked that place."

Five

A Boat

Our faith in wildness was born of water. When I was four years old, Dad built me a fishing boat. He had just finished four years as a carpenter in the Air Force, stationed at Paine Field north of Seattle, and he hand-built a two-person wooden dinghy in a room barely big enough to hold it behind the kitchen in our tiny apartment in Edmonds. It was his way to show me we didn't belong to apartments and air bases and war, that no matter how things went with him and Mom there were rivers and mountains without end. Edmonds is on Puget Sound, and about twenty miles of suburbs separated our apartment from the foothills of the Cascades, but that little boat carried us straight into the cedar forests on flows of sea wind and emerald snowmelt and the shadows of deer, and off we went—me, Mom, and Dad. A family made of the hunt.

Mom and Dad looked to the wilderness for a love that wasn't in them. All families come together through a certain amount of happenstance, but Bruce and Nancy might have passed each other by if it weren't for me. When Dad was stationed at Lackland, he wrote letters to Nancy, but he wrote letters to other people, too. After he moved to Paine Field in Washington, he was having sex with lots of women. He came back to Michigan for pheasant hunting with his brothers every September, because no force on heaven or earth could have stopped that, and when he did he saw Nancy. In the summer of 1963 he came home to Zeeland for the month of June, and shortly after he went back to the base, Mom found out she was pregnant. With me.

"When I told your dad that I was pregnant with his child, I got a letter about a week later. He stated in that letter, 'I don't know that I can marry you. I have someone else,' " Mom said.

Mom shared this with her family, and everybody knew what this meant: If he wasn't marrying her after dating for years, then he already had another woman pregnant. Bub and Dot told her to forget him; she'd be fine living with them. After a few weeks, another letter came saying Dad was rethinking the whole situation.

"Evidently, she, I think, miscarried, or had an abortion or something," Mom added. Dad told other people that he had actually asked to marry the other woman, but her parents wouldn't have it. They thought he was too much of a hick. Mom didn't ask too many questions. She was a nineteen-year-old nursing student at Grand Rapids Junior College who wanted a father for her child. In a universe of unnervingly random choices, Bruce chose us.

Bruce and Nancy were married that October at the old South Olive Christian Reformed Church, the Nienhuis's creaky pine-board sanctuary. They had handsome photos in the paper and were genuinely happy to be wed. Dad was delivering a new car from Detroit to a fellow airman on the base, and they packed that car directly after the service and said good-bye to everyone standing at the church and drove one hundred miles per hour all the way to Seattle.

When Mom settled into Dad's apartment on Thirty-Fifth Street in Everett, where the base was, she saw a pile of letters from some other woman in the closet. But she never read them, and one day they disappeared. I was born in March 1964, and we moved to a trailer in Marysville, and as soon as I could walk, at nine months old, Dad disappeared, too. We had just moved to an apartment on 113th in Everett, and Dad took off with another woman for three months or so. He left no word and no money. Mom didn't have a job or a car, so it was just her and me sitting around the apartment, slowly strolling through downtown Everett, hoping Dad would come back. Mom was homesick to the point where she was physically ill a lot of the time, so we went home for Christmas and stayed at the Nienhuises for almost a month. Mom didn't want to go back to Everett, but she felt some obligation that Bruce evidently did not.

"I thought: Doesn't he have a conscience?" said Mom. "To leave a wife and child? He just didn't seem to feel guilt. He acted like he was allowed to do this, like it was his right, and no one could tell him any different. He never said he was sorry for any of it. Not ever."

Dad's supervisor on the base was Roy Sutter, a civil engineer and a civilian, and he and his wife, Vesta, knew what was going on with Dad. They were a little bit older and became a second set of parents to Bruce and Nancy, and grandparents to me. They didn't approve of Dad's girlfriends, but they didn't judge him, either. When he came back, they were glad he was back. Vesta was especially important for Mom, as she looked after me when Mom started working, and she would take us up to their small farm in Arlington on nights and weekends when Dad was off chasing some other lady. Lots of times that chase began at one of the bowling alleys where he moonlighted. Paine Field had a bowling alley on the base and Roy was a part of the bowling team, so Dad started hanging there, too. He and Roy saw eye to eye on a lot of things and neither of them drank. Roy and Vesta were fairly strict Seventh-day Adventists and mostly vegetarians and didn't even drink coffee unless it was the roasted grain substitute Postum. Dad might take a cigarette now and then, but he probably hadn't had a dozen beers in his life. He told me once, much later, he didn't like the feeling of being "out of control."

A bowling alley was just a bar with games in it, though, and a lot of ladies came to have a cocktail, and there was handsome, brown-skinned Bruce. Through the bowling alley, Dad became great friends with Mac Lowry, a master sergeant in the Air Force who was also a pro bowler and owned Leilani Lanes and Sunset Lanes. Through Mac's connections, Dad got a second job working in a bowling alley in Edmonds. He even bowled in a few pro events, but bowling wasn't why he was there.

Mom never knew when Dad might leave for good, so in 1966 she took a job in the Inventory Office at Sears and bought a white VW Bug. A co-worker named Cheryl befriended Mom and came to live with us in Everett to help Mom cover the rent; Dad wasn't around, so Cheryl moved into my tiny room and I moved in with Mom. The wife of one of the other officers on the base babysat me whenever Vesta wasn't available, but they both had to be paid.

Dad didn't pay the rent and all he did was chase strange: Why not kick him to the curb? Mom believed one day his conscience would awaken and he'd fly right, but Dad himself didn't even believe that. He could have sex with anyone he wanted, for however long he wanted, and Mom would open the door when he got back. So he kept at it. When he returned to the Everett apartment, he was mad that Cheryl was there and kicked her out.

After he finished his four years in the Air Force, Dad worked construction and started in on a degree in building trades at Everett Junior College. Constantly running away from his misdeeds, we moved to an apartment on B Avenue in Edmonds and the insult continued. The owner of one of the bowling alleys where Dad worked had a gorgeous teenage daughter, a woman four or five years younger than he and Mom, and he shacked up with her for between three and five months. At least this time Mom knew where he was: the bowling alley owners sanctioned this affair and gave Bruce and their daughter a place to live. They were supposed to be friends, but they were only friends to Dad. The money stopped again and Mom was desperately lonely, and this time she bailed. She boxed up most of our stuff and shipped it Greyhound to Holland; she had to borrow eighty dollars from Grandpa Bub to get it there. She booked a plane ticket for the two of us and quit the apartment on B Avenue and gave her two weeks' notice at Sears, then moved in with Roy and Vesta until she could fly home. Bruce got wind of this and showed up before we could leave. He was always secretive about where he was sleeping and who he was with, but like a true creep he kept close tabs on Mom's movements.

Once again, he convinced Mom to stay and they got the apartment in Edmonds back and Sears was happy to have Mom return to work. Grandpa Nienhuis put their stuff right back on the Greyhound. The next year went okay, and Dad ran around a little less. The economy in Seattle was starting to flag in advance of the base reverting to civilian control in 1968 and Dad was having trouble finding work, but Mom's job was solid. He needed her to survive. It wasn't too long and Mom was pregnant with Brett, and in August 1968 they decided to move back to Michigan together.

~

I was a kid and what I knew was water. Dad was obsessed with fishing, so my first encounter with the sentient wild was the native cutthroat trout. Roy Sutter was a fly fisherman like Dad, and he showed Dad his secret trout spot just up the road from their farm in Arlington, a gorgeous small piece of Cascade Mountain water called Ebey Lake—now called

Little Lake. We started going there when I was just an infant, but by the time I was three Dad had me set up with a little closed-face spin-casting rig and we fished together.

I have dim memories of this lake, of emerald water ringed with tall, straight cedars moving in the wind, of the shallow banks picketed with dead snags and muck. I don't believe there were any structures or houses on the lake. My fish stories from this time were legendary with my grandparents and uncles and aunts back in Michigan, and I have photographs of me telling them, age three, in the Seattle train station. Out on the lake, Dad sent his fly line whistling back and forth, dropping dry flies among the hatchling insects resting on the surface, among the cottonwood seeds and the milkweed down that seemed to float without actually touching the water. I watched my bobber. I knew that fly-fishing was too difficult for me, but dunking worms almost always works better than flies anyway. I'd catch panfish, but Dad only really cared about the cutthroats: elegant, rare, with a slash of red behind the gills that gave them their lurid name.

I knew other animals. The Sutters had a cat and usually kept one feeder calf, and I went to an amazing preschool in Lynnwood called Maple Bar Ranch, which had sheep and goats and other animals and cost Nancy sixty-five dollars a month, which was a fortune. But I understood more about the fish because I was trying to catch them, and to catch them I had to think like them. I understood that they were thoughtful about their choice of bait and how much splashing and disturbance they would tolerate. I had to learn their watery culture. Fish mated and communicated and had a way of being when we weren't around, and they mostly liked doing that in the good places like Ebey Lake that were clean and wild. I internalized that from Day One: these fish needed the isolation of mountains. I had dreams about seeing what the fish saw from under the water—I am unsure of their provenance and it's possible I had these dreams later and they simply attached themselves to Ebey Lake, but I still have them today: looking up at Dad's flies landing on the water, legs in waders seen from underwater, the stumps of old snags, water that was unnaturally clear but always green. And the underside of our boat.

The dinghy may have been Roy's idea. It may have been a bid on his part to reconnect Dad to me and Mom. Dad had already left the service when he built the boat, so I don't know how he steamed and bent the wooden pieces to the appropriate curve, but Roy would come over to the apartment in Edmonds and help him put each rib and strake in place. I was very aware that this was *our* boat, not just Dad's. We painted it an ugly forest green, for when it needed to lie hidden in the brush along the shore, and took it up the mountain.

Even the boat had to fit the habitat. We were constantly assessing the Cascades environment, learning how we were related to the color of the water and the plants and birdsong. When we weren't fishing we were hiking up the fire roads or up to Ebey Mountain, and I liked hiking but only if I couldn't fish with Dad. Vesta foraged a fair amount of the food for their vegetarian diet, and I remember her telling me about ground cherries, a fruit that she grew or found somewhere. The Sutters had extensive gardens. She picked berries for money now and then, and when I was with her I sometimes took my afternoon nap in a big blackberry patch.

Roy and Vesta invited Mom and Dad to their Seventh-day Adventist Church, and Mom did go a few times, but Dad was skeptical. He and Mom attended Everett Christian Reformed Church for a while, and then Dad started probing around, trying Baptist, Lutheran, even Episcopalian. Then he quit going altogether for about a decade.

Real memories from the age of four are rare, but one distinct memory of our time in Seattle is being on Ebey Lake and looking at my bobber in green water and the dull shine of that water and the reflection on the water of tall conifers moving in the wind.

~

We left Seattle when I was four and a half, and Dad threw his Air Force dress uniform into a Salvation Army box. He had achieved the rank of Airman Second Class—now simply called Airman—and he was done with that and he almost never mentioned his military service again, except to tell me it was no good. Lots of other dads flew away to the Philippines and to Vietnam, but he didn't. Mom regretted leaving her good job at Sears but Dad was eager to make a fresh start. He had an honorable discharge, the GI Bill, and a two-year degree from Everett Junior College, and he was ready to go back to Michigan.

For the move, we bought a Volkswagen bus that Dad fitted with a big, comfy bed stacked with a thick foam-rubber mattress and heavy cloth sleeping bags whose flannel linings depicted hunters and pheasants. We towed Mom's VW Bug behind the bus at first, but after the bus wheezed and chugged all the way over the Cascades with the dinghy on top, Mom had to drive the bug and I went back and forth from vehicle to vehicle. We were rushing and didn't stop to fish. We rolled across the Clark Fork and close by the Big Hole, the Jefferson, the Beaverhead, stopping to look down into the Madison, the Gallatin, the Yellowstone, the Bighorn, waters that Dad called the "good rivers," hung with morning steam. We drove through the Upper Peninsula because the U.P. is the dream and slept in the van in the late summer, and anytime we stopped Dad would show me the rivers on the maps and say, "We're going back for those."

Dad was a good carpenter and he got work immediately with Dan Vos Construction out of Ada, Michigan, mostly building churches. But moving to Michigan didn't change his sexual appetites any, and because he was always chasing another job and another woman, we were on the move, rental to rental.

"The flip-flops went on from there," said Mom. "Lots of flip-flops."

~

The next fall, the fall of 1969, was the first time I ever saw my father and his brothers the way they saw themselves, easy comrades laughing together, men who had grown up farming and hunting together and shared a code. I'd never seen Dad so relaxed and secure, even around Roy. It was Dad and Vern, probably Jack, certainly Mike, and probably others I don't recall, standing in Henry and Gertrude's back lawn pulling guns out of fabric cases and handfuls of twelve-gauge shells out of paper boxes and stuffing them into their pockets. As they talked and loaded, they looked through a barbed-wire fence at a cornfield south of the house. A cock pheasant had flown across the dirt road from the river and into that cornfield and nothing else mattered. Down in a steep gulley between the yard and the corn, heifers ate around the bull thistle. Others drank at the cow tank on the west edge of the yard. Heinie stood among the men, muttering, "Boys, boys." The wet had cleared out of the blue sky because summer was ending. There was the metallic tap of cartridge brass seated in the chamber and a double-barrel snapped closed. Pump actions ratcheting.

Mom had baby Brett, and Vern and Sally had just had their first child, Sarah, so Grandma chatted away with them in her high nasal voice that was like a bluegrass song as they moved in and out of the house. My father had a beautiful Ithaca Model 37 Featherlite shotgun that I'd never seen before, because I'd never seen him holding a gun. If he was issued a gun in the Air Force, neither Mom nor I had ever seen it. The Ithaca was an elegant slash of dark wood and blued steel, long and thin like he was, with a very fast and loud pump action. The pheasant we'd seen had set its wings and tugged all the purpose in the world after it. Enough of each man remained in the yard to turn and grin at me, and I grinned back, and Mom and Sally grinned, and Heinie and Gert grinned, but theirs faded quickest because once again their boys were hustling away from them into those fields. Some of the men were still stuffing shells into the feeder slots on the side of the guns as they went through the barbed wire, quickly down a cow trail through the gulley, up past the old bag-swing tree, over another fence, and into the corn and gone.

Grandpa and I sat in the fall sun on a tiny concrete apron off the back of the brick house among the empty boxes of shells and listened for the dull thud of shots. Which thrilled me so when they came, I had to run to the maple tree in the yard and piss on it.

∼

Mom and Dad bought me a yellow Huffy Cheater Slick, a stingray-style bike with a fat rear tire and a little bit of a sissy bar. We had moved to an apartment complex on a big sweeping turn on Butternut Drive in a Holland neighborhood called Pine Creek, and my buddies and I had few restrictions on where we could ride. Just across the street was a barber-shop with a gumball machine. One afternoon I was straddling my bike next to a couple of other guys in the gravel in front of that shop, on the big curve, when we decided to get some gum. I didn't have any money and I laid my bike down without a thought and ran straight across the road toward the apartment. Almost instantly, I was hit by a station wagon moving at speed.

When I replay the moment of impact, I always see the grill of the wagon hitting me directly on the right hip. It makes sense, but memory is fallible. Mom, for instance, didn't see the accident but remembers me getting off the school bus and getting hit, but I distinctly recall that barbershop gumball machine. The impact, however, was certain: the car hit me square-on and I flew about twenty-five or thirty feet into the yard of the apartment complex. The guy who hit me was our postman, and he must have had a little speed up because as he braked, his momentum carried him into the yard, too, and the long wagon swung around, making almost a full loop in the grass, and slammed to a stop near a fence. I must have reconstructed the car spinning in my memory because I was too busy tomahawking across the lawn to have seen it. I found myself sitting upright on the ground, gripping at the grass as though to stop me from sailing away into the sky, awake and shaking violently.

The postman appeared beside me saying, "Are you okay? Don't move, don't move." Someone got Mom out of the apartment, where Brett was getting up from a nap, and she thrust Brett into that person's arms and ran out the door. They laid me down in the grass and checked me over, and I had scrapes in all the places where I had hit the ground—forehead, knees, elbows, palms, hips—as I ragdolled across the turf.

The poor postman! He offered to take me to the hospital, but Mom got me in the car and took me herself. Dad left a construction job and came to meet us. In the ER, they made sure I didn't have a punctured lung or need a splenectomy or anything like that, but I was fine. The next day the postman rapped on the door while he did his rounds and asked about me, and he was still pretty shaken up. I was at kindergarten, but Mom assured him I was okay. He had gone through a pretty bad night, thinking he might have killed a little kid. It was completely my fault. I was shaking too hard in the grass to apologize, or else I would have. No words would come out of my face while I looked at him with my eyeballs rattling around in my head.

I had already thought a lot about dying by that point in my life. Church people talked about dying all the time, 'cause that's when things were going to get good for them. I had thought about all the fish we caught and the pheasants Dad shot and the muskrats and mink my uncles trapped along the Black River and the moose Uncle Dale shot up in Canada. The animals didn't give up their lives easily and volunteer to go to heaven. They fought. They bit you if they could and gored you with an antler and clawed and wiggled and hightailed it. I wasn't ready to fly away to wherever God was in outer space, either. I had clung to the grass in the lawn with both hands while I sat there, shaking. My fingers were sore from it. I was like everything else that only had this life and then went into that ground. I wanted to live.

∼

Dad got into the building trades program at Western Michigan University, and we moved into a depressing cinder-block house in Richland, east of Kalamazoo. He worked construction when he wasn't at school and was gone all the time. Brett was just one year old, but Mom was pregnant again, and she was having a lot of trouble with the pregnancy. I didn't know much about it, I was only six years old, but she was gone to the doctor a lot and she'd take Brett with her. Her obstetrician was an hour away in Holland, so she'd drive up there for appointments.

In August, my brother Joe was born more than two months premature. He was about the size of a large guinea pig, weighing only two pounds, thirteen ounces, and he was kept in the Neonatal Intensive Care Unit—in the "*nick-you*," Mom called it—in Holland Hospital for six weeks. Mom had me and Brett to care for and Dad worked all the time, so Joe was alone with the hospital staff most of that time. His pediatrician called Mom with updates every day, and even if she did go up there, she wasn't allowed to touch him. Joe just lay there in his box, day after day, and developed infant depression because no one could hold him. I had a brother I had only seen in a plastic box with tubes and wires; the writer Rebecca Solnit once described preemies like him as a "half-written sentence." Dad didn't go to the hospital because he couldn't take it. When I asked him how Joe was, his eyes would well up and he'd say he didn't want to talk about it.

The doctors had warned Dad that Joe probably wouldn't make it, and if he did he might have some physical problems. He did have a double hernia, which was easy enough to fix. Mom didn't care what they said. She was never weepy because she never believed for an instant that he would die. She knew he would make it.

Joe did make it, and with a vengeance. You never met a kid who wanted more from life and who was determined to grow big and fast enough to get it. Later, when he was powerful and challenging every gallon of vodka to kill him, I thought about him lying in that little plastic box and I thought it unfair that a ravaging hunger would chase him from start to finish.

∾

That fall, we moved into WMU's married housing complex across the street from the sprawling campus, a series of maybe a couple hundred

white stucco apartments stacked three to a building and laid out in stag-
gered, faux-Mediterranean terraces. The place was overrun with kids so
I thought it was fine, but Mom and Dad were a complete shambles.

This was when I first became aware that my Dad wasn't acting right.
I had hundreds of other couples around me for comparison, and it was
easy to see he was up to something. On the weekends when people went
to Woods Lake or to Little League or whatever, he wasn't around. He
went to Western all day during the semesters and worked construction all
summer and on weekends, struggling to keep food on the table, but on
Saturday and Sunday nights he wouldn't come home. He'd come dragging in early Monday morning just in time to get some clean clothes and
bitch about how there was nothing to eat before he had to get to work
or to class, and then he and Mom would fight.

They would fight because Mom knew he was with one girlfriend or
another, and she was working like mad, too, babysitting as many as six
kids from the complex during the day to help make ends meet, so she
lived more or less in a state of rage. She was angry and desperate, but
she was quiet. She confronted Dad, but she didn't yell or scream or throw
things. She just blasted him with a terse righteousness. If she would have
slapped or screamed, Dad probably just would have laughed. He hated
any display of emotion. The two of them went into the bedroom to keep
the fighting away from us. Joe was just a tiny baby, but Brett saw their
faces twisted with anger and he was scared out of his mind, so I didn't
leave him sitting there alone. I would hang out until Mom reemerged and
then I was out the door.

I would disappear into a little savannah of sassafras and sumac and
honey locust that beckoned from the hillside up above the apartment
complex. I'd kick around in there looking for woodchuck holes and identifying the birds, and sometimes watching deer. The married housing
property went partway up Howard Street Hill and stopped at a chain-
link fence, but the scrubby, wooded savannah continued on the other side
of the fence and that was the property of the Kalamazoo Psychiatric
Hospital, or what everyone called the State Hospital. The heavy brick
buildings were visible at the top of the hill and its spooky medieval water
tower loomed over us.

The property beyond the fence stretched for about 150 yards up the
hill before it reached the hospital's grass yards. It had probably been open
fields not too many years before, as it was only lightly dotted with spindly

trees. I would cling to the fence with both hands and watch the residents strolling along trails through the goldenrod and milkweed and foxtail, smoking cigarettes. I watched one man stop and smell the locust blooms, which hung from the trees like bunches of cream-white grapes in the spring and smelled like honey. I thought heaven must smell like that, and I wondered if he thought heaven had a smell. Dad told me to stay away from these people because they were lunatics. Some of the walkers talked to themselves, but none of them ever came down to the fence to talk to me.

I couldn't be around when Mom and Dad were fighting, but I didn't think the tensions in our apartment were worse than anyone else's. We were living with several hundred young couples, lots of them with kids, and people were fighting like hell everywhere. They were sneaking around like crazy, too. We lived there from 1970 to 1972, from when I was six to when I was eight, and the gang of kids I ran with heard everything. We might not have known exactly what was going on, but the stakes were high for us—we were the *kids*—so we'd relate the fights to one another like they were TV shows. During the summers, people would put big fans in the windows and you'd hear people hissing and fighting and slapping, but in distorted, hacked-up voices that came through the fan. My friend Tracy and I had a whole routine worked out made of dialogue we heard through other people's windows. It didn't matter that we didn't know what half the words meant; we'd sit on the stairs outside and say them back and forth to each other:

"Oh, what? You're with that *slut* now?" I'd start.

"Shut up, *bitch*," Tracy said.

"Get away from me. I'll kick that dick and then see how you do."

That was our favorite: "I'll kick that dick." Down in the thickets along Stadium Drive we'd found that we could lift the manhole cover off a culvert and see Arcadia Creek gushing underground there, and we'd get down in there and if anyone threatened to put the manhole cover back on over our heads we'd bark out: "I'll kick that dick!" Our friend Bobby was younger and he had a tic that made him repeat everything you said under his breath, and he'd follow along behind us, whispering, "*I'll kick that dick. I'll kick that dick.*"

As far as I knew, all the apartments in the complex were identical inside, and all the families in them were pretty much identical, too, other than skin color or the stuff they had on the walls. I could walk into any apartment in the complex—they were rarely locked—and I knew exactly which cupboard the water glasses would be in or where they'd keep a cookie jar or toilet paper. Everybody kept their cheap silverware in exactly the same drawer and everybody was poor and everyone had Tang and bologna and white bread. One time I was going to visit Tracy and I absentmindedly walked into the wrong apartment and a man in a white tank top was fighting with a lady just wearing her bra and a slip, and they were in each other's faces. The man was seated at the table with food in front of him, but she was standing over him, and he was pointing at her with his butter knife. He looked at me and said, "Who the hell are you? Get the fuck out!" The lady barked, "He's just a kid!" as I backed out the door.

We were just kids. But we were paying attention.

~

Joe lived in a bassinette in Mom and Dad's room for a while and then moved into the second bedroom with me and Brett. Joe was a beautiful, towheaded kid, with blonde curls like a cherub from an old painting, and moms would stop Nancy to remark on how gorgeous he was. It was a little crowded in our room, with bunk beds and a crib, and I stayed outside as much as I could.

Dad wasn't around on the weekends to take us to the good places on the map, but Nancy tried to do it. We had friends one building over named Dave and Joy Meagher, and they had kids our ages; Dave was a skinny vet with sideburns and a mustache who had a chopped Harley and rode with some kind of motorcycle club. He was going to college on the GI Bill, exactly like Dad. One time after Dave had evidently graduated and Mom and Dad were really hating each other, Dave and Joy invited Mom to take us kids to their place in Milford, over near Pontiac. Dad wasn't invited, or couldn't go. I was probably eight. They had a house and a trailer and a big pond for swimming. We stayed in the trailer, and in the evening, some of Dave and Joy's other friends showed up. I was standing out on the dock with Dave, and one of his buddies came out there and took off his prosthetic leg and dove into the shallow water. And there was his leg, lying on the dock. I knew that some men lost their legs in Vietnam, but I thought we had left that in Seattle. I didn't realize that this loss had crept in everywhere, had stolen from homes right there in our part of Michigan. Dave and my dad had two good legs, and I was so glad. But I thought some other loss or madness had found my dad. No house was strong enough to keep it out.

I would ride the old Cheater Slick a mile up over Howard Street Hill, pedaling furiously past the State Hospital, and down to the YMCA on Maple Street. I took judo classes there and skipped swimming by hiding in the snack room and then taught myself to swim during the free swim that followed. I was mostly there on my own. The Y was a mix of every type of people, which is probably that organization's greatest legacy—women, men, blacks, Latinos, Jews, Asian kids, people in wheelchairs, more guys with fake legs, everybody was there. To me, that was the world.

Race mattered, though, and there was unease in married housing. I don't recall the circumstances, but one day a group of black boys threw me down and took off with my bike. Tall concrete walls separated upper and lower terraces, and they chucked the bike over a wall and then smashed it with big rocks, knocking the spokes out, bending the rims and the sprocket.

I ran back to the apartment and reported this to Mom through wailing and tears, and she marched right over there and yelled at those kids to get away from the bike and told me, "Go get it. It's your bike." I walked through them and picked it up, and she and I pushed it back to the apartment together.

The kids who had wrecked the bike came right along after us, though, jeering and swearing. They called us "white trash" and started to enjoy themselves more and more. It was a long walk and they came swarming right up after us onto the landing of our second-floor apartment, yelling and carrying on, and both Mom and I started to get scared. Doors were opening to other apartments across the way and people were peering out. Finally, Mom turned to face the boys as I hid halfway in the door of the apartment, wondering how in the world I was going to get a new bike, since we didn't have any money, and how I was going to live with a new gang of enemies. Mom scolded them for wrecking my bike, and one of the kids yelled out, "Lady, my mama come over here and put you in the hospital!" and another followed up and yelled, "White bitch!"

Mom smashed him across the face. It wasn't a "Look here, kid" kind of mom-tap, it was a full windup slap that turned his head halfway around.

She leaned in on him and said, "Don't ever say that to anyone again."

Everyone was quiet then. The boys stood there, openmouthed, looking at me, looking at her, absolutely stunned to see this white lady staring them down. Then they all took off running like they were scared to death.

I didn't know what to do. I was proud of my mom for sticking up for me, but I was also horrified that she had just started a race war.

Later that night, the police turned up and got Mom out of bed and took a statement from her. The mother of the kid who was slapped wanted to press charges. The police made it clear that that lady didn't know the kids had wrecked my bike, or the words they'd said. But when Dad got home, he basically took that lady's side. He didn't want any trouble, so he threw Mom under the bus. We saw how it was, then: if anyone ever threatened us, Dad would betray us. The truth must have come out about the bike, however, because that other lady dropped the whole thing.

I stayed away from that crew for the rest of the time we lived there. But a couple of years later I was playing Little League baseball and realized one of the kids on the other team was the guy my mom slapped. He was a good ballplayer, and after the game when the teams shook hands he smiled a huge smile at me as we shook and chucked me on the shoulder. I played against him a number of times down the line, and it was always that way. We were fine.

Six
Muskrat Island

Dad graduated from Western Michigan University, and he decided things could be different with Mom and him, so he bought a white, aluminum-sided, three-bedroom ranch home out in Texas Corners just southwest of Kalamazoo, a short block away from the summer-warm waters of Crooked Lake. The lake was ringed with houses and there were kids in almost every one, and surrounding the lake in every direction was farm country. We had a twenty-acre forest of red oak and slippery elm and sassafras out the back door and sprawling vineyards and cherry orchards and asparagus fields and undeveloped land across the street to the south and to the east. I didn't have to commune with the lunatics anymore to be in the woods.

Dad was working construction for Jerry Stifler and he was hardly ever home, but one day he brought us a dazzling black-and-white English setter puppy. I named her Brandy, probably because of that song by Looking Glass, as I listened obsessively to WLS-Chicago on the AM radio. That dog became one of the best bird dogs of our lives, a gentle genius. Mom and Dad still fought, but I stopped paying much attention because they'd basically installed me in paradise. I could fish for bass and panfish in Crooked Lake and pick leeches off my feet and swing from the wild grapevines like Tarzan and I didn't need Dad around.

Stopped paying much attention, that is, until September 1975. Mom and Dad had been out with friends on a Saturday night, and all day Sunday Mom was in a state, like she had grabbed on to an electrical wire. She moved slowly and five-year-old Joe wouldn't leave her side. Finally, in the afternoon, someone came to stay with us and Dad told us he was taking her to Borgess Hospital. She would stay there for three weeks, having what was then called a "nervous breakdown."

I didn't know some of this until much later, but the couple they'd visited on that Saturday night had finally shattered Mom's incredible state of denial. Earlier in the summer, she and Dad had visited these same friends and Mom had walked into the kitchen to find Dad making out with the woman, whom we know but shall remain nameless. True to Mom's tragic style, they remained friends, and when they went to see them again in September, the woman grabbed Dad and said she was taking him for a ride in her new convertible Volkswagen. Mom sat there in the house with that woman's husband, both of them knowing full well what was going on, making small talk for an hour.

"I just don't need this," she said to Dad when they came back from their ride. All four of them were standing right there. No crack across the face. No tears. She had finally decided she was done with him.

Vern's wife, Sally, allegedly took us up to the hospital to see Mom once, but none of us remember it. Maybe Mom dreamed it. Sally was a nurse and had tried her hardest to smooth things for Bruce. For years, she had called Mom and told her, "Try to find it in your heart to forgive him," and recommended that she take a hot bath. All of us remember her taking a lot of hot baths, and Brett and Joe used to climb right in there with her.

But Mom had left Dad in the house with us, and he didn't know whether to shit or throw up. He was pissed at Mom for going to the hospital and disrupting his life. He walked around the house, barking, "Fuck! FUCK!" He didn't know what to do. When he wasn't swearing he seemed distant and quiet, like he knew whatever was happening was his fault. We just kept searching his perfectly shaved face for clues as our faith slipped away morning after morning. He cooked what he would cook if we were camping: boiled hot dogs and canned baked beans and boxes of doughnuts. He bought hot, handmade pizza from the Crooked Lake Market, which we craved and rarely got. He didn't know how to do the laundry or how to make lunches for school or do our homework, and after a day or two Joe asked if he could have something other than toast for breakfast and the look in Bruce's eye told us he was going to get mean if that kept up.

We were sitting around the dark-brown Formica table in our little kitchen, with the harvest-cornucopia-themed wallpaper with fruits spilling out of baskets in brown, yellow, and orange, and Joe kept on asking. Mom always made waffles. Why couldn't we have waffles and syrup? And when was she coming back?

"Pretty soon," said Dad, standing at the counter leaning on his fists with his shoulders up around his ears, staring straight down into himself.

"WHEN?!!" screamed Joe, bursting into tears.

We didn't try to hush Joe because we had the same question, and we didn't care if he hit us or smashed something because our mom was in the hospital and he was in on it.

"She's taking a rest," he said, but he told us no more. The next day or soon after he went back on the road selling steel for American Buildings and aunts and neighbors came to stay with us. I was eleven and Brett was six, so I learned how to make pancakes by reading the Bisquick box and cooked breakfast until Mom got home. I never did learn how to make waffles, though.

I was worried our mother would never come back or, if she did, come back as someone crazy. I imagined that she had gone to a place like the State Hospital, where people had to be locked up because they were insane. I knew that there had been trouble in other people's houses up and down the block, and that some of them went to Parents Without Partners or had big church interventions when ministers showed up at the door, but suddenly that became real. That became *our* house. The home we lived in broke open and wildness rushed in like floodwater; I didn't know what would come riding in on that, but I feared it would be strangers and madness and loneliness. There was a difference between parents fighting and real, permanent trouble. A couple of the kids I had known on the block had left when parents split up and never came back, sometimes even separating brothers and sisters.

Little things Dad had done took on new meaning. I knew he could be a mean son of a bitch, and I wondered if that's just how he was with Mom all the time. A few months before Mom disappeared, all five of us had been driving in his Electra 225; I was dwarfed by the giant front seat and Mom was in back with Brett and Joe and all of us were screaming happy to be with Dad; then he looked in the rearview mirror and gave her the finger and smiled. She looked away. Mom just didn't know how to respond to a bad man. I thought maybe they were playing, just teasing each other, but after she went to the psych ward I knew it wasn't a game. He was telling her he could do whatever he wanted, and his boys would still love him.

But that wasn't true and he didn't know. It's hard to hate your dad but that little fire can become a conflagration. When Mom was gone we suddenly knew she could die or go nuts, and Brett and I, at least, began to turn against him, and we had no intention of turning back.

One day in October she was standing in the kitchen again, a pale and thin version of our mother, wearing clothes that looked like a tent on her. She had done some group therapy in the psych wing, and talked to a few doctors, but mostly what she'd done in there was read a paperback copy of *The Paper Chase* and not be anywhere near Dad. When he came to get her, he hoped she'd come home and take care of us so he could be seen as an upstanding guy and get back to chasing women, but she told him, "I want you to get the hell out of my life."

She had spent so much of her life deflecting attention away from herself, and she knew she could change that in a heartbeat if she wanted. Mom was the most beautiful mother among all our friends' parents, and we knew that the dads noticed her. We saw it happen all the time, and in less guarded moments or after a few beers they would even say things to us like, "Your mother is a nice-looking lady." But she pushed that attention away. She would sit in the bleachers at my baseball games and radiate a mild disinterest toward the men who stared at her tight jeans and see-through blouses. She got a job as the bookkeeper and assistant manager at Osco Drug, and she focused on starting a career and raising three boys on her own. Dad behaved like it was kind of a joke and that it would end soon, but Nancy had actually put him out in the street. He moved out, and he acted like he didn't know what the plan was anymore.

After he'd been gone a couple of weeks, Dad took me out to Bilbo's Pizza, a J. R. R. Tolkien–themed place on Western's campus, and he had a beer. It was such a rare event I took it as a sign. He was a guy who would open a bottle of $1.99 wine for guests and keep it in the refrigerator for two years and then throw it away.

"Your mother wants me to stay out of the house," he said, treating me differently, treating me as if, unlike during her stay in the hospital, I needed to know what was going on.

"Are you getting a divorce?" I said, hoping he would say yes. I felt sorry for him and I wanted to crack off the end of his beer bottle and stick it in his face. I had seen that on TV.

"I don't know," he said. "Your mom wants that, I think."

"Why?"

"I don't know," he lied.

"You fight all the time," I said.

"And I guess she just needs a break from that," he nodded.

He drank his beer.

"Can I still get a shotgun for my birthday?" I said.

He looked at me and nodded. "You're probably going to need it," he said.

"I definitely need it," I said.

~

When the lakes iced over that winter, Dad and I started our muskrat trap line, and I bought handgrip strengtheners and one of those chest exercisers with three springs on it so I could get strong enough to set my traps. I got books on trapping and on fur-bearing animals from my school, Mattawan, and from the Kalamazoo Public Library. Mom was big on reading, and when we lived in married housing she used to take us to the libraries at WMU and to the public library's Central Branch on Rose Street, and the Bookmobile would come out to Texas Corners. In one of these books I read the Anishinaabe creation story, in which muskrat is the hero. The Anishinaabe include the Ojibway (Chippewa), Ottawa, and Potawatomi people who occupied western Michigan when white people first arrived.

According to the story I read, sometime after the Great Spirit (Kitche Manitou) created the world, the humans started fighting with one another and the Great Spirit punished them with a huge flood. The only person left, Nanaboozhoo, gathered the surviving animals together and declared that he was going to create dry land by diving to the bottom of the flood and getting some dirt. But he couldn't hold his breath long enough to reach bottom. All the other creatures tried—the beaver, the grebe or helldiver, the otter, and others—and they all failed. The muskrat said he would try, and the other animals mocked him. They said he wasn't a good-enough swimmer. But down he went and he stayed under so long that he drowned. And when his body floated up, in his little paw was a bit of dirt. The other animals cheered: muskrat had sacrificed his life so that others could live. The turtle told Nanaboozhoo to put that dirt on his strong back, and thus Turtle Island was formed, which we know as North America.

It was wrong to call it Turtle Island, when clearly it should have been Muskrat Island! I already felt bad about killing that one muskrat and not eating it, but after I read this story I was done being a trapper.

I kept quiet about it, though. My gigantic white Christian family had no sense of humor about creation lore from the Ojibway or anybody else. It was Genesis or nothing. More important, I didn't want Bruce to think I was done with hunting or fishing because I figured that was how I was going to spend the rest of my life.

~

Dad got an apartment in the town of Oshtemo, just west of Kalamazoo. It was a ramshackle mock-Tudor place with white shag carpet and fake half-timbers. There were two bedrooms: one for Dad and one for his office, with a drafting table and flat files and such. There was no bed for us, because we weren't going to be staying there. Or if we did, we had to throw some sleeping bags on the couch or the carpeted floor.

Every place we'd ever lived, Mom and Dad had furnished for us as a family, so it took us a minute to understand that this new apartment wasn't for us. What he'd created here was a pussy palace. He had a real component stereo, with detachable wood cabinet speakers for that preternaturally intimate sound, and his stack of fifty or so sexy R&B, Motown, and lady singer records. I was practicing to be a drummer in school, and I would put on George Benson's *Good King Bad* to listen to Steve Gadd and Andy Newmark play drums, imagining the different parts of the drum kit with my head against the cabinets like a speaker freak. Dad had a queen-sized bed in his room under a giant macramé wall-hanging, and a bottle of Riunite white dawdling in the fridge. There were notes in women's handwriting on the counter. Brett and Joe found *Playboys* stashed in the end table and I saw his shaving kit was full of condoms. I was happy there wouldn't be any half siblings, but it did make me worry. I was obsessed with sex myself, and I was confronted with the evidence that my Dad was doing it, in this apartment, probably every night, deploying technologies like condoms and macramé. If someone moved in with him, where would we go? What happened if he married someone else and just moved away?

I never met any of his lady friends, but Joe did once, when Dad took him ice skating at WMU's Lawson Ice Arena and one of his dates came along. Joe was about six or seven and he told us, "Oh, she was real nice."

During the winter, Dad built me a room in the basement of the house by Crooked Lake, so that Brett and Joe could each have their own room upstairs. My room was behind the furnace and with only a tiny little casement window I'd never fit through. He said, "Well, there's no way you're getting out of here in a fire, so you better sleep light," which I took seriously. For Christmas I got a blue plastic Sears record player for listening to my first album, Aerosmith's *Toys in the Attic*, and one day I ran down into the basement and heard music from my room, so I crept up and Mom was in there, dancing all by herself to my forty-five of Barry Manilow's "I Write the Songs." I split without saying anything.

As promised, Dad delivered a shotgun for my twelfth birthday, a Montgomery Ward Western Field Model single-shot youth twenty-gauge, which he bought from Vern. It was already about twenty-five years old, and it was exactly what I needed. The price, I found out a couple of months later, was I had to paint the house. So I spent most of that summer up on a ladder, scraping and painting the wood trim and over-hangs, listening to WKMI and WLS with the dog, Brandy, sitting by and panting in the shade.

Dad did make a point of running the dog that summer, and luckily Brandy needed almost no training, because Dad lacked the patience to properly train a dog. He figured out the basic commands to tell her to hunt freely, hold point, flush the bird, or fetch it up, but she mostly knew what to do. Dad would yell and gesticulate in frustration. Somebody had told him that when you wanted the dog to come, you said "here," but you screamed it at the top of your lungs as a distorted, two-syllable "HEEE-YAAH!" She'd work the field back and forth but then get too far out in front of us and he'd be screaming, "HEEE-YAAH, Brandy, HEEE-YAAH!" She'd amble back and fix him with a withering look. When she put up a bird, she snapped at its tail feathers as it took flight, and when she got on a rabbit she was hilarious, running full blast and leaping high above the tall grass to track the dodging bunny, *sproing*-ing through the fields like a gazelle, and Bruce would break form and shout, "Leap, rabbit dog, leeeeeeeeaaap!" and we'd all bust out laughing. The rabbits always got away.

I took my state-mandated hunter's safety course that summer, which was taught according to a curriculum designed by the National Rifle Association, and Bruce told me resolutely that I would not be joining that organization. He was a conservative person, but early in his life he mostly didn't vote and shunned activism of any kind because people took ideologies as excuses for bad behavior. He explained to me that joining the NRA sometimes meant giving sanction to those people who abused their rights and became slob hunters. Hunting was hugely popular and not threatened by legislation in any way, but gun enthusiasts made a show of hunting using guns meant for killing people—for instance, going "full auto," using a machine gun to hunt deer or bear—in order to make a statement. Bruce told me those people had crossed a line. Politics had turned them into slobs. Slobs made animals suffer and turned the public against hunting. Being a slob showed a lack of expertise and restraint, and it was the worst insult he could bestow on anyone.

Of course, Dad's sex life was totally slobby. But about hunting and fishing and trapping he was a purist.

On the first day of my first-ever small game season, we stepped into a farmer's fallow hayfield, and Brandy instantly flushed a quail out of the fencerow right in front of me, and as it hammered away like a leaf-colored heartbeat I put up my gun and dropped it. It was my first shot at anything. "Good shot," said Dad. "Go help the dog find it." That was it, and I wasn't expecting anything more. He just assumed I'd hit it, I guess, since he and my uncles always did. Dad joined us for dinner that night and the four birds we'd bagged that day made us a family again for an hour or two.

∾

The oaks beyond the backyard fence were the color of dried blood as Dad stood in the kitchen at the house and announced with a grand flourish that he had found a new place for us! That pulled me up short. I thought he meant that we were all going to get a new house together, and I didn't want him and Mom to be married anymore. Joe was kind of excited about it because he really missed Dad being in the house, but Brett looked absolutely panic-stricken. Mom seemed shocked, too.

"I found a great place for us to *hunt*," Dad continued, and then told us that his customer Bernard Card, a steel building contractor up in Rose City, had invited us to his deer camp.

"Right by the Rifle River area, and just thick with deer," Dad said, triumphant. "If this turns out good, it could change everything for us."

I got excited about this, even if I didn't really quite get it. Hunting at Card's wouldn't have anything to do with his relationship to Mom, which we thought was the most important thing to change. But that was the way Dad's mind worked: a new river or a new piece of land held the promise of a new way of being, even a new way of thinking. He was going to take his boys to this new hunting camp and prove to Mom and everyone that he was a great dad, that he could be saved by works, that the world was going to give him another chance.

Old Bernie Card knew what was going on at home; he bought a fair number of steel buildings from Dad and knew he was out on his ass and maybe he even knew some of the other women. Bernard was the father of four boys around Dad's age and their wives and kids hunted, too, and he told Dad to bring me up to his 120-acre camp to see how it all worked. Whatever Bernard knew or didn't know about Dad, he doted on me. Bernard treated me like he and I were in on something that my father didn't need to be part of.

As his white Cadillac Eldorado squeaked and rolled along the sandy two-tracks through his hunting property, he'd stop to point out game trails and places where big deer had been seen recently and the cabin of an "old bastard" he was having a shooting feud with, and I could see Dad inscribing this stuff furiously on his brain. He'd only been deer hunting a couple of times and he wanted to do it right. About halfway to the back of the long, narrow parcel, Bernard parked next to a corn crib and told me he wanted to show me something. He opened the trunk and pulled out a lever-action .30-30 saddle gun and showed me how to load it. I was too young to hunt deer, the legal age was fourteen then, and I could see from the look on Dad's face they had not discussed this, but it was his first year there, too, so he deferred to the older man.

And Bernard's face shone. With his big twinkly grin, ample belly, and red hunting outfit, he looked a little like Santa, if Santa were to wear a gray, freshly mown flatop, and a little like Sorrell Booke as Boss Hogg because of the Caddy. He was clearly enjoying himself.

He told me to grab a tin lid from an old Masonite grain barrel and set it up against a stump about sixty yards off and then gave me the gun. I peered through the iron sights and hit it dead center and tried to act nonchalant about the fact that it had just about knocked my dick in the dirt.

"Well, that's damn well good enough to hunt in my camp," he said, clapping me on the back. "Bruce, you have him carry that gun. He'll probably shoot one before you do."

The next morning we were at the gates to Bernard's camp just before five A.M., and the black was smeared with cold stars. There were ten or eleven hunters, and we all loaded quickly into Bernie's son Jim's pickup in thick winter hunting suits and rabbit-lined trapper hats and ski gloves and scarfs, sitting on the edge of the truck bed with our guns between our knees. Almost everyone wore red with blaze orange vests and hats—even Dad suddenly had a red-and-black Buffalo plaid hunting outfit. I had on my ski gear. We squeaked and rolled through the camp, ducking over-hanging branches, watching the headlights play over funny wooden signs Bernard had put up like DOES A BEAR SHIT IN THE WOODS? and BERNARD'S DREAM. Warm breath streamed out behind us.

Jim stopped at each blind and hunters stepped off and said "Good luck" as they disappeared in the red of the tail lights. When our turn came, Bruce whispered to the others in a voice you could barely hear, then the truck creaked on down the line. Dad told me to pee before we got into our box. We sat in the gorgeous and nourishing dark for more than an hour before the light started coming up, and as soon as we could see we both sat forward in our chairs. We perched there on the edge of our plastic seats, crouched all day over the little propane heater that we'd turn on once in a while, seeing dozens of deer eating, lingering, sprinting past, both of us hardly moving. My quads were twitching badly from only sitting on about four inches of the hard plastic; I didn't want to sit back because that would mean sliding up and making noise if I needed to put the gun up. Dad said the same three words to me all day, in a half whisper: "*There's a deer.*"

When full darkness finally came around again, he slid back in his chair and exhaled fully. I felt his body sag. I was totally exhausted and relieved, and in my exhaustion I saw something else: I felt better in the dark. I loved being out in the blind, but I had been worried all day I was messing up Dad's hunt. We had gathered ourselves for the light, screwed ourselves down like tight coils with the sunrise, loaded, forcibly projecting ourselves outward toward the deer in a kind of mental casting that took immense focus. I had worked hard to maintain that focus all day, and I hadn't been able to shake the idea that I was doing it wrong. But the dark was more forgiving. Dad acted like I was okay in the dark. When the light drained away, Dad had receded and whatever was out there came toward me. I was surrounded by a kind of wholeness. *Oh,* I thought, *I am enough. It accepts me.* We had been watching the habitat all day, and sitting in a box had made it perfectly clear the forest was watching us, too; but in the dark I had the sense that I had my own relationship with the place, and it knew me. Bruce tolerated the dark as a cover from which we could spring out into the light and surprise our prey, but I felt like the light was where we were most hidden. The cold night was when I could be who I was in the woods.

We ducked out of our blind, stretched, and started walking down the dirt two-track toward the gate, talking about what we'd seen. The night was for talking, and we shared details for a while before Jim's truck came around and picked us up. In the bed of the truck, the vibe was completely different, everyone laughing and chatting loudly. The night was for celebrating. I definitely wanted to eat a deer, since that was the point, and we couldn't shoot one in the dark, but nighttime after an unsuccessful hunt wasn't full of disappointment. The habitat had filled everyone with humility and peace. Everyone seemed very satisfied to be riding home in that cold truck after a day in the field. Bruce was smiling and goofy and rode part of the way with his eyes closed. Hardly the guy who'd been on the edge of his chair all day.

Bernard didn't have a cabin then, so we went back to his house in town and Dad could barely stay awake. It was cold as death outside, and Bernard announced that he and I were going on an errand.

"Bruce, I'm taking your boy to go see a friend," Mr. Card said. "We'll be back in little while."

Dad didn't want to go; he smiled and told us he was going to bed. It was just Bernie and me in the lead-bottomed Eldorado, rocketing down the dirt roads toward the hunting grounds, chatting away. He slowed as we approached the farm gate to his hunting camp, but then drove on just a little farther to a grand, western-style log ranch gate with a name overhead: Grousehaven.

Grousehaven was a legendary hunting camp, three thousand acres abutting the wild Rifle River State Recreation Area and owned by Harold R. "Bill" Boyer, a former General Motors VP who bought the place in 1926. For decades, he turned it over every fall to the progenitor of modern bowhunting, Fred Bear, and select hunters and guests of Bear Archery. When Bernard and I bounced through the gate I found that Grousehaven shares a fence—and the swamp Dad and I had been watching all day—with Mr. Card's parcel, and it was just as raw and undeveloped. The leaf springs of the Cadillac *squinch*ed and *oomph*ed over a series of two-tracks winding through a forest of oak and beech and jack pine, with a grass landing strip for aircraft and a tiny old farm-house, which Boyer had turned into a kind of lodge.

Like on Bernard's place, the trees were hung with handmade wooden signs, most of them trail markers with names I would only understand later, like Arthur Godfrey Drive or Hoyt Vandenberg Circle. Boyer was a titan of American motor transport, the head of GM's Cadillac Cleveland Tank Division and the organizer of its Air Transport Division during World War II, when he was in charge of aircraft for the U.S. War Production Board. He oversaw all aircraft production during the Korean War and supervised tests on experimental vehicles later used by GM to build lunar rovers for Apollo missions 15, 16, and 17.

The Grousehaven crew included at various times Fred Bear; the TV personality Godfrey; General Vandenberg (after whom Vandenberg Air Force Base is named); Larry Bell of Bell Aircraft; Harley Earl, GM's chief stylist who designed so many of its cars, including precursors to the Cadillac we were in; and loads of other military figures such as General Curtis LeMay, former head of Strategic Air Command and U.S. chief of staff, and inspiration for the character General Buck Turgidson in the film *Dr. Strangelove*.

The farmhouse glowed with low lights and was wreathed with hanging smoke from a fieldstone fireplace. As we stepped out into the lung-burning cold, I loved the place immediately because it was just an old pineboard house, small and unimproved. From what I was told, Boyer could afford to build a forest palace for his friends but he didn't, and I loved that. I liked cabins that were old and piney. There were some other outlying buildings with more bedrooms and a garage with some cars and a tractor in the open bays, but none of it was fancy. This was the Michigan that emerged in the wake of the first wave of lumbermen, when the sawdust returned to earth and the rivers were restored by the Civilian Conservation Corps, the Michigan for me of the Nick Adams stories and the poetry of Jim Harrison and Thomas McGuane's *The Sporting Life*. I understood from what Bernard was telling me that Boyer was an important man, but out here it felt like we were all equals, all watchers taking our place in the dark.

People were talking inside and we let ourselves in. Fred Bear was standing silhouetted in the light and was deep in conversation. It was rifle season and his crew had already been there for much of October for bow season. I was introduced all around, and many of the guests lit up at the introduction of a twelve-year-old hunter. We all immediately fell to mapping the deer movements across the two properties.

I relayed what I had seen moving in and out of the swamp, and I was peppered with questions about deer numbers, size, sex, direction of travel, distinguishing characteristics. I was astonished and thrilled; these grown men and women wanted to know about everything I had seen, every snowy owl flapping slowly through the understory, every black squirrel that Mr. Card treasured, every turkey raking at the leaf litter. They wanted to know about a bent sheaf of reeds where the whitetails were passing in and out of a thumb of swamp to cross the fence, where I imagined they were bedding down, which trails they used most heavily, and any scrapes and rubs. All of them regarded my information as valuable intelligence.

We stayed long enough for Bernard to have a drink and we toasted Grousehaven's fiftieth anniversary. Then we were back in the car drubbing over the confusing tangle of narrow two-tracks with the headlights playing across the hard, cold darkness.

"I don't know why Dad didn't want to meet those guys," I said.

"You go easy on him, he worked hard to get you here," said Bernie.

"Yeah. He seems mad about something."

He looked at me. "Is it him who's mad or you?"

"He didn't say one word all day."

"And look at what you learned. I heard you back there. Your dad's a hell of a guy and the two of you will figure it out."

When we hit the two-lane blacktop, he said, "You write all this down. We'll stop at the grocery and get you a notebook and you make notes. You and your dad come back every year and you keep track of what happens. Pretty soon you'll have a good story about this place and everything in it, and you'll have a good story about yourself, too."

~

By the second summer of Mom and Dad's separation, when I was thirteen, I started keeping my shotgun propped up in the closet with two shells handy in the fold-down writing top to my dresser. The house was getting weird. Joe had horrible screaming nightmares about giant spiders, and if you went into his room to wake him he'd fight you like you were one. He had taken to sleepwalking, too: I'd be reading on the couch downstairs at night and Joe would float down like something I saw on Shock Theater, his eyes wide open but blued by another world. One time he sat down in front of the TV, which was turned off, and just flipped the knob through the channels. I said, "What you watching, Joe?" and he turned and looked at me with eyes that turned my skin cold. Then he got up and peed on the doors to the downstairs closet.

Men would show up at the door looking to talk to Mom. Word had gotten out that she and Dad were split, and no Olivia-Newton-John-looking lady was going to go unnoticed in tiny Texas Corners. Some of them were the fathers of my schoolmates, and even though I wasn't the man of the house, I was the man who was there.

I had a full-time summer job on a gladiola farm down in Three Rivers and to get there Dad had bought me a used Kawasaki 100 enduro, street legal, and through my workplace I got a farm license so I could ride on the road. Since I had a license, Mom would also send me to the store in her '69 Chevy Nova. Dad had finally sold the VW bus, which Mom had hated, and bought this Nova off a hot-rodder who had lifted it in the back and put on big slick tires. It would idle at about forty miles per hour, and I could barely see over the dash to drive it.

I came blazing home on the Kawasaki one late afternoon, and you could hear me coming from a mile away. I'd yanked the baffles out of the muffler when they got gummed up with carbon, so the bike whined like a deranged lawnmower; tests a few years later would show it cost me 30 percent of the hearing in my right ear. There was a strange car in the driveway, so I parked in the yard and banged through the screen door from the garage to find the father of one of my eighth-grade friends sitting with Mom at the kitchen table. She was demurely holding her shirt closed at the neck with one hand, and he had a cup of coffee in front of him. His ugly mug was frozen in a kind of rictus smile, but his eyes were darting around like he was about to jump out the window. The loud bike had given him plenty of time to escape.

"HEY JEFF!" he shouted, not getting up from the table. "I JUST STOPPED BY TO SEE YOUR MOM, WHAT DO YOU THINK ABOUT THAT?"

"Hey," I said, putting my thermos and lunch box down on the counter. "I'm just getting home from work."

He was yelling because he was nervous, and we all knew I could bust him. I hung out with his kids and his wife all the time at his house. I knew he wasn't sleeping with my mom, but something drove him to knock, to come in, to ask for a cup of coffee. He was sniffing around.

But that was enough for me. I was filthy from dusty farm work in my greasy Irish Setters, jeans with the knees torn out and a Mattawan football T-shirt, and he could see from the look on my face I already knew enough to be a threat.

"JUST TO SEE IF SHE NEEDS ANY HELP WITH ANYTHING."

"Well, thank you, that's nice."

"PRETTY MOM LIKE THAT."

I jerked open the door to the refrigerator. If I had been one of the Dutch kids from the Netherlands who worked on the flower farm, I could grab myself a beer. They were my age and their dad bought them a case of Budweiser every weekend. I slammed the door and looked at him. He had become my problem.

"WELL, I BETTER BE RUNNING! REAL GOOD TO SEE YA!"

I told him to say hi to his kid who was in my class. He brushed past me, and within fifteen seconds his car was lurching out of the driveway with the tires squealing.

"What was that all about?" I asked.

"Who knows," Nancy said wearily. "What was I supposed to say to him?"

"How about: 'You can't come in.' "

"It's fine. I can handle it," she said.

There were plenty of others, and we knew it wasn't Mom's fault; like dogs they homed in on the scent from everywhere in southwest Michigan—neighbors, friends of Dad's, guys who knew us from school or sports teams or cub scouts. And of course, sadists and psychopaths. Mom had not started dating, but she was thirty-three and blue-eyed and wanted to be as pretty and desirable as any other modern lady, and things took a bad turn.

For quite a while Mom had a regular phone caller, a man we knew and who knew she lived alone with her kids and made all kinds of threats about what he was going to do to her. Even worse, he would mutter, "Do you know who your husband is sleeping with tonight?" and spew out names. He *knew things* that only a real stalker could know. Sheriff's deputies told her to leave the phone off the hook and put pillows over it to drown out the "hang up" beeping. But, they said, unless he came to the house and tried something, there was nothing they could do. I was not a violent kid and I had never once been in a fight, but I used to pray that God would give me one clean, twenty-gauge shot at this guy.

Mom was no stranger to violence and predation. At Osco Drug she worked at the service desk in the evenings, handling the money. One night a man came in and put a pistol to her head and made her empty the safe and then ran off into the night.

She seemed to weather this okay, but that's because it was clearly about the money. All he wanted was to rob the store. The idea of the Phone Caller coming to her house, where her kids were, had her jumpy and sleep-deprived, constantly peeking through the curtains. One night she was in hysterics and ran around the house turning all the lights on and waking us all up, shoving shoes on our feet, and walking us down Q Avenue to the home of our friends Jack and Kay Brininger to spend the night. She wouldn't tell us what she saw, but it must have been an imminent threat because she herded us down the shoulder of the road like a mother duck.

"Mom, my gun," I said.

"No," she said.

"Why not?"

"NO!"

I needed that gun, but Mom knew better. She knew if the Phone Caller pulled up to us I would not hesitate to give him a face full of pheasant load, and then what are you? A teenaged killer. Mom couldn't live with that. She didn't want any of this to affect her kids, even though it obviously already had. It wasn't long before she started thinking about taking Dad back.

~

Other than not being permitted to shoot the stalker, I was treated like an adult. I got up at four A.M. every day and Mom made me breakfast, and then I drove south to the flower farm, where I set irrigation and built bulb-drying boxes and crawled along mile-long rows of gladiolas on my knees pulling nutgrass. Because I had a job, Dad treated me differently. Offered me coffee instead of milk. Took me to a bar on the WMU campus called Waldo's, where we could look at the waitresses and play pool after work.

That summer I started having sex, too. Mom hired a high-school-aged woman to look after Joe and Brett when she had to work at night, because I was desperate to see my friends at the lake and I was unreliable as a baby-sitter, anyway. One night after the sitter put them to bed, I was in my room in my robe listening to records and she just slid into bed with me and after talking for a minute put her hand in my underwear, and when she felt what was going on there she said, "I knew it. Horny as hell," and proceeded to shimmy out of her skintight jeans. I think I helped a little. She showed me what to do, but I don't believe I said a word. I was thirteen and she was probably fifteen or sixteen and I know these things would be seen differently now, but I was neither scared nor sorry. She was kind and seemed to delight in showing me the ropes, despite my sweaty silence, and I was as grateful as a puppy pulled from a well. I was sure she'd forget about me afterward, but she didn't. For a few months, it became a regular thing. Mom would make me my breakfast and I'd casually ask, "We have a babysitter tonight?" and if we did I'd dream about that all day.

The days belonged to Fred W. Nagle and Sons, flower farmers, but the nights were mine. I would drive the Kawasaki down to Crooked Lake and float around with friends in flotillas of boats and look at the fuzzy stars, or dodge the drunken dads cruising the lake on their pontoon boats shooting bottle rockets and black powder cannons at one another. The adults behaved much worse than we ever would. I was not in love with the woman I was having sex with, and she wasn't in love with me, either, and I was a little relieved we didn't run in the same circles, but the summer air felt better because she was out there somewhere.

The neighbors across the street, the Stevens, had a two-hundred-acre farm, and I took to walking their vineyards at night. They wouldn't care; their mom, Judy, was like a second mother to me. They had five kids and their oldest, Matt, was one of my best friends. I'd go over to their place in the mornings before school and sometimes eat a second breakfast, and Judy always seemed delighted to see me there. I felt good walking onto their place at night, and I especially loved going way to the back of their farm, near the center of the block under towering red oaks and maples. It was buggy but cool, and there were always deer back there. In September the grapes would be ripe, and it would smell like you fell into a vat of nirvana. Even Dad used to laugh at how much I craved that smell every fall; I'd ride in his car with my head out the window gulping at the air. The grapes were destined for the Welch's plant in Lawton, where they were made into grape juice, and sometimes they'd stay on the vine into October for added sugar. I'd walk through the vineyard in the dark with my mouth open like I could taste every berry.

I was secretive about my aesthetic and sensual fixations. If I went walking with other people in the grapes, it inevitably turned into a grape fight, and I didn't need that. I didn't want people to know about the babysitter. When guys in school talked about scoring with this girl or that girl, I would cringe, even though I would have loved to have been doing the same. I didn't want their beauty cheapened. The girl they'd be talking about would have a little thing about her that I absolutely adored, like the smell of her hair or her laugh or the way her jeans looked on her hips. I couldn't stand it when people fought. I couldn't stand it when someone went out of their way to run over a possum, or when hunting and fishing were regarded as an excuse for promiscuous violence or savagery. One of my best friends in school was a foaming fanatic about hunting, and one Monday he swung into the school hallways yelling and laughing as he told the story of his first deer over and over, how "I saw horns across the field and I started gunning with that twelve-gauge, *BA-WOOM! BA-WOOM!* And I hit it, and blood was flying up, and it got up and I was running and reloading! *BA-WOOM!* And I was falling down in the field and it was falling down and I thought I was never going to kill it!" Everybody was laughing as the *BA-WOOM* echoed down the hallways and I was laughing with them, and I hated this story so much. He told it for years afterward and I moaned every time. "What's the matter, Kuips?!" he'd roar. "You don't like the blood and guts?!" I didn't want my good friend to sound like a slob. He made hunting sound like it was all about frenzy and bloodlust and testosterone, like it was a revenge killing. I wanted it to be holy.

Sitting in the dark at Card's had raised a feeling in me and I hunted it everywhere. It was a complete picture made of black. I could think differently out there, experience a kind of wholeness, because the thoughts weren't all mine. Only a couple of them were mine. Maybe Dad was so quiet in the blind because he was listening to those outside thoughts, too. The thoughts belonged to the world. It was a feeling that everything out there owned pieces of my imagination. I couldn't disrespect them—trees, stars, mosquitoes, grapes, dirt—because they formed my own thoughts. I didn't have good enough words for it. It was an ecology of mind.

~

In the inky darkness, a noise like a heavy footfall shook the forest floor. And then another, with a shock like a tree slamming to earth, a *thud* I felt in my chest. The hair stood up on the back of my neck and I picked up my deer rifle.

I peered through the scope and saw pure black. It was my third year at Card's and my first sitting in a blind alone. In the dense dark, branches were snapping. *Thud.* The ground under my boots quaked. Even a huge bear would not stomp that hard. My heart was pounding as I took little sips of breath.

The trees were rattling and the stomping accelerated. *Smash thud thud.* The thing was charging, it was coming like a storm, all fang and claw, *Thud THUD thud thump-th-thud.* I twisted the little latch on the door to the blind, hands shaking, and hauled myself outside so I wouldn't be just a snack in a sheet-metal box. I raised my gun to the darkness.

Thud whump thud—Chok!

What the hell?

Chok chok chok chok, came a chalky cackle like the low talk of a giant chicken.

An idea slowly formed in my mind: turkeys! The gun shook as I held it up.

All around me in the moonless dark, wild turkeys jumped down from their roost in a tree right over my head, awkwardly cracking off small limbs on their way down with wings too wet to fly, maybe forty or more twenty-pound birds each landing heavily on the ground with a rubbery bounce. *Thump. Whump.* I could hear them flapping and clucking in the darkness.

Adrenaline boiled in my body, and I started to laugh out loud. I rushed over to a tree and took an urgent shit. The darkness around me sparkled with frost and magic. Why were these birds jumping down in the darkness? They usually waited until daybreak. Maybe they didn't like roosting over me; maybe I had called them down. I thought I knew what to expect in the woods, but this discovery took my breath away: a piece of pure imagination had become real. The monster under the bed had turned out to be a turkey. What else was out there? Or, rather, what else was *in* there? The thoughts inside me were somehow related to the reality outside me. They manifested one another. They made one another.

That night, Dad said he heard someone laughing in the woods when they were all trying to be quiet, and he wondered if it was me. I said yeah. "What was so funny?" he said, irritated.

"I got scared by turkeys," I said, and told him the story.

He and Jim laughed so hard I thought they would fall over.

~

Dad wanted to move back in with us. He hadn't wanted to leave in the first place. He wanted to have his wife and kids but also other ladies on the side. Sally kept lobbying on his behalf and Grandma Gertrude also put in a call or two. Men run around, they said. Don't split up the family. The whole time he and Mom were separated, Dad would come over to the house quite a bit. Sometimes they would disappear into the bedroom and I thought they were having sex and maybe they were, but then you'd hear their voices rise and they would be having a fight. He would be begging Mom to take him back and she'd be saying no. Joe sometimes stood with his ear to the door of their bedroom. Brett and I didn't want Dad to come back, but Joe did. Dad whipped open the door once, and Joe was standing there and said to Dad, "Why are you crying?"

"It's okay for dads to cry sometimes," Dad said.

Joe and Brett didn't have much of a relationship to Dad at that time, because he'd been put out the door when they were five and six, respectively, and gone for three years. Lots of times, he didn't know what we were laughing or fighting about, and when we did fight he wanted to immediately snuff the conflict with violence. Brett hit Joe once when Dad was around and Joe started to cry, and our father pounded down the stairs in his pointy-toed Tony Lamas and kicked Brett in the stomach, lifting him off the ground. He kicked the wind right out of him and Mom screamed that he might have broken Brett's ribs, but Dad just pounded back upstairs and prowled the hallway up there, stewing.

He started taking Joe and Brett to the North Branch of the Manistee during those years, but I didn't go because I had started working. My fishing abilities fell off for a few years, but Joe and Brett got quite expert. There was nothing else to do but get expert: Dad didn't go fishing *with* them, just like he didn't go hunting *with* me. We had to teach ourselves. It was more like dropping us off and hoping we got something out of it while he struggled with his own relationship to the Other.

He was gone for three years, and for two and three-quarters of those years, Mom never went on a date. She worked and took care of us and worried about the Phone Caller. Then she started talking to Tom, the wine rep who serviced the Osco where she worked. He was extraordinarily kind, athletic, mustachioed, single. He had been a high school tennis star. He made her laugh. He worked for Paw Paw Distributors, an influential beverage company run by a family in one of Michigan's few wine towns, and shortly after they met he invited Mom to the wedding of one of the owners' children. It was a strange first date, but she was intrigued and had a good time, and even danced with David Braganini, the president of St. Julian's winery.

Somehow Dad got word of this and rushed over to Vern and Sally's and collapsed. They talked for hours, and then he got angry and called Mom and she agreed to let him come over. He was as straightforward as only a true shit-heel can be. He never apologized for any of his infidelities or even acknowledged they'd happened, but said he absolutely would not stand for her to be out in public trying another man. He bullied her, and she wasn't going to be bullied. Everybody in town knew about his pussy palace. She told him to leave. And went on another date with Tom. But Dad kept coming back.

"He was pretty persistent. He'd cry and say things. After quite a few weeks, he said, 'If you don't come back to me, I'm going to kill myself.' Which is not like him; he values himself more highly than anyone. So that scared me," Mom said.

Behind her back, Dad had also visited Mom's parents and her siblings up in Holland, trying to solicit their help. He lied and insisted that Nancy had emotional troubles, trying to get them to make calls on his behalf, but not one of them would take the bait.

As summer 1978 was coming to a close, Dad came over to beg some more, and he and Mom went into the bedroom. It seemed serious. Joe had just turned eight and he posted up at the door. Brett was nine and he ducked outside and stood underneath the windowsill, listening to their voices as they argued and hissed. He clutched his once kicked stomach and mouthed, *No, Mom. No. Don't let him come back.* I was downstairs with the stereo turned up loud. Dad had been working constantly and had saved some money, and he told Mom he'd already been scouting around for a piece of property where they could build a big custom house. He wanted to get away from the house by Crooked Lake and the man he was there, leave that all behind, and leave behind all the people who knew about it, too. Start fresh. After hours of talking, Mom relented. They'd try again. Brett crouched down under the window and sobbed.

Seven

God in the Many

Dad came back singing and goofing into the house by Crooked Lake that August with his stereo and his condoms and saying, "Yaaasssss! Yaaas-ssss!" and he already had a huge plan in motion, a grandiose, overblown plan that relied entirely on place as a conveyance for a new life. We got no family meeting, no explanation of what that three-year gap was about or why it ended. He was loose and silly like he was when we started our trap line, singing Tom T. Hall's "Sneaky Snake" with Joe, but he was entertaining no questions. We asked what was going on, but instead of answers we got a threat, thinly wrapped in a smile: "Well, we're not going to talk about that right now."

Not later, either. Instead, we would move another ten miles out into the country, to a remote seventeen-acre parcel in Schoolcraft that Dad had scouted as the perfect place for the new house. He bought it from a guy in Detroit and Vern ended up with an adjoining piece of the woods that also included an old hayfield. We were trading the sweet lake life we adored and all our schoolmates and neighbors for this buggy ridge of shagbark hickory.

I told Mom I thought this was a bad idea, and she said, "I know. I don't know if it will work. But your father loves you."

Her life got worse almost instantly. Within days, Dad went into the Osco Drug where Mom worked and told them, without discussing it with her, that she was quitting. She found out he had been shopping at Osco's during their separation and buying ammo and groceries and whatnot with her employee discount. Just after their reunion, Dad had gone in to buy a gun he had been looking at, and the manager, who had finally become aware of his separation from Mom, told him he'd have to pay full price. He said that Dad had abused her privileges there. Dad told him he could stick it up his ass and that she didn't work there anymore. She loved that job and had worked there for a couple of years but the manager never called her to confirm that she was, indeed, resigning. He took Dad's word without question and canned her.

"Right then, I realized I'd probably made a mistake," Mom said. "He was going to control my whole life again."

I was set to work full-time on the flower farm again the next summer, but even before break rolled around my working life got amazingly complicated. Dad said I could work on the farm, but he also wanted me to clear our new land so we could build a house. I'd have to do this on weekends, evenings, and any days I wasn't absolutely required to be at Fred W. Nagle & Sons. This would mean getting up at four A.M. to get to the farm and then heading straight over to the property on the way home to work there until dark.

On a Saturday before school let out, Dad and I drove over to the property. We had our red Homelite chainsaw, cans of gas, a sharpening kit, and logging chains, and we had some of Dad's carpentry tools in his handmade wood carrybox and lunches and thermoses of coffee. We parked alongside the road, and there in the makeshift driveway was a used, red Farmall 400 tricycle tractor that seemed as tall and gangly as a giraffe. "How'd that get here?" I said. "I drove it here," he said. I forgot that he knew how to run equipment like that. The front piece of the hill had been logged for hardwood a few years earlier and all the slash and stumpage heaped a dozen feet deep in a little ravine that was exactly where the house's walkout basement was supposed to go. The thinning of the canopy overhead had resulted in an impenetrable riot of under-growth that had taken over the whole spot.

A man with a bulldozer could have cleared it in a couple of hours, but Dad's romantic idea was that he and I were going to do this work together. We spent most of that first day just figuring out how to untangle this natural mess, what to cut, what to yank out with chains, where to pile the mess so we could get rid of it. He was excited about the prospect that I would salvage and sell cords of good oak firewood out of that pile. "We'll split the profit," he said, and then seeing me glowering said, "Okay, you keep it. I guess that's fair."

When summer break came, my old jeans and boots stiff with mud and grime from working on our building site, I motorcycled to the farm, sore and already dead tired from working weekends, and weeded mile-long rows of glads on my hands and knees. It was going to be a shitty summer.

That Saturday, Dad drove me out to the land and dropped me off at the curve in the road where the muddy driveway stabbed through an enormous thicket of blackberry. We'd cut the brambles back the previous weekend and they oozed an acrid, burned smell like someone had scorched a field of ragweed and tomato and Queen Anne's lace. It stung the nose and I loved it, the smell of summer. I unloaded the tools and Dad told me he'd be back later. As he drove away, I knew that was it. Those first weekends had been about the extent of our working "together." For the next two months, I worked there mostly alone in the soggy summer scald and sometimes way past dark in order to get a bit of cool. There was one neighbor within sight about three hundred yards down the road, a Dutch farmer named Polderman with a brick house and a small barn and one baby boy and a few beautiful daughters my age I knew from school.

At dusk, when it was too dark to see what I was chainsawing, Mom would swing by to pick up the tools with her hotrod Nova. Dad was still at his office, but he didn't want us to leave the chainsaw or any tools out there because "some hillbilly" would steal them, and I couldn't carry everything on the motorcycle. Dad and I hardly saw each other for those months. Dad would come home late a lot of nights, and I'd be out on Crooked Lake, slapping mosquitoes as I lay on Fenstermaker's dock or one of my friends' rafts where he couldn't find me. The stars slowly turned to the soft banging of the oil drums under the raft. I didn't want to be home discussing the next day's work with Dad. I didn't want to talk to anyone about what I was doing. I just wanted to float.

I was angry about the isolation but not the work; most of my friends also worked, pitching bales on family farms or taking seasonal jobs detasseling corn or tying grapes. I was fifteen, but some of the kids I knew had turned sixteen and could work in shops. Day after day it was me at the farm, or me and that slash pile, or both.

Every morning on the property would start cool and fresh with dew, with my T-shirt clean and my Red Wings and Levi's stiff from drying out overnight. I'd sharpen the saw blade with a raspy round file and fill the tractor, conscious of the morning breeze off Little Paw Paw Lake below and the patter of birds and the light drilling of tree frogs. But after I started that saw and the sun rose overhead and the sweat started flowing, the cicadas and peepers seemed to shriek to make themselves heard and the mosquitoes and deerflies swarmed in clouds; the woods and I seized each other in a fever of carnality. I'd be knee-deep in steaming black muck, jeans and shirt soaked in abrasive grit that tore my skin, rolling some swamp-stinking piece of stump against my chest and arms. As the rotted bark slid off I'd mash fat white grubs and termites and earwigs and slugs against my body, wolf spiders an inch and a half wide running up my face (and once into my mouth; they're sour), wrestling with decaying wood in a drenching sweat, trying to muscle it, mostly losing, feeling myself merge with the rot and muck itself.

It was a hassle to climb up and down off the tractor to chain out heavy logs, so I'd just try to roll them and more than once I collapsed under a section of oak that was simply too heavy to carry, maybe two hundred pounds, and I had to lie out on the cool muck for a while until my back would stop spasming. The work was brutal, and it was a brutality I created myself. The more the pile talked to me the deeper I went. This was the part of my day I really liked and I still like now, when my body is hot with work and wanting the next chunk of wood, when the air throbs with electric insect bombination, when time becomes irrelevant and everything is blurry with sweat and gasping, and there's not a square inch left to keep clean.

In this state of altered consciousness it was easy to make a slash pile become a house.

There were few words for the experience because there was no one to talk to. Mom felt bad and borrowed an AM-FM radio that I could set on a stump, but after a few hours I'd always turn it off. By midmorning almost every day I had transformed into something a little other-than-human— clothes so wet they bagged and slipped and even a hot wind would raise goosebumps, talking to myself, my imagination ringing with a huge chorus of voices, a standup version of the rot that lay under the bark and burst white grub guts and the jeering of crows.

The crows were the sign: when I was deep in it, crows and jays would come down from the tall hickories above and sit on a stump and bob their heads at me and dash in to pick grubs and escaping insects. Once I was a muck-thing they lost their fear, I guess. I saw a little of what they saw through their eyes. I learned in biology that the word *human* comes from the Latin *humus*, meaning soil or earth. The intelligence of the place opened itself within me.

At lunch I would sit on a stump and think about the muck. The life in the moldy, slimy stumpage was rich and black. The bugs and fungus and salamanders there seemed loud. The pile stood in direct contrast to the sterile fields I walked all day on the flower farm. Everything in that gray-dun soil had been killed except for the crops. It was dead silent.

The old patriarch of the flower farm, Fred Nagle, had separated the world into useful and nonuseful species, and for him, farming was a cosmic battle, an apocalyptic war between a God who fed his people and a Satan who commanded legions of weeds. "That nutgrass is from the Devil, and we battle Satan for our very lives," he would say, as the Nagle kids all rolled their eyes. But I thought about what he said as I walked and drove those fields, where all the fencerows had been long torn out and even the ditches were mowed and sprayed. I thought about how many people felt the way Grandpa Nagle did, that we were at war with nature. That it was our mission as a species to eradicate all the others. My mind tore at the surface of things.

Dad would come out to the land on weekends, sometimes for the day and sometimes for five minutes, and he was delighted to see the hole in the forest growing. He would power up the chainsaw and swing it like a scythe, mowing down brambles, then usually get back in his car and leave. We once spent one whole weekend pulling out flowering dogwoods with the tractor because they form an understory and he didn't want anything to block his view.

"I want to see through the trees," he said. He'd also take down big sumacs and slippery elm and tulip trees and others he thought were no good compared with hickory and oak and beech.

Somehow, Dad and old Nagle both agreed that God wanted them to clear the land, to reduce its complexity, to banish the useless species as a way to make way for clean thoughts and deeds. I was finding the opposite. Working in that rotten slash pile, I thought it was perfectly obvious that nature favored more-ness, not less-ness. More species of tree and frog and bug and fungus, not less. More exchange or communication between them, not less. Everything in that slash heap was very explicit about its desire to live. All you had to do was grab onto a little dogwood tree with both hands and pull and you would feel it tugging back. A place was richer or poorer because of the number of exchanges that went on there, all of which fired the imagination.

I wasn't sure what God was or if it existed, but if all things were an extension of God, then its fullest expression was more, not less. I was starting to talk with the minister of the new church Dad had joined, Pastor Stulp, and I understood there was a tension in God between one-ness and many-ness. The one-ness, God as a unity, I might never see. But God as many-ness was right here before my eyes. Life and God and nature expressed itself through difference and diversity. There had to be differ-ence in order for two things to talk to each other—two different people, for instance, or one tree talking to the other tree through the white threads of fungus that connected trees so they could share nutrients and chem-ical signals—and if there wasn't any communication between things, then there was no world. The world wasn't actually made of things: it was made of the communication between things.

Working in the woods, I was like a demolition expert defusing a bomb, cutting the wires one by one. Diminishing God a little at a time every day, and making the world too safe. Every farmer, and pretty much every human being everywhere, was doing the same thing: clearing their little patch, not thinking it will matter much, replacing the chatter with silence. It got to where I was disgusted with myself and my role in this treachery. I wanted to make the world louder. I wanted to sneak a couple of wolves or pumas into the thicket and watch imaginations explode all over the township.

~

Only a kid absolutely desperate for company would think these things, and I was desperate. I was communicating infinitely more with this slash pile than I was with my friends or family. Between the flower farm and clearing Dad's land, I wasn't getting much lake time. I'd either go straight to the land or come home and get Mom's Nova so I could carry the chainsaw, but I was running things all on my own.

Then the summer took an amazing turn: suddenly Dad announced we were taking a trip out West, and for three and a half weeks we drove the Rockies in a rented Winnebago on a mission to fish the Yellowstone and the Firehole and Madison and a bunch of other good rivers, most of the ones we'd skipped when we left Seattle a decade earlier. Joe and Brett and I fished so close to elk that we could hear their bellies rumble as they watched us warily through glassy black eyes. At the Sun Canyon Lodge in Montana I was thrilled that the horses would walk right into the dining hall and take carrots out of the cook's hand, and a mule climbed into our RV. That was the only time someone else cooked for us, as Mom had planned and provisioned three weeks of meals. I felt like a real fisherman again when I caught one decent trout out of the ankle-deep Sun River, but I seem to recall that Brett and Joe were hauling in fish by the bushel. On the way back, we hit rivers in the U.P.

It was the best trip we had ever had as a family, a kind of miracle, but there wasn't much summer left when we got home. Dad was in a panic to get the contractors to frame in the house before the snow fell. Two-a-day football practices were starting soon, so even though he was worried about how it might look at his new church, he had me on the building site seven days a week.

One afternoon when it was about one hundred degrees Fahrenheit I walked through the ditch and down the road toward the neighbors, trailing a wake of deerflies behind me. I don't know that I agonized about it at all, I just started walking. I was thinking about the Polderman daughters. I crossed over their yard and went to the front door in my filth-encrusted jeans and black, sweat-soaked shirt and rang the bell. Mrs. Polderman opened the door just a crack.

"Yes?" she said. I had never met her but I think she knew who I was.

"I just wondered if the girls wanted to go for a swim," I said. They had an above-ground pool in the backyard. I didn't have a swimsuit, so I guess I just imagined we'd all swim naked in the name of health or something. I had no idea how this would work or why I was even asking.

"Oh, our girls don't swim on Sunday," she said, and closed the door on me.

Sunday? Was it Sunday? I walked across the street and into the trees. The days all seemed the same. I guess I had no idea what day of the week it was. But then I started to think: she didn't seem mean or angry that I had asked. Would she have said yes if it had been a Monday? My dreams started to expand.

~

I was standing in the ooze, chainsawing a tough, knotted crotch of red oak and blinking the mosquitoes out of my eyes when suddenly the saw blade bucked back and cracked me in the shin. I fell forward trying to get my leg out of the way and stabbed the sizzling saw blade into the dirt and rolled over it in a somersault. I felt myself rush back into my human mind on a wave of adrenaline. I arrived fresh; I didn't know where I had been moments before. I had been somewhere in orange roots and insect whine. I blinked and blinked and then flipped the power switch on the saw to "off" and pulled myself onto a log and got back into being human.

My pants were cut and there was blood. I figured I had sawed my leg half-through and needed to act fast. There was no way to call for help. It was twenty years before my first cell phone. I fished a bandana out of my lunch bag to make a tourniquet and tried to gauge how far I'd have to crawl to the Poldermans. I imagined they'd rush out in swimwear, dripping pool water on me while loading me into John's truck. I felt very calm about the whole thing.

With a deep breath, I pulled up my wet pant leg and wiped the black sweat off my leg to find a groove about a millimeter deep. Maybe one sawtooth had gotten in. Somehow I'd swung my leg out of the way or the bar and its singing knives had bounced off my shinbone at the wrong angle and missed me.

I was surprised by the jump of the saw blade, but I was more surprised by how far away I had been when it hit me. Weeks and weeks of communion with this place had erased the boundary formerly marked by my skin. My self didn't end there. When the saw hit me, I had instantly imagined that what was wet within me was just going to bleed out and become muck, and that seemed fine. I don't think I was depressed or suicidal or anything, but it just seemed easy to transform into some shape other than human. I lay back on the log for a long time while my leg stung with sweat. It was like dying and being pulled back across by wild nerves, so I let myself soar on the nerve juice, to fly up where the crows and jays and cowbirds were waiting high in the canopy for the sawing to end. They were not surprised to see me show up there.

～

Football workouts had already begun in the muggy, still days of August, and I had assembled a pile of stumps and uprooted dogwoods and slash as big as our old house, a heap about forty feet across and twelve feet high. I am a hell of a worker and I'd done a hell of a job. I had really only moved the pile about fifty yards and greedily cut out all the usable firewood, but it took several months. I'd probably sold two full cords of wood at forty bucks a rick, so it didn't pay. The spot where Dad told me to make this pile was where the new garage would sit and the heap was ready to be trucked away or buried. But he saw a cheaper and stupider alternative.

"We'll burn it," he declared.

"I don't think that's a good idea," I said. Our one-acre clearing stood in a hardwood forest of several hundred acres, most of which was owned by other people.

"What?" he demanded, challenging me. "What else you going to do?"

"Get your excavator to bury it. Or truck it over to the gravel pit."

"Ah, horseshit. We'll burn it and it'll be gone."

Everything in the pile was wet and caked with mud, so we picked up used motor oil and old tires from Mr. Purk at the Marathon gas station in Texas Corners. We loaded them into the Jesse, which Dad had just bought for the construction of the house. We added enough petrochemical energy to the pile to melt that black forest soil into glass. Dad leaned in wearing a white T-shirt and his straw cowboy hat and put a match to it and the pile exploded like a bomb, puffing his hat off his head and sending an enormous fireball boiling up into the sky far above the fifty-foot-high treetops.

And then the old tires caught fire, puking black smoke and twenty-foot flames into the lower branches of the overhanging trees.

Within a minute or two, we had a crown fire. I imagined hot ash raining down on the girls next door in their pool, ruining my chances forever.

Dad started shouting, "Well, FUCK! Fucking trees! Get the goddamn saw!"

I ran to the Jesse and retrieved the saw and Dad jerked it to life and started cutting down the trees as they burned, running from one to the next. I had worked all summer to protect those trees, to clear a place between them where the new house could be built to look like the trees had grown up around it, but down they went. Dead and flaming limbs crashed down around us as he kept shoving his cowboy hat down on his head, grimacing in panic. One whole snag about sixty feet tall burned like a flaming sword. He hunched under his hat as if it were a helmet, like it would stop a three-ton limb from crushing him. It was so *not* funny that I burst into laughter from sheer terror, running through the forest putting out spot fires in the dry leaves with a shovel, barely able to contain myself. I had worked like a slave for months to make this place for us, and now Dad was going to destroy it in ten minutes.

As he sawed, the fire pile roared with the sound of a wheezing jet fighter, getting hotter and hotter. He cut through the flaming snag and I helped him push it over, burning branches raining down on us as we felled it smashing into the fire. It kicked up clouds of sparks and hot ash billowing skyward. I ran through the woods giggling idiotically, extinguishing hot ashes.

When I didn't see any more wisps of smoke coming up from the forest duff I sagged back toward the fire. I was exhausted and a little hysterical. Dad and I were forced to stand far back from the inferno. He looked at the tears running down my face and shouted, "What's so funny?!"

"YOU!" I screamed. "You and that stupid hat!"

"What?" he shouted, his eyes flashing anger. His mouth twisted into a snarl and held there, and then broke into a smile. His shoulders dropped and he bent over at the waist, and it was like he was vomiting he was laughing so hard. He knew he had completely botched this and almost lost the whole woods, maybe even killed us. He had botched *my* job. His hat was scorched and smudged with black ash and fell off his head again. His white T-shirt was ripped and black. At one point he had fallen off a downed tree he was sawing and got a big bloody cut. Both of us were banged up and looked like we had a bad sunburn. The saw was so hot it ticked.

He straightened up and tears streaked his dirty face. I was fifteen and he was thirty-five and we seemed to be the same age, like two teenagers who had just run through the middle of the night after stealing beer or a live chicken.

"I was going to send you to John Polderman's to get the fire department," he said, holding his breath in order to get the words out, heaving. "OH God!" He couldn't stop laughing.

"Oh, that would have been great: 'Hi, I'm the new neighbor. We never took the time to introduce ourselves before, but we've set your woods on fire,'" I said.

"Oh, I know! I know!" he roared. "Shit, oh dear! Ha ha ha! We just about burned down the whole damn township! Oh, son."

The heat of the fire dried our eyes; the furnace-like blast of the pile belched a column of black tire smoke that blotted out the sky. Little puffs of white smoke curled off the downed trees. The cicadas and tree frogs were hushed in horror. We stopped laughing after a while and drank all our water and then went back to looking for spot fires in the woods.

The fire burned all night and into the next day, and we took turns watching it round the clock, sleeping in the Jesse and getting replenishments of bag lunches and water and thermoses of coffee. There was nothing else we could do: the fire was white-hot in the center and you'd need one of those oil-well-fire specialists like Red Adair to snuff it. In the morning, we fired up the tractor and started pulling ten-foot dogwood and red maple saplings and throwing the live trees on the fire, where they disappeared like they were paper.

A couple of weeks later, I got a job in the meat department at the Hardings grocery in Portage. Brett and Joe were ten and nine, old enough to swing an axe, and I didn't work for Dad anymore.

Eight
Animal Talk

Dad had come back to the church as part of his reunion with Mom, but we didn't talk about it. It was just presented as a fait accompli. Dad bought me a brown tweed suit and Florsheim tassel loafers and then it was church twice a day every Sunday, but he wasn't really into Bible discussion, per se. We didn't talk about his new job selling building components for Peachtree Door, and I don't believe I ever saw the inside of the office he got on Centre Street after he gave up his apartment. We didn't talk politics or sports or catechism and never, ever, not even once discussed my schoolwork. We never talked about why Brett would shoot at Joe (missed) with a .22, or what to tell the folks around Crooked Lake about why Dad basically ducked them the rest of his life. I never went to him with a problem about girls or anything else. Our house was loud and chatty and crackled with gunfire, but we never talked about those things.

What we talked about was animals.

I knew that other families were not like this. I had been at friends' houses where the parents swore openly at President Carter on the TV, or the daughter defended her drug-dealer boyfriend, or kids shouted at their father for being a drunk. Those topics were impossible in a Kuipers house.

I was riding out to the new house one night on my third motorcycle when a big buck whitetail came out of the ditch on the run and jumped clean over me, one of its back hoofs smacking my metalflake orange helmet with a sharp *TAK!* as it went over. Life is a series of near misses.

I told Dad and his first words were, "How big was it?" He hustled me out to the Jesse and asked me to show him the spot, and he put some flagging tape in the tree there. I guess so he could talk to the owner about hunting that spot. But he never asked me if I was okay or whether I ought to be driving motorcycles. Whenever I'd start to tell the story, he'd hijack it and say, "He thinks it was an eight-point, and it went into that little bit of pines there by the house down the road. Now, I talked to that guy and he said he'd seen it," etc., etc.

It wasn't Dad's fault, exactly. He and his brothers had learned that the way to avoid conflict with Henry—or anyone else—was to immediately talk about wildlife. It was neutral territory. Nonemotional. I cannot exaggerate the degree to which this subject dominated our lives, at the expense of any other topic that concerned human beings. Like a blue-hot star, the observation of nature stood at the center of the clan, and everyone's orbits fell continually toward its gravity. There were no family arguments—unless they were about knowing the difference between a teal and a widgeon on the wing, or the amount of drop on a .300 Win mag at four hundred yards. Any subject that would generate *feelings* fell into this devouring fire and was made smoke. No one asked what books I was reading, because Kierkegaard made them nervous. Years later, no one ever asked what was up with Joe; the implication was it was better to know nothing about his drinking or drug taking, even if he died. That way, no one would have to feel embarrassed about it.

Since animals and the way they lived were the stand-in for everything that could not be said, family cohesion among the Kuipers was actually very high. But how Nancy stood this for two dozen years, considering the other things that needed to be talked about, I don't know.

As one of my cousins put it, "The family's interests are sort of an inch wide and a mile deep." At a mile deep, however, the expertise in the room was formidable. And there was nothing that the uncles valued more than good intel on game or weapons or tanning hides or making jerky or, holy of holies, secret hunting spots. With my five sets of uncles and aunts, sixteen first cousins, and Grandpa Henry and Grandma Gertrude, we were thirty-three people at the Kuipers Christmas talking as fast and loud as we could about whether the grouse were in high cycle, and that was before the cousins started having babies like crazy and not counting any straggler relations. God help you if you didn't have a take on this year's Juneberry crop.

No one escaped this stricture. At a family dinner one year, Grandpa Henry replied to a political comment with, "Well, the Democrats are Communists, and so allied with Satan." One of the uncles immediately countered, with a bowl of mashed potatoes in his hand: "Dad, the elk herd is doing so good up by the Pigeon River that they're going to start issuing licenses on 'em again." Grandpa glowered at the obvious denial of his bid, but that door came down, heavy and impenetrable.

Bruce may have known how to fly fish and how to catch mink, but in this company he was still intimidated. These stories were the life of the whole family, and he had learned to defer to Dale and Vern and Mike, who all spent a lot more time afield, and principally to Dale.

Dale's work as a Baptist missionary took him to Thompson, Manitoba, where he served for pretty much his whole career. Before he had a church building there he held services out of his house. Thompson is a nickel mining town at the end of the paved road going north, and he ministered in town and to the Cree villages farther out over muskeg and tundra. He was popular in those villages even though he could only reach some of them in winter, when he'd drive his station wagon over ice roads marked by pieces of pine tree. His oldest, Lisa, is my age and told me she loved making these trips with her dad, because he'd go as fast as he could along the ice roads and then slide out, with the car spinning into the snowbanks. She loved the way people responded to her dad. The tribespeople trusted Dale because he'd drive out with supplies and drive back with a kid headed for juvenile court or high school or a mother who needed medical attention. On at least one occasion a kid with a badly broken leg lived with Dale and his wife, Sandy, and their five kids for a month or two until he could go home.

He hunted moose out in the swamp and would take the family on the mining train out to a friend's fishing camp at Standing Stone, where they would catch stringers of walleye so endless that my father raved about them as a quasi-religious experience after his own trip there. Dale was a powerful man whose brush cut and charismatic smile always reminded me of Muhammad Ali; he was also an old-school snake-oil salesman who would blubber over you with snot coming out of his nose if it meant he could add your soul to his tally. When he shook your hand he'd hold it for a long moment, and then he'd try to put some God on you with that smile of profound mischief, like the two of you had already agreed that you were going to come over to his side. "God has a plan for you," he'd say to me.

Dale did what the other brothers could not: he seamlessly merged his love for the creation with his religious fervor and made it okay to talk about God.

"I went out ice fishing on the lake by us," Dale said one year in his raspy voice, always hoarse, I guessed, because the rougher the town the louder you had to yell to keep people thinking about the Lord, "and, boys, a wolf come out of the trees, and started coming my way a bit, to where I was sitting on my bucket, but she wouldn't come all the way over. She watched me for a while and then she left.

"And the next time I was out there, she came back," he said, his eyes gleaming, "and she came a little closer than before and I said, 'Hallelujah.'"

The brothers and cousins had circled round, and he paused for effect and looked each one present in the eye. "And then I caught a nice walleye and I wanted that fish for the pan and I never told Sandy"—he raised his voice then so Sandy could hear him, and some of their kids who were in the room—"I never told Sandy I threw that nice fish to the wolf. And she took it and trotted off. Heh heh. Boys! I said, 'Lord, let me catch a mess of fish so it's not just the wolf that's going to eat tonight!'

"I went fishing pretty regular and she always came out, and I'd throw her a fish. Until one day she got close and I lay down on the ice and she got the message and she come over. She was taaaallll and she was wild and she stood across the hole from me but she did not take her eyes off me and I got a picture."

"And then I threw her a fish. I was thankful for the fish, but God sent the wolf, too."

For all Dale's TV preacher boo-hooing, lying down on the ice was an act of humility before the wolf. How many could do it? Dale was forever raising bear cubs in his garage and sending us joke trophies like a taxi-dermied moose nose. The fact that he was the minister of Burntwood Baptist Church made him the de facto leader of the whole Kuipers clan, and even Grandpa Henry deferred to him. He wrote rhymed poems about his ministry and animals that were published in church publications and Sunday morning bulletins all over the country, which my father saved in a file.

Sandy was from Holland, Michigan, and she didn't want to live on the edge of the boreal void her whole life, but she was as deeply involved in the ministry as Dale was, and they both tied their usefulness to the raw wilderness. It seemed God was needed more in the wilder places. My mother and all my aunts were living some version of this. Vern's wife, Sally, and Jack's wife, Jane, both hunted pretty seriously and enjoyed it. Mom even tried sitting in the blind once with Bruce, but he was so put off by her presence there that she never did it again. My aunt Rita, a year or two after she'd married Mike, told me at one of the family gatherings: "I don't really like going out in the woods, but if I want to be with Mike, that's what I have to do, because that's where he is."

~

Animal stories had to save us. It was all we had. That, and hillbilly "hold my beer" stories about the neighbors. When we all lived in the big new house in the woods, dinners were excruciating unless Joe, Brett, or I could whip up a show about the guy down the street mistakenly gunning his snowmobile up the woodpile and hanging it from the eavestroughs. Dad would generally eat his dinner in total silence while we tried, and when he was done eating, he'd look at Mom like none of us were there and complain, deadpan, "No dessert?" No dinner she ever cooked was good enough. But if we could get him laughing, the night would be saved.

The story of Dad's crown fire was an instant classic and would usually have us in tears. Or the rabbit Dad bought to train our beagle that immediately bit the dog and started chasing it around the yard. Dad wasn't prickly about being the butt of the joke. He would forget the details in between tellings, so every time he heard these tales he would be dumbstruck.

"Remember my underwater hunting apparatus with Terry Purk?" I started one night at the table.

"Yeah, with the air compressor?" Brett said.

"Yeah, Terry and I wanted to be able to spear rock bass, and we had that three-pronger trident spear with a long handle, a frog spear I guess, but you could never see anything from the dock that you could hit. We figured that if we could stay underwater we could lurk in the darkness under the dock and just stab fish when they came by."

"Oh, ha ha ha, that is a good one," Dad started. It was just that easy to steer him away from evil.

"So we wanted to make like a diving helmet out of a bucket or something, but then we realized we didn't need one. We just hooked the garden hose up to the air compressor, and then duct-taped the other end to the top of a snorkel—"

"Oh Lord!" said Dad, already wiping his nose.

"—and you'd crank that thing up and the air would come blasting out of the purge valve on the snorkel, so all around you the water was like boiling and this froth would blow your mask off and everything. From up on the dock it looked like a submarine was going to the bottom. But we'd be down there like Poseidon, armed with our trident."

"HAW HAW HAW!"

"Oh, but that air!" Mom said, making a face.

"It was full of oil. It tasted like car exhaust. We couldn't stay down very long because it made you dizzy. We did see fish, though. Some big ol' fish would come by, but none of them ever came close enough that we could poke it."

"HAW HAW! How could you get enough arm speed to throw the spear?"

"Well, you couldn't. It was always like slow motion. Your best bet was to try a kind of straight-ahead jab."

"Gosh, you'd think Marge would say something about that air," said Mom.

"Oh, HAW HAW! You probably could have died of carbon monoxide poisoning!" roared Dad. "Ach du lieber! Ha ha ha!"

Mrs. Purk was one of the lunch ladies at school. She never said anything about not using the compressor. What the hell, this is what kids did. And I don't think we knew anything about any carbon monoxide or whatever.

"Oh Lord, you boys are crazy," Dad said, beaming, and then he went downstairs to get into an episode of *The Love Boat* all by himself, feeling he had the greatest family in the world.

~

Dad asked me once at the dinner table what my favorite story in the Bible was, and I gleefully told him I loved the Witch of Endor. He never asked me again.

"The New Testament makes such a big deal out of Jesus raising Lazarus from the dead and then the resurrection, but the Witch of Endor makes it clear that pagan people did that kind of stuff all the time," I went on. My brothers were listening keenly.

I combed through the Bible obsessively looking for evidence of God in the many rather than the one—the powers of nature, the talking donkeys, the small gods, which are all over the Bible like so many chalk outlines of bodies on the street.

The story is in I Samuel 28, when Israel under King Saul was about to be destroyed by the Philistines. Saul needed battle advice but Jahweh wouldn't speak to him, so he disguised himself and went to a witch in the town of Endor. He asked her to "bring up" the beloved prophet Samuel, who had recently died. I loved this story so much because, no matter which modern translation you read, her abilities are completely unremarkable: she brought up Samuel out of the ground without any difficulty, and he stood in the room and barked at Saul, "Why have you disturbed me?" Evidently it's torture to be among the living once you've tasted again the original dust.

King Saul goes out of his way to assure the witch that God is not displeased with her, and even though the Lord is generally wrathful she wouldn't be punished. Rather, Saul needed her and the old pre–One god ways. And she seems nice. When she figures out this visitor is really the king in disguise, she insists on killing a fatted calf and making bread and feeding his whole entourage, because it's clear he has starved himself with worry. And he eats.

"It's so normal," I said. "He sits down and eats with her."

"Ha ha! Oh boy! I don't know," said Dad.

"Well, I like to read stories like that," I said.

"Okay. Well," he said, and he got up to read the paper. End of talk.

∼

Of course, this is partly why we never talked about anything but animals. But I was not cynical about the church; I embraced it, I squeezed it with both hands. I simply wanted to fall in love, like any kid. I wanted to fall in love with the dirt that held the living and the dead. I wanted the world and the people in it to be beautiful and not something to be judged or doomed to fire. Our pastor, Jack Stulp, figured out I was a mad reader and fed me books by the Calvinist philosopher Dr. Francis Schaeffer, the prophet of the church militant and a principal architect of the modern evangelical movement, who zeroed in on the singular push to reverse Roe v. Wade as the focal point of their crusade. When I was sixteen, I told my father I loved the people in our church but that I "loathed the political institution" because people acted differently in their political lives than they did at home.

I prayed in Pastor Stulp's study and traveled with him and his wonderful wife, Jan, to attend Bill Gothard's Institute in Basic Youth Conflicts seminar in Grand Rapids. The Stulps had the sunny joy I associated with Grandpa Nienhuis, and they were among the first church people I knew who actually read books and weren't threatened by ideas I might read out of the ecologist Paul Shepard or, for that matter, the Old Testament. I craved hanging out with them because it was okay to ask questions. In Gothard's big seminar, a multiday event that attracted many thousands to a big hall, the evangelist made a show out of telling women how powerful they were as an influence over their men, and in return they had to submit to the husband's authority. Men around us had tears streaming out of their eyes. I thought this was a terrible idea. I was trying to get with the program, though, and I asked the Stulps about this on the way home, leaning in between them from the back seat: Do women have to be subservient to men? All I could think about was my dad. Jan Stulp assured me Gothard didn't have all the answers. I was so relieved that there was room to disagree with Bible bigwigs.

I was starting to read a lot of ecology texts at this time, beginning with Shepard's work, and the interests overlapped. I had this passage from Psalm 19 taped to my wall in the big new house, right next to my worn-out copies of *Quadrophenia* and *Outlandos D'Amour* and the sweet 1960s Gretsch drum kit I'd borrowed from the neighbor; the poem was about the true nature of reality, the speechless speech, as the psalmist described it three thousand years ago in Mesopotamia:

The heavens declare the glory of God;
the skies proclaim the work of his hands.
Day after day they pour forth speech;

night after night they reveal knowledge.
They have no speech, they use no words;
no sound is heard from them.
Yet their voice goes out into all the earth,
their words to the ends of the world.

In the Hebrew Bible, the original phrase for "voice" in that passage was "measuring line." *Yet their measuring line goes out into all the earth.* The other-than-human world takes its own measure, judges the conditions, and responds according to its own purposes, using its own sensory information. The world winks at us through the language, as the psalmists in the time of King David harnessed the old pagan animism to pull for the new One god. I guess it's good to have the old gods on your side. But the skies themselves were obviously still keeping their options open: *Day after day they pour forth speech; night after night they reveal knowledge.*

I understood that, without the voices of the wind and stones, even the super-promoted Semitic storm god Jahweh could get no traction in the mind. For the imagination is built of this speechless speech. The small gods carried the original instructions, the user's manual for the nonideological way we actually live on earth.

One night I found a little sticky note from Dad stuck to that Psalm where it hung on my wall, and it said, "Very nice."

∾

In the fall of 1981, Dad and I were driving to the house in the Jesse when a buck ran across the road in front of us, plunging into a field of drying corn. Bruce thought the deer would stop in a small plantation of red pines at the top of the hill, and we roared the quarter mile home, grabbed deer rifles (which was illegal, it's shotgun-only in that part of Michigan), and roared back, with me loading both guns as we drove (also illegal). We left the truck on the side of the road and ran through somebody's corn and up the hill, and sure enough, the buck trotted ahead of us into somebody's pines.

We separated a bit and stalked into the rows of trees and face-first into a blazing fall sunset coming over the top of the hill. The sun's rays were perfectly horizontal and seared the eyes, leaving long black shadows that swept toward us and projected down onto the cornfield. I saw the deer step into a dark stripe and disappear. I put my gun up to look at a nose, then a rear leg, then nothing. The deer stepped quietly from tree to tree. It was toying with us, and I started to smile so hard I wept. I was seventeen and cried over just about everything.

"*Where the hell is it?!*" Dad hissed.

I pointed at the tree where I had seen it, tears splashing down my front, and we flanked the tree, but there was no deer there. The plantation was only a couple hundred yards long, and when we reached the far end we turned around and saw the deer's ass departing right where we had come in. He took one step down the hill and was gone.

At Christmas that year, I felt like I had a good story to tell to the Kuipers crew, but Dad stopped me. "They don't want to hear that story," he said to everyone.

Later when we were driving home I asked him why I couldn't tell that one.

"Those guys don't care about how beautiful the sky was or any of that," he said. "The deer got away. That's what matters."

Nine
Back to the Cabin

When Bruce, Vern, and Jack finally got their deer camp from Ike in 1989, it didn't change Dad's life the way he'd hoped. I wouldn't hunt there. Joe had gone the first two years and then quit, and Brett managed three, and in 1991 Brett even shot a decent deer there. That gave him rights to name the blind he'd been in, which sat on the miasmic edge of the bog and was prone to fogs and spookiness. It was only fair, since Brett had also built all the blinds as a job for Dad. He named it "Gonzo" after the writer Hunter S. Thompson. Then he stopped going, too. It was just no fun.

So Bruce got very lonely in the cabin he had built, even though it was full of other family members. He was lonely to the point of paranoia and weird behavior. I started to get reports.

"Dad called me from the cabin and said he wanted me to come up there because he was finding these drag marks all over the place," Brett said. Brett and Joe had lived in San Francisco for a couple of years while I was there, but both of them ended up back in Kalamazoo.

"I said to Dad, 'What do you mean, "drag marks?"'" Brett said. "'Like someone driving out there and dragging out trees for firewood or something?'

"He said, 'No, like someone was dragging a body. Exactly the weight and shape of a body. It's that goddamned poacher. He's been shooting all the deer off our place for years, that's why we never get any big ones.'"

The poacher was a real person, or a real family of persons, but I'll withhold their name because the only thing they'd ever done for certain was ride their ATV across the Kuipers camp. One or more of them did go to prison for growing a lot of dope over in the USA, but I don't think they ever poached off our place.

Brett continued, "So I said, 'Are you following the drag marks?' And Dad said that's why he needed me to come up there. He said the drag marks meandered all over the property, looping back on themselves. They went out into Mr. Carter's corn and then back onto our property. They went all over hell. Dad said you could see the heel marks, so it's a person on foot, but the poacher would have worn himself out dragging a deer that far. He couldn't figure it out.

"So I said I'd go up there, and I did. Dad and I walked the property and he was right: it sure as hell looked like someone had been dragging a body around. I followed the marks, and I couldn't figure it out, either. It might not have been a deer—you know how paranoid Dad was about that—but somebody was dragging something. Knocking down the bushes, running over stuff, dragging something heavy through the sand.

"So then Dad's pissed, and he's going to call the sheriff. But first we go over to Joe Carter's to ask him if he's seen anything. And Joe says, 'Oh, sure, that's not a poacher, Bruce. That's a horse!'

"Joe Carter says, 'There's a lady named Jeanie Mannor to the east, right there on the corner, she puts her horse out in the lawn so it can eat the grass. And instead of staking it, she ties it to a tractor tire so it can pull the tire and go to a new spot. The idea is that it wasn't supposed to go far, but it's been down here in these hayfields across the street and even over across the next road, which means it's more than a mile from home. That horse goes all over this section dragging that tire. Poor horse.'

"Well, then Dad felt kind of foolish because he'd been raving about the damn poacher! And what are you going to do to stop a horse? They don't have a fence around the deer camp. He never did go see that lady about it, though. Too intimidated."

∽

Dad ended up on the place alone. In 1997 Jack and Vern both quit the Kuipers Hunt Club because they needed their own camps. Grandbabies were popping up everywhere and the previous Thanksgiving there'd been twenty-some people jammed into that tiny cabin, and of course with the rules being what they were about minimizing the disturbance outside it was crazy-making in there. Plus they shot everything that moved so there were hardly any deer, much less porcupines or coyotes or cranes.

Dad had to either buy them out or sell the place, and he was leaning toward the latter. He effectively had 215 acres, if you included the USA adjacent, but he was dismayed that the deer weren't like they were over on Ike's across the road. And we were boycotting, so how was he going to police all those acres? He'd be overrun with poachers, for sure.

Dad and Joe were driving somewhere in Michigan that summer and they called me from the car.

"Kemosabe!" he shouted. "Hey, Joe and I were just up north looking at places that might be on a river, and I wondered what your vote would be: Joe wants some land on a fishing river, and Brett wants swampy woods for grouse. I'm more interested in bowhunting now. So you might be kind of a tiebreaker. What do you think is most important?"

"I don't even know what's going on," I said. "Are you getting a new hunting camp?"

"Well, that place by Ike's is no good."

"What? The cabin? You've been trying to get me to go there for years! I thought you guys all loved it so much."

"Well, maybe we can get a better place where there's more game. You know we never see anything big there."

"That's because you had like a thousand people hunting it. Anyway, I wouldn't know."

"You gotta come this fall," Joe interrupted. "We're going to kick around the place and see if we can put up some birds."

"Brett wants to do that," Dad said, dejectedly. "I mean, we really should leave it be and bowhunt it now that it's quiet there."

"We're going to bowhunt, too. We can find some birds and still see deer," Joe said, reassuring him.

"If there's birds there, why aren't you keeping it?" I asked.

"It's just all that stinking sand," said Dad. "Nothing grows there. The deer don't have anything to eat. Jack tried to put in rye but it won't even come up."

In the spring of 1990, with the cabin under construction, Jack had bounced through First Field in his Astrovan pulling an old stretch of chain-link fence around, weighted with granite boulders to rip up the crust of moss and prickers. The windshield wipers slapped back and forth at a brown cloud of ant lion chitins and lichen fibers and sumac berry dust and stink bug stink that rose up like the column of smoke from a forest fire and blew into the interior of the van. He scattered fifty dollars' worth of rye seed over the five acres and figured something would come up. The magnetism was there. "You felt like you had to do something," Jack told me. He did this spring and fall maybe three years in a row and got nothing more than a green fuzz to come up. So he quit.

Vern did better with his spruce trees. He liked to plant conifers and had put white pines all around his home out by Dad's—I had mowed his yard for years and saw those pines grow into giants. That first year at the cabin, he bought hundreds of spruce trees, mostly Norways, but anytime you buy spruces there are some blues mixed in. The uncles and cousins had themselves a planting party at the cabin and whacked those into the sand all up and down along the road, for privacy, and in sun-scorched drifts here and there around the property. Most of them survived and by the time the uncles and their families decamped for more rivery cabins elsewhere, the spruces were head high and had already formed a dense wall four or five trees deep along the road. All three of the Hunt Club's original members were thrilled with those trees, not just because they kept prying eyes out but because the trees flourished and the flourishing was satisfying no matter what you believed about your responsibilities here on earth.

"Have you looked at good places?" I prompted.

"We saw one place on a river we liked, but the guy said the family was selling it out from under him and he'd only leave as a corpse," said Joe. "We decided not to get involved with that shit."

"You both sound excited, though. And Brett's looking at places, too?"

"Yeah, he's looked at a few. We're focusing mostly on river places, but they're so much more expensive," said Joe. "Maybe we can get a forty bordering on some federal. It would be great if you come out in the fall—"

"I'll be there," I interrupted.

"But you gotta talk to Brett," Dad broke in. "We're going to run all the deer off by thrashing around out there and it just makes me sick, we've worked so hard to keep everyone out of there. We could go in the federal land—"

"I'll be there," I repeated. "Can you look at my Wingmaster to make sure it's not a pile of rust? It's still in the box somewhere in your house. I've only shot it a couple times."

Dad went on explaining how bird hunting was going to wreck the place, but no one was listening. We'd never before agreed to all go to the cabin together and it was unlikely we'd find another time that would work for everyone. Bruce would probably end up selling this place, or hunting it on his own. But at least we'd get a couple of days hunting together.

~

We got out there for Thanksgiving, and the oaks were already bare and the sky cold and brilliant gray. As we stood around the Gonzo blind, a boggy wet breeze fluttered the few gold leaves that were left on the aspens and the yellow-bronze leaves of the beech trees. Leaves were banked up against the trees in ankle-deep drifts. We wore canvas jackets and gloves and stocking caps, and our words puffed out in little nebulas.

Most of the aspens were small but we came across a towering mature aspen about fifty feet tall that beavers had chewed halfway through. The beavers had felled a whole row of them so the tops fell into the bog. They chewed them into sections bitten to pencil points on both ends and dragged them down their slides. It was only my second time on Dad's deer camp, and I'd never seen this corner before. The twelve-gauge was heavy and unfamiliar in my hands.

I watched the remaining gold leaves shuddering on the aspens and I thought of Van Gogh's *The Mulberry Tree*, which writhes before your eyes. It is at the Norton Simon in Los Angeles, and I made a habit of seeing it about once a year. While we talked, the leaves burst off the trees with the least touch of fall wind, and the forest constantly unmade and remade itself before us. Writhing and stripping down.

"The prime habitat is already gone in here," Brett was saying. "Aunt Sally took a picture of me here when I shot that deer in '91 and this was all understory as thick as dog hair and just a few old mature trees. They logged it about five or eight years before you bought it and now it's been fifteen years and everything's shaded out. Pretty soon you could get back in here and take them down again for pulp and they would sucker like crazy and then we'd have some really good grouse and woodcock habitat again." He'd been talking like this on the whole walk out.

"If they screwed it up, nothing would ever grow back," said Dad.

Brett looked at me and said, "And this is why we've never been involved up here."

He turned back to Dad. "Damn, Dad, I just—look around! The guy who owned this logged it, and look at how it filled right in. The aspens are clonal, they—"

The trees boiled over.

Drubbity drubbity drubbit. A ruffed grouse thundered out of the leaf litter. Everybody jumped out of their boots. It doesn't matter how prepared you are; you can be staring at a bird at the end of a dog's pointing nose, and when it flushes you're still going to jump. In this case, we didn't have a dog and everyone's hair stood on end. What looked like a flying fistful of bracken fern twisted madly through the trees, and Brett and I shot simultaneously and down it went. I never got my cheek on the stock and shot over it by at least five feet. It had been fifteen years since I'd touched this shotgun and I didn't even remember how to load it: back on the porch I had twisted the cleaning nut off the end of the loading tube and sat at the picnic table trying to figure out how the shells went in and Brett stuck his finger in the loading slot and said, "In here, dummy. Jaayzus. Want me to shoot 'em for you, too?"

He had. Brett found his bird in the dry leaves and walked toward us holding it tenderly and smiling a smile I'll never forget. He had been waiting a full decade for that grouse. The beech tree above us roared.

"This changes things," I said, touching the bird's warm plumage.

"I knew they were in here," said Brett.

A half hour later Joe shot another one as it erupted out of one of Vern's neck-high spruce trees on the west side, over by First Field. We had two fresh grouse to go with canned baked beans and burgers Dad had brought, and Joe let him cook even though Joe actually was a cook and had worked at a hip diner on Kalamazoo's downtown mall. We'd already had a big family meal with the Kuipers clan, but this was our real Thanksgiving. It was one of the best of my life, just the four of us sitting at the table. We left the curtains open and watched the darkness fall on the aspens and the bright red of the swamp maples beyond Cabin Field. The sweet meat tasted faintly of sandy muck and gray dogwood berries and it was perfect.

"Are we going out tomorrow to look at other places to buy?" I said. "Because I'd rather just go across the road to the federal land and do this some more."

"Me, too. We're just wasting our time looking at other places," Brett barked. The words burst out of him like he couldn't hold them back. "We got everything we need right here."

"Okay, okay," said Dad, calming him. "Vern and Jack found good places."

"Not as good as this, for what we do. None of the places we've seen so far are anywhere near as good as this, with all this federal land here, and with this great cabin on it. We're far from a river, but if you really look you see that this place has crazy good habitat."

Joe agreed, saying, "The cabin makes a huge difference. Most of the places we've seen are either some Chicago millionaire palaces or just shit-shacks."

"We're not seeing lots of birds or big deer here because this place needs work," continued Brett. "We got pine plantations that are about useless and miles of sand. But we can change that. Dad, I know you don't want to hear that."

"It doesn't matter if I want to hear it or not," said Dad. "Nothing will grow in that sand."

"I'm serious," said Brett, the cords standing out on his neck. "I'm not going to commit to this place and then find out I'm not allowed to cut down a funky old Scots pine or plant a crabapple. I have to be able to come up here on my own and run the dog. It's not a deer museum."

"I don't like being scolded, Brett," said Dad, his face clouding.

"But something has to change. Today is one of the best days we've had in way over a decade, and there's no reason it can't be like this all the time. I don't know why you wouldn't want that."

"Oh, it's been like that the whole time we've had this place. We've had so much fun, but you just didn't see it because you weren't here," said Dad.

"But we weren't here exactly because it *wasn't* fun for us," Brett said, leaning in. "I don't want to speak for Joe and Dean, but I was dying to come here. It was just that my ideas weren't welcome."

Joe and I weren't saying much. Brett pursued his true interests to a point of high expertise, and I had realized that day while walking the property that he had very specific changes he'd like to make to the habitat, and to our dad.

"I'd like to do some work here," I added. "Now that there's room for other opinions."

"You guys were always welcome to come here and do anything you want," Dad said, trying to head off a fresh mutiny. "You were just too busy."

"I'm not going to get dicked around," Brett said. "This place could be great. If we want a cabin we all love, let's keep this one and fix the place up."

"But why not look at some other places? We could find something perfect," Dad said.

"Because this place is an opportunity for us," said Brett. "We don't need perfect habitat; we can *make* it."

Then we didn't talk about it anymore.

Cold gray clouds foamed over the treetops. We moved out to the picnic table on the old porch so Brett and Joe could smoke; the porch had no roof then and was open to the falling cold. The dew came with the sweet watery taste of aspen and raised the odor of pine duff. Brett went out to his truck and got a pint of whiskey and Dad didn't protest. The presence of whiskey and cigarettes made it the most decadent day the cabin had ever seen. No one had agreed to stay on this property, but it seemed pretty clear we were staying. Joe and Bruce pointed out into the trees to indicate where their new bowhunting tree stands should go.

≈

The next morning, before dawn, I went out to sit in a blind to watch the forest. I hadn't done this in a long time. The blinds were out there holding their piece of the darkness and their tug on me was tremendous. I hardly knew where I was going on the camp but I navigated by headlamp and I had field glasses and a notebook, but no gun. It was November and the leaves were wet and spongy as I walked. I had three coats on and Dad's old Sorels and crappy leather work gloves. I was so new to the place that I was nervous and my stomach shivered.

I walked through the south twenty to a blind called Shouldabeen. Dad had sat in this blind quite a bit. One day he went in for lunch, which he almost never did, and Jack sat in the blind for an hour and shot a nice deer. Shouldabeen there. It stood on a little knoll in the middle of the aspen stand where Brett had shot the grouse. The aspen and red maple there had shaded out most everything else and it was easy to see through the trees.

Dad was a little pissed off that I wouldn't take a gun, but he was happy to have someone sit in the blinds, demonstrating to the poachers out there that we were defending our place.

I was hunting other things. When you sat in Shouldabeen and looked south, toward the bog, you looked right at that porcupine tree that stood about twenty yards away. We had stopped and examined it right after Brett found his grouse in the leaves, and Dad said you could hear the porcupines mewling in there when it was very quiet. The tree was a yellow birch snag, hollow and broken off about twenty feet up, with porcupine shit flowing out of it like it was vomiting out of multiple holes. I had seen it on my one previous visit years earlier. When you had a flashlight, Joe said, you could shine it up inside and see porcupines looking at you. They had obviously lived there for decades. We had followed their narrow trails leading from that tree to the dark hemlocks forty yards away, which is the porcupine's favorite winter food.

Joe named all the porcupines Wendell. He was reading Wendell Berry's *The Unsettling of America*, a book about the abuse of land through chemical and mechanical farming and how soil degradation has led to the disintegration of American culture. The book had everything to do with the restoration potential we saw in this camp, and it seemed a fitting tribute. The porcupines were nearly impossible to tell apart anyway, except by size, and we weren't sure how many there were in that tree, so one name was fine. When you saw one, you saw Wendell.

I set up in the blind and let the darkness settle, but I never did hear Wendell. Not this time.

The old feeling I knew from Card's place came back fast, though. I was smiling. I was comfortable in the dark, wide open, feeling a woods that was heavy with creatures. I didn't have to guess they were there; I had walked out to them because they were always there. The swampy woods implied the deer, the porcupine, the coyote, the crane. If they decided to show, like the turkeys bombing out of the pines, I would be so pleased but not necessarily surprised. It felt wrong to look past the blue-black shapes of trees as though they were just a container for something to eat; the aspen and highbush blueberries and witch hazel were enough. Watching them was to watch that whole implied community. Geese that hadn't yet gone south were honking on the pond over on the camp next door, which belonged to a nice guy named Landheer. An owl was crying from the spruce island in the middle of the beaver bog. Every puff of wind shattered the pale lights of the aspens and sent a shower of night-grayed maple leaves to earth. I wasn't straining to bring things into range. Rather, I was slightly overwhelmed by everything in the forest coming toward me like it was reaching out, wanting to be acknowledged. I felt the leaves would bank up against the blind and flow in and bury me in an outburst of affection.

About five minutes before sunup, chickadees and crows started their wailing, then the sharp scream of cardinals, and the forest was different. It receded somewhat. It took a step back and assumed a more standoffish daytime posture. I let the sun come up into the treetops to the east and then walked back to the cabin.

"See anything?" said Dad, in his robe.

"Everything," I said.

~

We took to calling the place "the cabin," as though it were ours. It had bloomed within us and we talked about it whenever we talked, which was suddenly all the time. Even Mom was jabbering on about our cabin and she had never seen the place. She had reason to dislike the camp, since Dad probably bought it with money that should have gone to her, but she let go of that. She wanted us to be closer to one another and closer to Dad. She responded to our enthusiasm, as the cabin had occupied our minds. It was hard to say whether this occupation was going to be good or bad. Dad would call up to make little announcements every few days:

"We have to get a new coat of stain on the cabin, especially that south wall over the porch."

"Brett says we should look at a wood-burning stove because those baseboard heaters are expensive to run."

"Brett wants to put up a barn but I don't want to."

"There are a few trees that need to be trimmed to open up the view into Cabin Field. I can't see a damn thing."

"Joe says we should put in some apple trees, we need some apples."

"Hey, Aunt Sally and Aunt Jane left us pretty much everything but we need a new can opener."

Any time he had an idea to change one blade of grass at the cabin he reached for the phone. I could trace the calls like a map leading into the dirt. They started with things like can openers and camo makeup remover and turkey license deadlines, but with every call his focus drifted earthward, and he talked more about the needs of the land itself. He detoured right into talking about those two big fields of sand and how to get deer food plots on them, what the turkeys eat, how he wanted to plant wildflowers. The land was swarming up into his mind.

Bruce was a builder and all day long he fitted metal and concrete to the earth. It's certainly possible that he talked all day long about the land and what it needed, but he just hadn't done it with us. We hadn't had a specific place to talk about since we'd finished his house twenty years before. But he so obviously felt good talking grass and apples.

Why did grass and apples feel good? I figured that it reinforced images arising from an "ecological unconscious." Theodore Roszak had first proposed this idea in his book *The Voice of the Earth*, and one article about his findings described the ecological unconscious as "the voice of the earth expressing its own pain through our seemingly unrelated woes." If the earth is expressing pain, I reasoned it must also be expressing its needs, its joy, its everything. Carl Jung had theorized in the early twentieth century that humans pulled archetypal images and all manner of psychic material from a deep layer of evolutionary experience shared by all people that he called the "collective unconscious." Roszak had extended that vast repository of knowledge to the other-than-human world. This meant that images could spring up into your mind from all types of beings that have experience living on earth, from whales to trees to mountains.

Roszak's books were about ecopsychology, a burgeoning field of inquiry that addressed the mental health of human beings as a function of the mental health of the planet. Building off Searles's and Shepherd's and others' idea that a sick environment was driving humans insane, and vice-versa, ecopsychology proposed that the way to make human beings feel better was to make Lake Erie feel better. The standards for what constituted health—grass and apples, satisfaction and laughter—might arise in our minds via the ecological unconscious. If we felt a deep yearning for grass when we saw a barren field of sand, perhaps some part of that very human desire arose from grass or sand itself, or beyond. The universe, dreaming.

Perhaps the call I heard from the land flowed from the ecological unconscious. Joe, Brett, Dad, and I were all awake to it now. But our new awareness of that exhausted sand didn't mean things got instantly better for us. The more we engaged, the more we acknowledged our sickness. All our talking turned out to be the nervous chatter before a big fight.

Years later, the psychologist Robert Greenway sent me some e-mail correspondence about this. Greenway was a pioneer in the ecopsychology movement and had been studying it since the 1960s, when he used to refer to it as 'psycho-ecology'—an ecology of psyche. During his years at Sonoma State University, he took study subjects out into the wilderness to record the effects on the human psyche. He had left academia as an emeritus to run Corona Farms in Port Townsend, Washington, growing vegetables as part of a local food movement in that bioregion. Which meant that he was still very much involved in studying ecopsychological entanglement. When I pressed him for some shorthand about how working a piece of land could change a family, he e-mailed:

> Every Ecopsychology would probably have a different theory as to "what's healing" in terms of "working with land" . . .
>
> Here's mine: I'm with Paul Shepard, believing that humans cut off from "natural processes" are crazy (Cf., *Nature and Madness*). I also believe that "minds" (or "psyches"—or the sum-total of one's "mental condition") are improved with a certain degree of "natural stress"—that is, "survival-oriented" stress, or the requirements to plant and harvest a crop, to overcome "weeds," to deal with the HUGE needs of the plants we grow for food—especially if you care for the plants, and see them in their full, organic context. Keeps one awake at night! So, the challenge awakens the mind— both the "present mind," and the eons of past times still carried in the depths of our psyche. And the farming itself draws one into the systems and dynamics of "the natural world." Farming is not "nature" per se, and it's not "culture" per se—it's an amalgam of both—and so, there you have it—the bridge, the non-dual task!

And when you enter this as a family, you're all in the soup! Division of labor issues arise—ALL the family issues present will arise; the work can be brutal, interspersed with incredible moments of joy. It's like the cliché, "a rising tide lifts all boats." A family experiencing this—from the stress to the work to the joy—not to mention the products and the tastes—is like a common place, a common boat, and you're all on it, paddling like mad . . .

I liked the sound of "paddling like mad." I hoped we could get there. So far, we had just pulled the oars down out of the barn.

~

When Joe had come back to Kalamazoo from San Francisco, Dad helped him buy a house. It was a creaky old three-bedroom 1931 Craftsman at the top of West Main Hill, where a lot of the WMU and Kalamazoo College faculty lived. Joe was as astonished as anyone, because Bruce thought of himself as a bootstraps kind of guy and didn't give away down-payment money. He didn't believe people should borrow money. He had borrowed two thousand dollars from Grandpa Henry to buy our house by Crooked Lake, and even though he quickly repaid him he felt guilty about it for the rest of his life. He felt similarly conflicted about using someone else's tools, which is why he didn't just borrow a tractor from John Polderman for a couple of days to clear the land for his house but instead bought one we really didn't need.

Dad's rigid insistence on self-reliance even extended to medical issues. About three years after Joe got his house, he was over at Dad's and got stung by a bee or a yellow jacket. He didn't know he was deadly allergic, but he was, and went into anaphylactic shock. His lymph nodes turned bright white and his throat swelled closed to the point where he was choking, but Dad tried to put him in the shower. "Just take a shower; you'll be fine." Finally Joe had to push past our father and whisper to his girlfriend Chrissy that he needed to go to the hospital, and on the way he got so scared that she had to drive. He got an IV drip of adrenaline, which may have saved him, but Dad thought that was ridiculous. Doctors and EpiPens were for fancy people. Just a way to make you pay money or grow dependent. There wasn't anything a shower couldn't cure and there wasn't anything an able-bodied person couldn't pay for on their own.

But Joe got a house, and then Brett came back from San Francisco in 1996 and he moved into Joe's house, too. Joe always had renters there, living in the tiny upstairs rooms, and one of them was an ex-girlfriend named Shannon. Shannon had a friend named Ayron, and one night Ayron came over and she and Brett got a good look at each other, and she started coming over all the time.

Ayron was Irish as Irish could be, with prominent cheekbones and bright blue eyes and freckles and shoulder-length brown hair that she was constantly streaking and tweaking, a beautiful woman in her mid-twenties who cried when she laughed because she laughed hard. She was a nonstop talker and good listener and had been a high school sports star, and when she was talking she'd stand up every so often and do a few stretches and pop her hips. She had been an academic star, too, a Medallion Scholar at Western Michigan University, an award given to only a few people every year that paid forty thousand dollars in cash, which was so much cash that she dropped out after her freshman year to better focus on spending it.

Ayron's folks had split up when she was two, and she survived a chaotic and mostly unparented horror show that honestly made Bruce's cheating and control issues look quaint. She was tougher than any of us would ever be, and how that translated into burning through forty thousand dollars is her story to tell. The salient point here is that she had grown up mostly without a father and, when she was eighteen, reclaimed a relationship to her troubled dad through sheer force of will. She saw echoes of this in both Brett's and Joe's warped relationships with Dad, and started talking to them about ways to fix it. Things started to get really analytical around Joe's dining room table.

Brett was resistant at first to strategizing with Ayron because he was too blunt for nuance. He just wanted to tell Dad he was a total dick and say, "Change now." Whenever he didn't like something, he said it. For instance, Brett didn't care much for Joe's housemate Shannon, and one day just blurted out, "Shannon, I fucking hate you." So it would be hard for him to stick with any kind of long-term plan to slowly bring Dad to a new consciousness. Brett's directness, however, went both ways. He knew hate and he knew love, and he fell head over heels in love with Ayron and he said so, and she moved into Joe's house, too.

Joe had been in therapy for a couple of years with a private clinician in Kalamazoo, and also volunteering for a crisis services agency called

Gryphon Place, manning a suicide hotline at all hours of the night. He had a nice touch with the folks who called, though he had never used any hotline himself. He had known about it for years but never called it because he didn't think he should be taking up the precious time of a volunteer who might be able to help someone who actually didn't want to die.

Callers to Gryphon Place didn't have to know that, though. When folks called in the pit of the night, he earnestly steered them toward services. He could talk right through to sunrise if that's what it took. One of his regulars was more lonely than suicidal and ended their nightly chats with: "Okay, talk to you tomorrow." Believing in tomorrow is a kind of hope.

In 1997 Joe started taking classes in psychology at Kalamazoo Valley Community College, and Dad agreed to pay for them. He'd paid for Brett's tuition, too, so that seemed fair. Just like Brett, Joe had to pay for his living expenses. With Joe back in school, Ayron felt the kick, too, and re-enrolled at WMU, also in psychology. The material became superrelevant and drove them both back into school.

Brett was working in a bronze foundry downtown, pouring fine art sculpture, and he was frustrated because he was working his ass off but Joe and Ayron were living the student life. Dad paid the mortgage and both of them had student loans, which meant they had walking-around money. Joe didn't drink much anymore, but on at least one occasion in the previous few years he had smashed his car while drunk and Dad got him a new truck. Dad had given Brett a used GMC Jimmy when he was a student, too, and let him sell it to pay down student loans, but Dad was scared that Joe would go back to guzzling if he didn't prop him up. He would corral Brett and Ayron several times a week to talk about how to best help Joe, and when Ayron asked him about whether Joe should shoulder more of the responsibility, he was very open about his rationale.

"I'm too scared to put any expectations on Joe," Dad told her, "because I'm afraid I'll get a phone call that they found him dead under a bridge somewhere."

So Joe and Ayron would go rollerblading all day and eat ice cream, and when Brett would come home at night they'd be at the table shushing him because they had to do their homework until Joe had to go in for his shift on the hotline. Brett learned to see the positive: the schoolwork gave him opportunities to work on motorcycles or build fly rods or do other things he enjoyed. To have his own life. To Joe's credit, he didn't abuse the advantage Dad had given him: after a semester, Joe was enrolled simultaneously in both KVCC and WMU and maintained a 4.0 GPA.

Both Joe and Ayron started working for a company that ran group homes, and for a while they even worked in the same one in downtown Kalamazoo. Because of its long history as a center for mental health treatment, the city is absolutely chock-full of these kinds of facilities, especially after the Kalamazoo Psychiatric Hospital began "deinstitutionalizing" its patients in the 1980s and sending them out into the world. Ayron made friends with homeless and troubled people wherever she went, befriending folks she called "clinical strays," and had even had her mom and others hire them for part-time jobs, so it was no surprise that both she and Joe fell in love with their clients. They roared hysterically at their antics, but also went out of their way to help them in any way they could. Ayron would take clients out for errands or appointments when she was off the clock or bring them home for Thanksgiving dinner. But working with people who had mental issues brought up a lot of feelings for both of them, and they would tote these home to Joe's dining room table, where he and Brett and A-Lee, as they called her—her middle name was Lee—would smoke and drink coffee and crack it all open.

Their talks would wend inevitably toward Dad and what they were going to do about him. Or rather, mostly what Brett was going to do about him. Joe was as much involved in our saga as our middle brother, of course, and had suffered more than any of us, but he had no intention of making demands on Dad. Dad was helping him a lot and he didn't want any confrontation. He was pulling for Brett, though.

"That cabin is an opportunity, if you ask me," said Ayron. "You're being handed an opportunity. Because the changes you want won't happen here in town."

"You're right about that," said Joe.

"You guys see Bruce all the time now. And your relationship is awful. It consists of you guys asking him to help you buy a house, or to help you out with a job at Delta Design when you need one, or to let you borrow the boat, or whatever, but you have no real adult relationship. You're still kids. You guys haven't become adults in his eyes."

One of the conditions that allowed Ayron to create a new relationship with her own father, when she was eighteen years old and he was getting married again—he had been married multiple times—was that Ayron had been an emancipated, self-sustaining adult for years already. He'd never given her a penny and she wanted nothing from him but a father. And, miraculously, he agreed.

"Being an adult might not change anything," said Brett. "Dad has outrageous control issues."

They talked a lot about whether Dad had obsessive-compulsive disorder, a need for control that drove him to protect his ideas or habits even if it meant hurting people.

"That control is a deep personality trait, and I'll just slam into it every time I approach him."

"Don't try to change it, then," Ayron said. "If you want a different relationship with your father, then the only control you have is how *you* respond. So you need to start responding differently. If you want to talk to him as an adult and have an adult relationship, then *be* an adult. Be the change. Stop letting him pay for anything, and stop whining and bitching about what he does. Just start going bird hunting or whatever it is that you do, and let him catch up. Don't work for Delta, even when he wants you to. If you propose changes at the cabin and he says no, then show him on the map where you're going to be camped on the public land and tell him he can come there if he wants. Put it on him. Make it obvious that the life you're proposing is a life you're going to go live anyway, with or without him. What else can you do? You'll feel better."

Dad wasn't really ready to forge adult relationships with his kids. His own brothers were his adult peers, and when they left the Kuipers Hunt Club, he saw an opportunity for his kids to be his kids again, like Jack's and Vern's kids had. So he started roaring back and forth to the cabin on every occasion, going up there every few weeks all through 1997, '98, and '99 in order to make the place good for us, like a dad, bringing up an old windbreaker he didn't want in the house anymore, or a board game he'd found, or an old set of pillowcases, exhausted by the idea of all this change, sitting at the dining table staring out the window at Cabin Field all by himself. He put a lot of effort into fluffing up the inside of the cabin without acknowledging the obvious prohibitions that kept us from engaging with the outside.

Brett didn't start frequenting the place, but Joe did. He would go with Dad whenever he could. Dad and Joe didn't talk much about his work or schooling because they could talk bowhunting. Joe's new enthusiasm for bowhunting reinforced the old man's feeling that the property was for hunting deer and for that purpose only, and that relieved some of his anxiety. Joe started exploring the place in detail, studying the tree stands that had been put up by the uncles, reassessing them as he scouted the deer trails beneath them with his nose to the ground. He presented Dad with great new locations for stands, and together they'd walk those trails until our father was satisfied. With the other uncles gone, Joe could stay up all night at the cabin and drink coffee and stare out the windows if he wanted.

Dad was enthused and bought Joe a compound bow that I couldn't even pull without a comic spectacle of heaving and grunting, but that Joe pulled like he was brushing his hair back. One of the first times he used it, Joe fell out of a tree stand on the very edge of the bog. It was not a very good stand because it was low and the deer would look up and see you sitting there in the opening and run off. He and Brett had walked out there together, and Brett moved off into the federal land to hunt ducks on the edge of the bog—since he didn't care for bowhunting—and just as Brett disappeared into the predawn darkness, Joe fell. The drop of ten or twelve feet was enough to break Joe's ankle, even landing in shore muck. He'd pitched the bow so he wasn't impaled on his own arrow—you laugh—but he didn't want to interrupt Brett's hunt. Every time Joe got in trouble, it was always Brett who came to rescue him, and he needed to give our brother a chance to hunt in peace. So he climbed back up in the tree and sat there all morning with the ankle making him nauseous. Dad and Brett had to cut his rubber boot off that night because his ankle was huge. Four days later he finally ended up with a cast on his foot.

～

Not long after our first hunting trip to the cabin for Thanksgiving 1997, I was introduced to an artist named Meg, and our relationship got serious pretty quickly. She was brilliant and showed her work all over the world, and I was crazy in love. Trained as an anthropologist, she brought depth of insight to any subject we'd discuss, from local politics to culture to environmental stories I was working on, and her wit and charm lifted me out of a funk from my latest failed relationship, which had left me confused and a little freaked. Plus it was fun to be witness to her artistic process. We both felt we had found a partner we could respect and trust.

Meg was in her late thirties and wanted to have a baby without a moment to lose. The first time she brought it up I said yes without any hesitation, which was as much a surprise to me as anyone. I had absolute confidence in her. So we had started trying to get pregnant. She wasn't too thrilled when I said I had to go to our deer camp for a week or so in November 1998, but I hustled right back and got on with the baby-making and the absence was forgiven. I wasn't totally sure how the subject of hunting was going to go over, but she had grown up on Long Island and gone to college at Kenyon in rural Ohio, so she was at least familiar with hunting as a country phenomenon.

The trip to the cabin with my brothers and the idea of having a child had convinced me that I had to find a more direct connection to wildness. My work in the 1990s had me in action camps with forest activists fighting logging in roadless central Idaho, on a Sea Shepherd boat chasing shark poachers around islands off the Pacific Coast of Panama, hiking into the Nevada Nuclear Test Site with Greenpeace to sit on the bomb site and stop the tests, and in old-growth forests from Mendocino to British Columbia. I was always in some mountain redoubt, but often I had no deep and personal story in that place. I needed a cabin with my brothers.

A friend had recently given me a nice Aquatech longboard, and I started focusing on the wilderness in our backyard in Venice, the Pacific Ocean. I had been working for *Ray Gun* magazine and I was committed to living in L.A., and I was excited about life with Meg and a new family, so I surfed a lot that fall and winter. We rented a house at Rose Avenue and Sixth Street, where we could hear the big winter waves pounding Venice Beach at night, and in December we were engaged.

Meg and I threw together a trip to Michigan so she could meet my family, and Dad put on an engagement party in the back room of a Kalamazoo sports bar called Gallagher's Eatery & Pub. Mom and Tom came and Jack and Jane, as well as Brett and Ayron and Joe and some of my good friends from high school. Dad was in great form, making toasts and turning on the charm. He'd become fairly good at this kind of thing, and had once thrown me a tremendous high school graduation party. Mom mostly let Dad run this party. She enjoyed her life with Tom immensely and had even taken to having a glass of chardonnay or two in the evenings, and she gave a toast. In this setting, Dad presented himself as a patriarch, with his boys all around in a kind of rugged fraternity.

I realized then, seeing my family outside the usual context of hunting or fishing or skiing, that we didn't know much about one another—for instance, neither Dad nor Mom knew very much at all about what any of us had studied in college—but that didn't matter, did it? In the important moments, we would pull together. We could get married just like Jack's and Vern's kids, who were all married years before. Dad put on a good show and I was grateful.

Meg was happy to be welcomed into the family, such as it was, but she got the full Kuipers experience right away. Dad started talking about our grouse hunting trip the year before, and deer and turkeys, and fishing, and most everyone at the party took his lead. No one other than Ayron asked Meg anything at all about where she came from or what she did.

The next morning, we were at Dad's place, and he fell into the subject as a kind of afterthought. "What kind of art do you make?" he asked, as though it had never occurred to him. Conceptual art, she explained, for example, a performance piece about Marvin Gaye that included hundreds of drawings. It was a very well-known work.

"And people buy that?" he asked. It wasn't a critique. He was interested, and he had no idea how the art world worked. Meg tried to fill in the gaps for him, and after they talked a while, it became clear her work was shown all over the world and collected by institutions he had heard of, like the Museum of Modern Art in New York. "Really?" he said, suddenly sitting straight up, with his mouth open in surprise. It was part of Dad's approach to the world to assume people were not worth knowing until they revealed their expertise in something, and then he was astonished and rushed forward and took extreme interest. He talked for years about a guy he once met on a plane who invented what he called a "windless lighter," which Dad considered some kind of miracle cure for man's need for fire.

He leaped up and rooted around in his office and produced the duck stamp art he'd bought at a Ducks Unlimited meeting and wondered what she thought of it. Then he busted out pictures of the deer camp and the deer he and Joe were seeing. He'd exhausted what he could take in about Meg's life, and he wanted to get back to the animal stories that made him comfortable. Meg would only make two more trips to Michigan after that.

Dad brought up our wedding about once a week on the phone afterward, eager to know what the plans were and if he could host the ceremony in Kalamazoo, and about three months later I told him Meg was pregnant, and then his demeanor changed.

"Well, I guess you gotta move back to Michigan now," he said, serious as the Reaper.

"What? No, Dad, we live here in L.A. Meg is part of the art world here, and she works at great colleges. We both have a good community here. I'm not so sure they're hiring at the *Kalamazoo Gazette*."

"I'll come out and we can have a quick wedding and then I'll help you find a house here."

"That's not going to happen, Dad."

"I'll fly your mother out, too. We're friends now."

I told him I was happy about the baby and that we'd make it work. It wasn't a long conversation. Dad called back the next day.

"Well, how is he going to know about the cabin and all the fun we have there?" Dad asked.

"How is who going to know?"

"The baby."

"Well, we don't have fun there. I've only been there twice in my life. That last time was fun, when we hunted birds."

"Oh, we always have fun there. You've had so much fun there."

"Those were Jack's and Vern's kids."

"And Brett and Joe. They know."

"Look, if Meg says it's okay, we'll bring him out to the cabin. Or *her*—it might be a girl, you know."

"You spend every last penny to fly all over the world to spend time with those goddamned radical people, with that Sergeant Shit or what-ever he was called." Bruce's voice was calm but loud. I had told him once about Sergeant Sphincter, a guy I had interviewed who shut down the logging of an old-growth rainforest on Vancouver Island by sitting in a strategically placed tree platform. When the Mounties tried to bring him down, he got naked and smeared himself in his own feces, and they left him alone for days. When they did finally try to arrest him, he swung off into the forest like naked poop Tarzan and got away! I would much rather interview that guy than go to anyone's deer camp.

"But that's my job. I like to write about those people."

"You're not going to do that anymore."

"Oh, I hope so."

"No, you have to get a real job. You're going to have a child now."

"Journalism is a great job. Why would I stop doing that?"

"All your stories are about how nature is more important than people. I never told you this before, but that is obviously insane, son. That's evil. That's the Devil."

"Look, why'd you buy that deer camp?" I asked. "You bought it to protect a place for deer and porcupines to live wild. I'm so happy we're doing that; it's exactly what we need to be doing. But we can't just have our little piece and abandon everywhere else. You always say all the good rivers and good hunting are out West, in Wyoming and Utah and Canada. They're only good because someone kept it from getting turned into a Walmart, which you know as well as anyone because you help build all that stuff. You and I aren't doing that, but Sergeant Sphincter is. I write about them so people know the fight is on."

"You are insane."

"I never said that was more important than my family. I'm about to have a child."

"Totally insane."

~

This probably would have been the end of my relationship with Dad, if it weren't for the intercession of a new love in his life. Oddly, around the time we all started going to the cabin again, Brett, Dad, and I all met new partners who changed our lives.

In 1998 Dad started going to a new church in Kalamazoo, Calvary Bible, and he noticed a woman there who seemed powerful and intriguing. Her name was Diane and she was a tall Dutch beauty with a blonde bob and fierce blue eyes. He sat next to her in the pew and asked her to coffee, but she turned him down. That hadn't happened much in Dad's life. Even more interested, he persisted and finally they went out on a date. The loneliness he'd embraced for a decade suddenly felt wrong. He'd dated so many other women, some of them for years, but never seemed to take them or himself very seriously. He treated them like he'd treated Mom, like they were half a person. But affection illuminates the dualities we grip in our minds and suddenly makes them seem foolish or even damaging.

Diane was an intellectual and grounded in a blunt political and material reality, and he was absolutely stunned by her. She had a PhD in psychosocial nursing and a minor in history from the University of Virginia, and a postdoctoral degree in intellectual history from the University of Pennsylvania. She had published quite a bit in the field of psychiatric nursing, and she was one of the founders of the Bronson School of Nursing at WMU. She had retired as a major from the Air Force, and had been in the service around the time Bruce had been, but unlike him she served in Vietnam, working in a hospital in Cam Ranh Bay and in the equivalent of M.A.S.H. units in the field. She was recovering from cancer and had a deep understanding of what it meant to be wounded by wars of all kinds.

Bruce took in the full scope of the major and fell hopelessly, gorgeously in love. It took a woman who outshone him in every way to convince him that a love of equals was the thing he needed.

I was so grateful for Diane's influence. I had begun to dread Dad's visits to L.A. He loved to stay in Santa Monica and walk the bike path, and when he saw a woman in a thong bikini rollerblading toward us he'd scramble for his camera and click away like he was Avedon as she rolled past inches away, often giving him the finger or barking "Asshole!"

"Ha ha!" he'd laugh, watching her roll off down the beach.

"Dad, you can't just take pictures of people. They're not hired performers or something."

"Oh, they want you to do it," he said. "That's why they're dressed like that."

He had stacks of four-by-six candids of rollerbladers, waitresses, bartenders, women in sundresses on the Third Street Promenade or sitting at the next table in Venice restaurants. He was shameless. But after he met Diane it all changed. After meeting her, the hot locals didn't stand a chance. He deferred to the major like he'd never seen another woman before.

∾

That spring, the spring of 1999, Joe and Ayron both received a bachelor's in psychology from Western Michigan University, graduating with honors. It only took Joe two years to complete his degree. They both immediately enrolled in master's programs. Joe was still working at the group homes, and about halfway through his master's program he became a manager at Gryphon Place.

Dad continued to scour the Lower Peninsula for new camps, sometimes taking Joe or Brett with him, even though they had already put up new bow stands that became iconic at the cabin, such as Double Tree, which was on the border of the USA to the west, and a new blind we just referred to as Dad's about twenty-five feet up a red maple above a mucky swamp crossing to the southeast. Until he saw an increase in the number of deer, Dad simply wasn't convinced he wanted to keep that cabin.

I wasn't doing any work on the place and Brett wasn't doing much, but in Dad's mind, all of his boys were back. That land was talking and he was listening. The way he spoke of the place on the phone, all three of us were there busily working at the cabin, making vast improvements, rebuilding the place from top to bottom. But in reality, it was just him and Joe snipping a few twigs. They worked around their bow stands, clearing shooting lanes of every possible branch and leaf that might get in the way of a loosed arrow, and they talked about putting in deer plots sometime in the future. Mostly Dad was there by himself.

Every time Dad told Brett he was going to look at a new property, Brett saw his own involvement at the cabin become less and less likely. He took Ayron's advice and started training his talented English setter, named Gertrude after our grandma, showing up at Mom and Tom's rural home with live pheasants and releasing them into the twenty-acre hayfield that surrounded their house and letting Gertie find them and put them to flight. He took the dog up to Oceana County to run the public lands near the cabin, and invited Dad along. Sometimes Dad even went, but they wouldn't stop at the cabin. If they did go to the cabin, Gertie wasn't allowed out of the car. Brett had very good reasons to want to train the dog on the cabin property itself: there was plenty of room to run out on the USA, but he was scared to train the dog on those public lands because antipredator zealots had set hundreds of coyote traps out there that would kill or maim a dog. Dad had his own bird dog, a brilliant wire-haired pointing griffon named Rose that was badly neglected and needed the work, but Dad left Rose at home in her outdoor pen for years because he wanted to go to the cabin and she wasn't allowed. Brett was hoping to show by example that this antidog position was hurting everybody, but Dad just wasn't budging.

Plus all the other prohibitions: No friends, the constant hectoring about cigarettes. No bonfires or peering at the stars through a telescope.

Certainly no planting bushes or other gestures for the wildlife. No boogering up the place.

Brett and I were pretty much stuck, since both of us wanted to pursue the restoration project. I took what I could get. When I got out to the property, I would sit in the blinds, summer or winter, since that didn't involve disturbing the woods. Dad made it clear that he, personally, would never go out there without a weapon, what with all those horses dragging tires and such out there. He considered my version of watching to be esoteric and pointless.

Brett, however, wanted to hunt birds, and the more he talked to Dad, the more Dad took Brett's ideas as an affront to his authority. I tried to talk to Dad about it. We were in the car in Kalamazoo. I didn't mention the church, but that's where he went with it. "You guys don't go to my church," he said, the AC blasting out of his truck as if to push back the underworld. "The Bible says that's my fault, and I'm willing to accept that."

"What does that have to do with the cabin?" I said. "The Bible doesn't say there's anything wrong with planting berry bushes or running a dog."

"No, see—that's not it. You and Brett don't respect what Vern and Jack and I built there. You think your way is better. You want to tear the trees down and talk about your ecoterrorists and play your heavy punk music and read your books and smoke and drink. You're just doing that to show that you don't approve of the way I worship."

"What? That's totally paranoid, Dad. We're just enthusiastic about the stuff we like. If you think we're bad people, then you just shouldn't have us come up there."

"You sit in the blind without a gun to show me you're better."

"Sometimes I don't want to shoot anything."

"You guys are pissed at me and you want to show me I'm wrong about the land up there. I know that."

The asphalt under us melted in the sun. Everything eventually goes back to earth.

"Well, I really enjoy sitting in the blinds, but I don't have to do that at the cabin," I said. "I can just sit in the dark in my backyard in California, it would have some of the same effects."

Dad stared ahead.

"No it wouldn't," he said. He had been to my backyard.

"Sure. The dark is talky just about everywhere."

"No, because your brothers and I wouldn't be there."

"Hmm. Yeah, that's a shame, because that's where I want to be, too," I said. "That's the whole point. But what can I do? Honestly. If it's such a horrible conflict for you, let's just call it off. We thought this was about enjoying the woods, but obviously it's more than that."

We drove by the Saniwax Building, an old manufacturing building in downtown Kalamazoo that housed a bunch of artists' lofts, including the Alchemist bronze foundry where Brett worked. Maybe that's where we were going, I don't recall. Dad thought the art lofts there were romantic, and he often said he really thought the place was "neat." He was an enthusiastic and tireless shopper, and even though he'd never visited any of the other artists in the building he was pretty sure he would one day and he would buy some stuff.

"Oh, you should see some of the pieces they make at Brett's place," he said. "They are real art." We weren't talking about the cabin anymore.

It was hard for Dad to talk about the Brett who wanted to change his Hunt Club. The Brett Dad really liked, the one he talked about all the time, was the Brett who worked doing penurious physical labor in the foundry. That, Dad thought, was a real man, pitted against fire and metal, melting bronze in the heat of an un-air-conditioned Midwestern summer. The boiling hot work reduced Brett to a walking bag of ligaments and tendons struggling to keep even 140 pounds hung on his six-foot frame, but *that* was a good Brett! It was a job that didn't require any *talking*, it wasn't just a bunch of puffed air like psychology or writing; it was brute force, pouring and welding and hammering and grinding.

He was not-so-secretly thrilled that he could buy one of these bronze sculptures and thus shop for the Brett he wanted.

∾

Brett got the message. Late in the summer of 1999, he sat in the driveway at Dad's house in his rusty old Jeep Wagoneer sobbing his eyes out. Ayron was trying to console him, but he realized he was at an end. They'd just had another argument with Dad about the cabin. Brett was thirty years old and worked like a beaten dog, and he wasn't going to be tricked into putting any more energy into the cabin. It had been mostly his idea to give the deer camp a try, to make some bird habitat there, but he was quitting. He'd been a fool to get his hopes up.

He wasn't crying because he didn't get what he wanted. He was crying because Dad didn't see how easy it was to be free. Maybe they'd never hunt together again.

Ayron told Brett he'd only be disappointed if he kept this up. He needed to be his own adult, and if Dad couldn't get with it, then fuck it.

Brett and Ayron had their own life. They had bought a nice wooden 1937 house in Kalamazoo's beautiful Westnedge Hill neighborhood and they could focus on that instead. Ayron was working on her master's in social work and Brett had the foundry, and Dad's false impression that all three of us boys were up at the camp obsessing over shooting lanes and counting the number of times the deer chewed its cud just made it clear he wasn't paying any attention to Brett's life.

If Brett wanted to make himself perfectly clear, Ayron advised, he should write a letter. Put it all down in black and white. And then walk away.

So he did. With Ayron's help, Brett wrote a four-page letter to Dad, telling him he couldn't be outdoors with him anymore. It was just too complicated and painful. He wasn't allowed to express his own interests in forestry and dogs and birds. Worse, he and Joe were seen as the same person.

They had been treated like twins when they were kids, but now they were grown men. Because Joe was bowhunting at the cabin, Dad simply assumed Brett was, too. He didn't even seem to notice that Brett wasn't there during bowhunting season. Brett had bowhunted once at Card's when he was thirteen and hated it, because of course Dad hadn't spent one minute showing him how to do it, and his first day ended in bloody disaster and Bernard was angry at Brett for not being a more skilled hunter. Brett wasn't interested in sharing half a life with Joe like they were Castor and Pollux, spending half their time in the mortal world and half in the immortal. He was tired of begging for personhood.

The letter has been lost to time, but it started and ended with the words: "I love you." It wasn't an angry screed. It was a demand for change. Like Martin Luther's Ninety-Five Theses, it was the blueprint for a reformation. Brett needed his own relationship to Dad, and the path forward he preferred was our habitat restoration project. If Dad was going to stick to his rules and not let him actually inhabit the property in a way that was Brett-like, then there was no place for him. It would be easier to simply show up with a green bean casserole to pass for Christmas dinner and grow aspen trees somewhere else.

Bruce had written a lot of serious letters when he was in the Air Force, when phones were expensive, but only Roy Sutter and Dale really kept up the correspondence over the years. Dale would send him a photograph of himself from Canada holding a dead wolverine, with a caption: "I met a guy from Michigan with a wolverine on the sleeve of his jacket." Their letters were mostly jokes and family news and weather, but Brett's letter was like a Class 5 tornado; it swept up everything and flung it onto the land, leaving a shocking debris field. And so it seemed that the cabin experiment had failed.

Dad read the letter and called Brett. "Ha ha! I got your letter!" he cried.

"Don't," said Brett.

"Oh, son, you've blown this all out of proportion," Dad sang on. "I don't care about any *rules*, you can do whatever you want—"

"I'll just hang up and this will be over. I mean it."

There was a long silence.

Dad exhaled. "Okay," he said.

"Okay what?"

"Let's fix the place up for birds. Whatever you think is right. Let's see what happens."

∾

Meg gave birth to our son, Spenser, during small game season 1999, and I figured this would be the jolt required to get Dad out of his head. Spenser was his first grandchild and I thought that should matter. I didn't want to give up on my father. Lots of people would have given up decades earlier, but we stupidly stumbled on hoping to be accepted as adults. Every day I questioned why I should care. But I had to acknowledge that I did. The blood pumps round and round and longs endlessly to return to its source. Dad and Brett and Joe had just gone out to South Dakota to hunt pheasants on the family farm of some church friends named Veenstra, and had taken both Rose and Gertie. Dad was an enthusiastic guy and he'd evidently caught Brett's bird fever, but we didn't know yet if he'd allow that kind of hunting at the cabin. I yearned every day for the cold leaf-litter smell of Michigan and the wet lake wind that blew through its trees. I had a home with Meg and Spenser, but I wanted them to know why this other place called to me. The only way to do that was to get my own place in Michigan, and I knew it would be a long time before that could happen. We had to do everything the hard way.

Mom couldn't wait to get her hands on Spenser and appeared at our door in Venice the second we were home from the hospital, and Dad came out a few days later. They both cried tears of joy when Dad held Spenser close to his chest like a puppy. Dad put his face down on the top of the baby's head and said, "This is perfection. He's perfect."

"I can't wait to bring him out to the cabin," I said.

"Oh, it's going to be awesome. I'm going to get him some little camo," he said.

"We can build him a tree fort out in the woods there, so he has a place to play."

"Yep," Dad said through tears.

We walked around the block with Dad holding Spenser. Finally he said, "Well, we probably don't want a tree fort messing up one of the trees, but he can sit with me in the blind and we'll see how he does. All you kids were pretty quiet."

Mom was astonished. "Well, Bruce, Dean always had a tree fort at the Nienhuises, don't you remember? What do you have there, one hundred acres? Surely there's *one tree* where he can have a treehouse."

Dad was smiling. He was outraged that Nancy would refer to his deer camp using the same mouth that said "I want a divorce."

"Well, it's not that kind of place," Dad said. "We don't do that there."

"We can build a tree fort out at our place, then," she said. "We only have that one big tree in the field, but he can have it."

"Good! Perfect! That would be great," he said.

Ten

First Plantings

I was over at Mr. Carter's place and we were sitting on the front porch with his son, Andrew, talking about the fence line we shared and what neighbors had come and gone. Joe and Andrew farmed over three hundred acres, and, like a lot of things at their place, the house was no fancier than necessary.

"Well, this house here was built in the 1870s, early 1870s. And they said they brought a sawmill in," Joe said. "You go upstairs, I got white pine boards up there that big, don't we, Andrew?" He spread his hands to indicate huge boards.

Joe's house was originally built as a stagecoach stop on the line from Hesperia to Hart, and it was radically overbuilt with heartwood framing double the size used today, which is probably why it's still standing. There's a stairway going up the front that was for the women, and another going up the back for the men. Joe and his wife, Marilyn, moved in there in the 1970s when there was still a wall upstairs dividing the sexes, but Joe knocked it out and made it all into one big room.

"They brought in a sawmill and set it up," Joe said again. That meant the original builders milled the lumber from big white pines on this land.

"When you're out on the state land out there, you can look at those stumps that are still around that have been burned inside when the forest fires come through," said Andrew. "There's still a lot of that."

~

Joe Carter's story about his house confirmed for me that our section once stood in old-growth white pine. It was of immense interest to me because they'd never grown back. Surveyors conducting the General Land Office surveys of 1816–1856 had dragged their sixty-six-foot measuring chains from south to north across these acres, and their beautifully hand-transcribed notes for our section and those surrounding it indicate mostly white pine, hemlock, cedar, beech, and hard maple. They laid out the section line between us and Carter, at eighty chains to a statute mile, and every so often they'd record a representative tree that stood on the line, often at the section corner or the forty-chain midpoint, to give some landmarks and some idea of the vegetation. That particular line went right through the beaver bog, and the surveyor wrote: "Enter Spruce swamp . . . Hemlock 30 in diam . . . Leave swamp." As they walked north, the elevation came up a few feet, the ground dried out, and by the time they entered the western edge of what would be our spread, they walked under some big trees.

Like the giant Douglas fir or ponderosa pines of the West, virgin eastern white pine forests in Michigan could stand 140–160 feet tall and 3–4 feet in diameter at breast height. The old-growth red pines and hemlock were nearly as singular. The white pines did get even bigger: the tallest recorded by an early colonist on the East Coast was 250 feet. We don't even know what it feels like to live under that canopy, with the life up above more in communication with the air than with the ground. I grew up under second- or third-growth oak and maple topping out at roughly fifty or sixty feet, with the occasional yellow birch or hickory or a big ash maybe reaching seventy feet tall. That's what there is today east of the Mississippi.

A fellow named Valentine Carpenter homesteaded our property in the 1860s, and he had the whole north quarter of the section, 160 acres that included our property and also the 80 to the east now occupied by our neighbor Randy. By the time he paid his 1870 taxes, the first assessment on this property, he'd cleared at least the 25 acres required under the Homestead Act to take possession of the land. Maybe the big trees were already gone by then, from pirate logging. Maybe he was a logger himself, one of the steady stream of working men pouring into Michigan with crosscut saws in hand after the white pine forests in the East were cut over.

Carpenter fought for the North in the Civil War and then returned to the East Coast and married the former Mrs. Martha (James) Warner.

Martha already had a young son named Fred, and her father, Daniel Sharp, lived with her. All four of them followed Valentine's father, Rufus J. Carpenter, to Oceana County in 1866 looking either for trees or for the farming that came after the trees. Farming was going to be a challenge. A climate tension zone stretches across Michigan from roughly Muskegon to the deep inset of Saginaw Bay, dividing the state into warm and cold. Below the line, it was deciduous broadleaf trees and good loam for farming. Above, gargantuan pines and sand. We are just north.

As Carpenter moved in, half the land in the township that was deemed arable—meaning it was above water—was held by speculators selling off the timber, many of them later simply abandoning the land for back taxes after logging it. With an interior drained by scores of float-able rivers that could bring logs out to the Great Lakes, Michigan became the logging capital of North America between 1870 and 1890. Timber barons took every big pine tree in the state, and sometimes simply every tree. Photos at the Hartwick Pines Logging Museum taken from the banks of the Manistee and the Au Sable rivers show men standing on log rafts in the water and not one standing tree for miles. Just ravaged landscapes of bald dirt. The logging camps cut and moved; more big trees waited in Wisconsin and Minnesota just across Lake Michigan to the west. Valentine witnessed the peak of this activity as sleighs piled fifteen feet high with logs groaned along the wagon trail in front of his cabin in the winter, headed to mill.

We only really know what our place might have originally felt like because of one small stand of remnant old-growth timber expressly conserved as Hartwick Pines State Park, which is a couple of hours north of us. After blowdowns and fires, it still holds forty-nine acres of indig-enous glory. You are different there. You are incredibly small. As in a big redwood grove, the overstory is another tier of knowledge, an upper room, a life of birds and insects and epiphytes that most humans never see. The mystery up there belongs to itself and floats from tree to tree on the fur of flying squirrels. These soft, aromatic trees breathe the kind of air that humans can't help but think of as rare and even sacred.

Carpenter's farm became part of the new Leavitt Township in 1866, separating from Elbridge, which was then mostly Native Americans in the Ottawa Indian Reservation, and at the very first township meeting, Valentine was elected clerk. His father, Rufus, was a carpenter both by name and by trade, and he built a good-sized general store a mile south of Walkerville, which had an upstairs meeting hall for public business. It also housed the Bird Post Office and he became the postmaster.

By 1870 Valentine and Martha's household included baby Arthur and their farm comprised one horse, one milk cow, three swine, and crops of Indian corn and rice worth $125 and $20, respectively. For tax purposes, his crops and livestock were valued at $200. They were hemmed in by water. South of his acreage, the surveyor's notes for the section line in the General Land Office survey book read: "Land Mostly Swamp."

They say that it takes a thousand years for undisturbed forest to create an inch of humus, so the uplands there could have accumulated as much as a foot since the withdrawal of the ice sheet, give or take. Once Carpenter opened it up, that humus deteriorated fast. Beneath it was pure sand.

White pines are easy to grow, but they also don't seem to mind waiting. Michigan is marked with large and distinctive stump plains or stump prairies well known in the literature of silviculture such as Kingston Plains and Deward Pine Stump Preserve. These are fields of elephantine white pine stumps cut more than a century ago and still sitting there like it was yesterday, as if in protest, where nothing other than grass savannah will grow. Most of these stump prairies were burned in epic and repeated slash fires, consuming what was left of the humus and cooking the already xeric sand. Whether it's a matter of infertile sand or lack of seed stock, no forest has yet returned, not even scrubby sumac or sassafras. Intensively logged oak-maple-beech forests did tend to regenerate in swampy tracts like ours, but the large white pines that once stood in them did not. By now, 140 or 150 years after they were cut off our place, they'd be well on their way to maturity again, and towering above the forest. But they aren't.

Our place was exhausted and turned into a sand dune.

∾

The Carpenter farm folded in some kind of abrupt ending. The homestead patent was granted in 1872, but it went to Martha, who within a few years took young Arthur and her baby daughter, Lillie, and moved west, ending up in Kansas City, Missouri. It's easy to imagine that the poor soil was one cause. Valentine stuck around Oceana County and was a member of the local chapter of the Grand Army of the Republic, the society for vets of the Civil War. Martha sold the homestead piecemeal over a couple of years and from that point on, the land we occupy changed hands in rapid succession, sometimes yearly, as speculators looked for new profits.

Chief among them was the Ludington timber baron Horace Butters, who invented a steam skidder that could drag timber out of the woods without battalions of men and horses. Butters laid in his narrow-gauge Mason & Oceana train lines—known locally as the "Mean & Ornery"—spreading out spiderlike to glean what was left of the trees up through the early 1900s. A forty-acre parcel abutting ours, now part of the USA, was once owned by Butters, as were many tracts around us. The beavers across the road are still using the raised M&O railroad beds as dams.

A fellow named James Askins bought the seventy-five (then still an eighty) in the 1930s and built a house up by the road. His son told me they milled all the lumber themselves from beech and oak growing on the land, and like Carter's place they made them double-thick, so the studs are mostly four-by-fours. The place is indestructible. The land was crap, though, and in 1951 he put in strip pine plantations to control the blow-sand. He planted five acres of Scots pines in the middle of the place and more Scots along the property line to the west, reclaiming an old dirt lane that lead from a schoolhouse up on the road right down the section line to a long-gone house at the edge of the bog. Though it's full of trees now, that lane is easy to trace through the forest to where it hit the bog and may have connected to a dirt road on the other side. Askins put in a long stripe of red and Austrian pines ten trees wide and eighty trees long to the southwest and the slash of red pine six trees wide and fifty trees long that now shades the cabin. They all show signs of being trimmed and thinned. He owned the piece for almost fifty years and when he died, his wife sold off the house and the five acres around it, which is why we own a seventy-five and not an eighty.

Most significantly, Askins put in a small stand of white pines over to the southeast, which grew so slowly it was almost imperceptible. The land did not go racing into secondary succession in a bid to return to the stability and energy efficiency of its so-called climax white pine forest. Instead, for over 140 years it had remained what the great plant ecologist Frederic Clements called a "disclimax" community: a stable ecological community that had stopped in succession somewhere short of its former end-state because of human disturbance.

By the time Vern's childhood friend Ike Huizenga got hold of the land around 1980, it was just waiting. If it was working through succession again, it was moving at a pace not discernible on a scale of human lives. It was a quiet sand field covered in lichens with the occasional deer and a gang of resident porcupines.

"The guy who owned it didn't do anything with it, it wasn't farmed or anything, it was just sitting there and I guess he just wanted to get rid of it," says Ike's son, Iran Huizenga. He's the same age as my brother Joe and a partner in Huizenga Land & Livestock Corp. Across the street they ran fifteen thousand hogs, but they never put hogs on our place because it was too few acres for their operation.

"The only thing you could put in there was asparagus, and we weren't too into asparagus at the time, we only did hogs. It was just sand. And that's all it was, just sand with a couple little sticks that stuck out of it that looked like grass, but nothing would grow there."

Out in Buck One, I could smell the difference between the white pines and the spruces Vern planted, or the hemlocks in the black muck. Unlike the other conifers, the white pines have a peppery edge, like biting into an orange peel. Aunt Sally named that blind Buck One after she shot the first deer out of it. Askins's little planting of white pines stands between it and the cabin. Those trees gushed resin as though their interiors were overwrought with bigness, like a teenager who was destined to play center for the basketball team. But they had not grown tall; they were fat but not tall. What were they waiting for?

~

Dad and Diane came out to Venice during the summer of 2000 to play with Spenser. Dad doted on his new grandson and liked taking care of Meg. As we dragged Spenser around the block in his Radio Flyer wagon to get him down for a nap, Dad acknowledged that he wanted his grandson to love the ocean, to love the nighttime air in Venice, to love the good rivers and herds of elk in the Rockies, to love Michigan. He was eager to have Spenser and Meg come out to the cabin, but he recognized right away that the deer camp was no good for a baby in the summer: it was too buggy, too hot, no lake or river close enough to give it a cooling breeze. Instead, we spent a lot of time together on Venice Beach, and Bruce tried to be around enough to take part in the little milestones in

Spenser's life, such as buying Spenser's first pair of shoes at Harry Harris in Brentwood.

~

In the fall of 2000 Brett enrolled in a Master Woodland Management program through the Michigan State University Extension in Grand Rapids, wisely figuring that a credential would give him better standing to argue for changes on the deer camp. Dad was excited when he told me about it, though he doubted any of this total horseshit Brett was reading was going to grow any more grouse or turkeys or whatnot. He just wanted Brett to feel encouraged. Dad was pretty sure we couldn't really affect the natural cycles of wild game. You just had to leave things alone. He believed in Man's Dominion, that the planet and everything on it was ours to eat up, and even though he wasn't thrilled to be sharing that destiny with other human beings, he thought it inevitable. I think he was actually depressed by the thought of it, because he also held romantic ideas about the purity of wilderness. He had always told us that true wilderness could not have people in it. One hiker toting a bag of Doritos ruined it for him. I suspect he felt the same way about heaven: the other people there were going to really screw it up.

Brett was well aware of Dad's skepticism, and he made a move that probably changed our lives more than anything else we would ever try with Dad, including estrangement or tear-splattered letters or figurative murder: he brought his class texts over to Dad's house so he could read them himself.

People who don't want to change their minds about difficult subjects like global warming or evolution simply avoid reading the science. Dad had never read anything about game management. Brett was compiling a thick binder of management protocols for individual species from song-birds to moose, and he was only a few weeks into his class when he recognized that it was a powerful tool.

Managing Michigan forests for wildlife mostly meant growing ruffed grouse, as their food sources and habitat were also generally great for woodcock, bears, whitetail deer, and a whole raft of other game and nongame creatures. Brett had reams of publications from the Ruffed Grouse Society, and most of them talked about growing and cutting aspen, as grouse depend on the tender flower buds, catkins, and leaf buds of aspen as their primary food source. Secondary sources would be hazels, birches, and ironwoods, which were also abundant in our woods, and then the flower buds of cherries, apples, and a few other fruit trees. Bruce thought he was going to be reading about what berry bushes he should be planting, but most of Brett's pamphlets and texts were about trees.

On the first page of Gordon Gullion's standard text, *Managing Northern Forests for Wildlife*, he was confronted by this: "Also to be considered is the widely held concept that a forest undisturbed by fire or timber harvesting is best for wildlife. In many circumstances this is a false notion and the prevalence of this concept has led to marked declines of some wildlife over large regions of North America."

He took this like a punch to the gut and kept reading. Of course, Brett had been saying these things for a decade, but Dad worshipped expertise and these were the experts.

Like everyone else in the Kuipers family, Dad had always been taught that popple (a slang version of poplar or *Populus*, the family that includes aspens) was a kind of weed tree and needed to be eliminated. Compared with oak or pine, aspen had very little value as lumber and was used mostly for pulpwood or to make pallets or oriented strand board (OSB). When I had sold firewood years earlier, I guaranteed my customers that it would contain none of that punky aspen, because the mature wood didn't burn well and no one wanted it.

But Gullion's book was mostly about growing and caring for aspen.

> Ongoing intensive research is showing that ruffed grouse is only one of many species of forest wildlife closely associated with this [aspen] ecosystem (Flack 1976). Among the game and furbearing species fully as dependent upon this system are beaver, woodcock, snow-shoe or varying hare, and moose. Research in Michigan, Minnesota and Wisconsin has identified the aspen ecosystem as the key to successful white-tailed deer management. In Minnesota, at least, black bears make much use of aspen as a food resource and the fruit-bearing plants that are a component of this forest ecosystem are essential to bears and important to many other forms of wildlife.

Another study cited in the book found that aspen cuts attracted at least seventeen species of songbirds. Dad was sentimental about what he called "tweety birds," and he knew Diane liked them, too. He read about the predators that would follow, from badgers to bobcats to wolves, and as he read on through the hunting season and into Christmas 2000, the experts slowly began to emulsify the old man's defenses.

He and Brett were at the cabin in early spring, with some snow here and there on the ground, looking at the fields. Dad was still processing. These things just take a long time.

"So Michigan was the first state to have a game warden," he said to Brett, sitting at the table and peering over his glasses. He had been reading. "They had to bring in a warden to stop the market hunters from mowing down all the wildlife to feed the logging crews."

"Right, but it was the logging crews that created a lot of the wildlife," said Brett, sitting down with his coffee.

"See, I mean, that's just backward to me," said Dad. "I always thought the market hunting happened first, as they logged, and then nothing came back until the trees matured."

"Nope, it's the opposite. They'd log off an area and for about ten years the wildlife would be stampeding through there. 'Cause they like to eat all that new browse. Michigan probably didn't have that many deer until they started logging."

Bruce looked at him. "I'll be damned," he said and went back to his pamphlets.

"It's disturbance that makes the birthrates surge," said Brett. "Just like if you introduce a predator, too. Letting a coyote hang around probably makes more deer."

That spring, the forester teaching Brett's class, Tom Nederveld, was giving a talk about game management in Newaygo, and Brett convinced Dad to go. Nederveld, it turned out, was not only Dutch but from Byron Center, only a couple of miles from where Dad had grown up on the Kasslander Place. Dad was so relieved to be in direct touch with someone who was like him, and who was an honest-to-God state-certified authority, that he was overtaken by fervor. He convinced Nederveld to drive with them straight out to the cabin that same afternoon. All three of them walked the ninety-five acres together, and within a few weeks, Nederveld sent them a rough, page-and-a-half typewritten plan to improve the habitat. Dad was almost giddy with newfound faith. He envisioned giant whitetails pronging belly-deep through lush fields of alfalfa and clover and fat grouse exploding from a series of new berry brakes. The heart of

Nederveld's plan was to take out the five-acre Scots pine plantation and a couple of acres of aspens, but Dad just glossed over these ravages. He wasn't about to do anything like that. But berries! He was all about grass and berries, and that was all the start that Brett needed.

~

Ayron packed some sand around a hazelnut seedling six inches tall and watched Dad slosh toward her with a five-gallon bucket of swamp water, banging it against his legs as he heaved it along. Joe was leaning on a steel planting bar, his face white and clammy with the heat. It was May 2001, the first hot weekend of the year at the cabin, and the oaks hung heavy with catkins. Cottonwood down stuck in everyone's hair. Joe lurched like he'd passed out and dropped to his knees and then lay on his back and looked at the sky.

"What's wrong with you?" Dad barked. He loved mindless hard labor, believing it had value no matter what the objective, and he felt close to the kids as they labored under the blistering fusion of the sun. He was especially impressed with Ayron, who didn't have to be out there but who worked extra hard to demonstrate her support for Brett's restoration plan.

"I'm fat!" Joe shouted from where he lay. Bruce made no motion to help him.

"It's not *that* hot out here," Dad said.

"Bruce, everybody brings something different to the team," said Ayron. "Brett's got the plan, you are providing the means to buy all these seedlings and the muscle to carry the water—"

"And I'm bringing the fat!" Joe added.

Dad was skeptical. "You guys have been smoking that wacky tobacky again," he said. "I know you."

"Bruce, I swear to you that that is not what's happening here," said Ayron, half-laughing. "Joe is just big. He can't take this heat."

Joe moved to the shade for a bit and then kept planting, swatting deerflies away from his head. They had a lot of work to do: Dad and Brett had gone all-in on their first planting at the camp, trailering in six hundred seedlings in pots and trays and burlapped root balls—Autumn olive, multiflora rose, Washington hawthorn, arrowwood, nannyberry, blueberries, and hazelnuts. They were all quite small, maybe six to eight inches tall, but they'd bought as many as they thought they could plant in two days. Brett had welded up some steel dibble bars at the foundry that you could stomp into the ground and make just enough room for a seedling, and the four of them wedged plants into the sun-scorched sand in forest openings all over the seventy-five, starting on the mostly treeless rise full of dust and prickers between us and the hunting camp of Mr. Landheer to the southeast. Bruce took it on himself to water them by dipping buckets out of the blackwater swamp.

Ayron nursed the conversation along to keep Joe's mind off retching. "Oh, you missed this one, Joe, I think it happened after you left the group home, but there was that one dude who was always talking about Kent County? 'Kentcounty, baby, kentcounty.' I guess that must be where he was from or something, because he was always talking about getting back there."

"Yeah, I remember that guy," said Joe, bent over at the waist and hanging on his planting bar.

"Anyway, he said one week he wanted to go to church, so we found some liberal church downtown that we could go to and one of the staff took him down there and the minister was taking prayer requests, you know, polling the congregation for stuff that people wanted to pray about. This dude jumps up and he says, 'Yeah, I really need some PUSSY, man!'"

"Ha ha!" yelled Joe. "Yeah!"

"'Yeah, I really need some PUSSY, man!'" yelled Brett, who already knew the story.

Dad stumbled with his bucket, laughing despite himself. Ayron was encouraged; you never knew which way that would go with him.

"And so, the minister, he doesn't even miss a beat, he says, 'And we pray that this man may find a special friend!'"

"HAW haw! No!" said Dad, laughing.

"Yep, a 'special friend.'"

"Oh Lord!"

"I'm going to say that in church next time," said Joe. "'Yeah, I really need some PUSSY, man!'"

"You guys are definitely smoking that wacky tobacky," Dad said again.

Joe had graduated with his master's in psychology, magna cum laude, only a few weeks before, and I didn't even know. Dad, Diane, Mom, Tom,

Brett, and Ayron all saw him walk, but I actually didn't know anything about it until years later, when he mentioned it during a conversation. I said, "Wait, you have a master's degree?" "Yep," he said. I answered, "Really? In what?" I never knew what Brett studied in school, either (sociology). We were close as could be, yet we knew almost nothing about each other.

Joe and Ayron were careful about their client's private lives, and they never used their names or identifying characteristics if they talked about them, but a lot of these people became part of their lives. Ayron often found them jobs or would take them to doctor's appointments or to Social Security and things like that when she was off the clock. You had to laugh at the stuff that went on in the group homes because otherwise you'd go mad knowing these clients were going to linger in these facilities a long time, or maybe their whole lives.

"There was one guy you'd love, Dad, he was so sweet," said Joe. "A guy who loved cars and he had traumatic brain injury as the result of a car crash. He talked nonstop and he called everyone 'Sir.' He would sit in the back of the activities van and yell, 'Red-line it!' The house wasn't locked, it wasn't that kind of facility, but on two different occasions this guy decided he was going to run away and instead of walking out the front door, he leaped from the second-floor window and both times landed on the air conditioning unit below. One time he broke his leg."

"Anyway," Ayron picked it up, "one time me and Joe took the whole house to the movies. Just the two of us."

"We're in the middle of the movie and the jump-out-the-window guy started hissing behind us, 'Sir! I gotta go to the bathroom!'" said Joe. "I turned around and told him he couldn't go, because this guy loved to talk and he would just go out in the lobby so he could chat up the people out there. So he starts getting excited: 'Sir!'"

"Joe was holding out."

"I just shook my head and said no," Joe continued, "and he got more and more excited and finally, right during a quiet part of the movie, he just hollered out, 'SIR! I'M GONNA SHIT MY PANTS!'"

"HAW HAW!" yelled Dad, tears streaming down his face. "Oh, I just don't know how you do it."

"It's hard work, but look at you, Bruce," said Ayron. "You're not afraid of hard work."

"Yeah, but I'd want the patients to get better. Are they getting better?"

"Sometimes you see a glimmer of hope," said Joe.

"That's hard to take, isn't it? Isn't it demoralizing?"

"Sometimes it really is, but like everything else you have good days and bad days," Ayron said. "It's satisfying to know that once in a while they really have fun."

Joe had switched companies and his new job was overseeing five group homes across the street from the State Hospital, plus managing a bunch of other "independent living sites," meaning apartments, and handling about sixty-five patients and around one hundred staff. That earned him fourteen dollars an hour and the privilege of being on call 24-7.

Ayron was still working on her master's in social work, but Joe had managed a BS and an MS in psychology, with a final GPA somewhere north of 3.8, in three and a half years. His original plan was to start a private therapy practice, but once he grasped how long it would take to build a client base, the idea faded. He was increasingly disenchanted with the whole mental health field. Technically, he was required to be available on his company cell phone at all times, but there was no cell coverage at the cabin. It was one of the reasons we all liked to be there. Every puff of hot wind made the aspens hurrah.

"I wish we could bring some of our clients out here," Joe said. "It would do them a world of good to plant a shrub. They never get to do anything like this. Don't you think, Brett?"

"I do, but oh God, can you imagine?"

" 'Sir! Sir! I am gonna SHIT MY PANTS!' " yelled Joe.

" 'Yeah, I really need some PUSSY, man!' "

"Oh Lord! Haw HAW!" roared Dad.

"Bruce, it's fun working out here with you," said Ayron. "You're loosening up."

"Oh, we always have fun here."

"And it's not just because I'm fuckin' selfish and I want more game birds," said Brett.

Ayron burst out laughing. "It's all about you, Brett! You and those damn birds!"

"Selfish fucker!" yelled Joe.

Dad doused a little blueberry bush with swamp water. "I thought so at first."

"I know you did," said Brett, "and to your credit and everyone else's, there is some truth to that. I want to do what *I* want to do up here. But it just so happens that if we make it better for game birds we make it better for everything."

"Listen to you all, pretending to like each other," Joe said, his head soaked in sweat. Then he lay down again on the sand.

~

They sat at the picnic table at dusk and drank coffee and were hushed every few minutes by a ruffed grouse drumming on his log in the deep swamp to the east. The thumping slowly built to a buzz roll like the bird was somewhere inside your own chest. The heat died away in the spring twilight.

Flights of geese passed overhead, conversing not with the casual traveling honks of fall but the urgent, hungry cries of the nesting season. All four of the people present jabbered away with hearts inflated by hope, talking about where they were going to plant the several hundred seedlings that remained. Brett and Ayron threatened to bring not only their hunting dog, Gertie, and their Lhasa apso, Jimmy, but also their cats, Mooker and Little.

"You're just going to freak out, Bruce!" Ayron cackled. "Oh my God! A cat!"

"Don't tell Vern or Jack. It's sacrilege," said Joe.

When Brett was in the shower, Dad said to Ayron: "You and Brett are really great together. You laugh together. That's so important."

"That's a nice thing to say, Bruce. You know if Brett's laughing that he feels good."

"He's like a totally different guy. He's really relaxed today. Usually he's so absolutely rigid."

"But it's not acting out. You know that, right? He's not just being an ass, there's intention behind it. It's like we were talking about earlier: he wants to make this place into something he really enjoys, so it feels like him, and then he knows he's going to feel better and you'll all have a better time together. The bottom line is that he wants to have a better relationship with you."

"He doesn't say it as nicely as you do," said Dad, fastidiously scrubbing a dish over and over.

"No, I know it. He can be harsh. But the harshness has the best of intention behind it."

"Well, he's sure lucky to have you, even to interpret things like that. I see that the two of you are really friends."

I wasn't there that day, but from the way all of them described the planting to me a few days later, the feeling had changed. The land was no longer an abstract; it had seared their brains with its absorbed solar heat and stabbed them with hawthorn and Autumn olive thorns and gone under their nails and shot itself through them. They weren't just walking the land; they had opened it up. As a family and as a project, we were now in its very guts. Working shoulder to shoulder had scrubbed most of the charge out of the air between them; it was as though everyone in the planting crew had just had a massively satisfying conversation, though really the banter hadn't been much more than group home yucks and whether someone should see if Joe was okay. Dad didn't know if anything good would come of this planting, but he went with it. Trust is effective in truly microscopic amounts. The dirtier they got, the happier they got. They walked around the kitchen in their work boots and Ayron watched Dad, looking for anxiety, but the old man seemed simply pleased to have them all working there. The outside came in.

They were out on the porch again at daybreak downing an outfitter's breakfast of coffee and Ibuprofen and listening to the drummer. Dad was the first out in the field to plant for a second long day. If he could have, he would have worked all night.

The more they planted, the more they were all irritated by the sunbaked sand in Cabin Field and First Field. They didn't put bushes in those fields because they were just too dry and exposed, but the new plantings increased the barren effrontery of those dunes covered in gray dust. Their emptiness stood out like an open sore. Dad pitted himself against them. Soil tests Brett had sent to MSU showed those fields had almost zero organic matter and the acidic pH of the swamp. Their weekend plan hadn't included working on those fields, but they had opened the soil now and the berry bushes didn't even seem as important. Before they left on Sunday night, they agreed they had to get into those fields and plant buckwheat as soon as possible. The place was making its own agenda.

~

The first planting really had me itching to get my hands in that dirt, but I had an infant son and a partner who weren't going to go on a working vacation, so I got as close as I could. Michigan had filled my consciousness—even if we didn't actually go to the camp, I wanted to be immersed in those trees and the smell of sand and lake water. Dad understood so he rented a house for us in Saugatuck, about two hours south of the cabin, in the shade of huge sugar maples high on a bluff overlooking Lake Michigan.

Dad was conflicted about that fancy cottage. He worried that we'd stop going to the deer camp and start doing this instead, lying around in the dreamy shade. Vern's new place was right at the mouth of the Manistee, where the grandkids could play in Lake Michigan, and Jack's cabin was on the nice kayaking waters of the Sable. Dad, however, just wasn't cut out for that kind of leisure. If he couldn't hunt, or fish, or ski, or hike, he was a little lost. I don't remember us ever going kayaking or canoeing together. Saugatuck is at the mouth of the Kalamazoo River, and he asked if I wanted to go on a guided trout trip; he and Brett went out that summer with Fred Lee from the shop Fishing Memories in Portage, and the river was right there. I declined, but Dad did take Meg and me out on Lake Michigan in his Lund boat with its big Mercury motor and Bimini top, and we fished a little, but the lake was rough and we cut it short.

Finally we just played with the baby. Mom and Tom had a great time with Spenser, leaping from bed to bed with him as he giggled like mad. His eyes would light up when Tom would say, "Spense, let's wrassle!" Spenser was walking and we'd all mob down the steep trail of exposed roots to the cool of the sugar-sand beach. Lake Michigan is a wide inland sea, but the tiny green waves sloshed without the detonation and rocky gargle of the ocean. Meg and I bought a kiddie pool and Spense slapped at that water in the shady yard as Grandma Gertrude, Uncle Mike and his second wife, Barb, and some of my college friends came by to talk and eat and have coffee. At night, big thunderstorms rolled in like the shards of lightning were spokes on a wheel pulling the clouds across the lake and the big maples slapped their branches on the ground. The mornings broke clear and the mosquitoes gathered in the shade, and it was strange to be in a cabin where there weren't berry bushes to plant or shooting lanes to clear.

Dad liked being a grandpa, but he was just biding his time. We talked about what would happen the next summer, and he made sure we understood that beach life wasn't going to be a regular thing: "If we want a cabin where we can actually hunt, it's not going to be like this," he said.

Eleven

The Other Kuipers

Dad and I walked the edge of First Field a couple of days before the deer season, kicking at the dust, carrying a ladder between us. The sun brought the temperature up to about fifty and the old man was in his glory, smiling as if he could see heaven. Spenser was in the cabin with Diane, and Brett and Joe were clearing brush from their shooting lanes. We were setting out to do that, too. Both this field and Cabin Field had been planted to buckwheat, which came up fairly thick but was mostly like ground cover rather than the twelve- to fifteen-inch-high plants we had expected, and in this season a patchy green fuzz of winter rye about two inches tall poked out of it.

"This field is still struggling," I said.

"Oh, nothing will come up here," said Dad, his smile dimming only a little. As long as he had separated himself from the place, it didn't bother him. "The buckwheat we planted in the spring only got that big, too, and then we disked it under. I showed you pictures."

"Gradually we'll get some organic matter in that sand."

"Well," Dad said. "It's just a different place here. There's a reason Ike and all them never farmed it. Carter throws corn in the ground and it flies up eight feet tall—you can see it from here—but over here nothing will grow. That's just the kind of place it is."

In July, after planting all the seedlings, Dad spent thirty thousand dollars on a brand new John Deere tractor with a bucket loader, a disc harrow, a big mower people generally refer to as a brush hog, a broad-cast seeder, and a snow blade. Of course, we could have borrowed or rented that stuff from Mr. Carter, too, as he had all kinds of equipment, but that's the way Dad was. Brett had gone round and round these fields wearing a respirator, disking up the reindeer moss and prickers and raising a choking dust storm that swirled around him as thick as the Eighth Plague and then peeled off in the prevailing westerlies. With the buckwheat they had put down fertilizer, which is a salt and makes the pH more acidic, so that required amending with lime, too.

"You don't want to put down too much fertilizer, though, or you burn the fields," Dad said as we walked through.

"What does that mean?"

"That fertilizer just fries the plants."

"I guess you'd have to really overdo it to make that happen."

"Oh, no, even if you use the suggested amounts it happens. Your grandpa Henry used to say that all the time. You burn the fields. So I told Brett we should only use half of what it said on the seed bags. That's probably what originally happened to this place: it got burned. Now it won't come back."

We left the west end of First Field and entered a tractor trail that led to a blind called Desert Storm. I didn't care for the name as it commemorated the first Gulf War, but it did make local sense since it sat on a sand ridge. All around it were small red and Scots pines and open pits of blow-sand that looked like sand traps. Or desert.

Dad and I had restored a shooting lane from this blind that followed a heavily trafficked deer trail about one hundred yards through the oaks into Mr. Carter's field to the west. But it was overhung by branches at the far end of the lane, in the old roadbed that ran along the property line. Dad didn't want to use the bucket loader to get up in those trees, or use the chainsaw, either, as they made too much noise for the day before Opening Day. So I went up the ladder with a handsaw.

"I want to walk around and see all those nannyberry and blueberry and stuff you planted in the spring," I said. "That's going to make a big difference."

"Oh, those all died."

"All of 'em? All six hundred?"

"Yeah. I think a couple of the Autumn olive survived, but they're like a foot tall. This is just a different kind of place. Nothing grows."

"Damn," I said. "There must be something we can do about that."

Dad didn't worry too much about it. Or if he did, he wasn't letting it ruin his hunt. He was smiling. We were all there. His towheaded two-year-old grandson was there, proudly stomping around in his own blaze-orange hunting cap. Even Diane was there, which was the first time he'd ever invited a woman to camp. He'd had long-term girlfriends before, but none of them ever made that cut. I figured then he'd marry her. All those years when Sally and Jane and their kids and grandkids were there, he'd been alone. In a way, Dad finally had what he'd always wanted from this camp: a place where his partner and kids would hang out with him, just like his brothers' families had. He had closed the gap between himself and his family, and that allowed him to widen the gap between himself and this place. It didn't matter if the place was shitty; he was going to maintain just enough interest to keep us all coming back. That kept him from seeing how serious we were about the restoration project.

I scrambled up and down a half dozen trees, and as each limb dropped through the canopy he greeted them with a "Yes! Now I can see something!" and dragged them off the deer trail. He loved limbing trees and so did I; the harder to reach the better. Working in the trees was the best thing in the world.

"You going to take down those Scots pines by the cabin?" I said from my perch, full of logging love.

"What? No way."

"I thought that was part of the plan."

"No way in the world. You can see for yourself that nothing grows. It would turn into a sand dune."

∿

"I can't even talk about it," said Brett. "This is how it's been all summer."

We walked out to a blind Dad called the Taj Mahal, which Brett had built high up in a gargantuan beech tree that overlooked First Field. The tree sprawled like a baobab, its bark a smooth gray elephant skin, emerging fat from a vast mat of gray-brown beechnut husks. Brett had built it as a gun blind, a little too high for good bowhunting, and he would sit up there perched in the canopy and whisper to the birds. This was before Ayron started coming out to sit with him in the blinds. Brett was putting some cushions up, and, just like Dad, he had been happy to focus on the next day's hunt until I mentioned the habitat plan.

"Nothing grows here because he'll only agree to use half the fertilizer and lime that we need and the rain just washes it right through the sand. He won't cut the trees. He bought all this great equipment but it sits in Kathy's garage except for a couple of days a year. We planted seedlings in the spring that were way too small and they withered, so now he thinks bushes won't work. We do a little clearing around the blinds and that's about all the change he can handle."

Kathy was the neighbor who owned the five acres up by the road, and she let us store the tractor in her utility building for a while.

"And why's Joe so jumpy?"

"Diane has Joe in a rage."

Diane had always been very warm to me and Spenser and had taken a particular interest in Meg as a fellow academic and intellectual—they both had university positions—but she took one look at Joe and decided that he was her personal problem. She couldn't hide her disapproval. Diane was a psychiatric nurse, and she understood that Joe was depressed, but she thought Joe took advantage of Dad, letting him pay for a house and university fees. She didn't see any reason why Joe shouldn't be doing that himself, and more. He was an able-bodied man. One reason she got along so well with Dad is that they both had just about zero tolerance for neediness. But when it came to Joe, Dad was a dad, and she was appalled. Diane confirmed all this in talks with me later, saying, "All you guys have your own bullshit, and all of you manipulate Bruce in your own way, and I'm just not going to entertain bullshit."

I could take that kind of talk. As a reporter, I talked to people who didn't like me all the time. I actually think Diane and I liked each other just fine. She was nice to me and nice to Spenser. Joe, of course, fell apart in the face of criticism of any kind and thought that she'd turn Dad against him. I don't know if that ever happened, but Dad was deadly allergic to any kind of conflict, so he mostly said nothing.

None of us, including Dad, minded if Joe needed extra care. Ayron, in particular, had talked Joe through hundreds of bad nights, over thousands of hours of deep distress, and every time he called, she still took the call. Joe would show up at Brett and Ayron's house in the middle of the night, and all three of them would talk it out. It was the relationship Brett and Joe had had all their lives, and Ayron was a much better listener and reflector than Brett had ever been. She thrived on it. Joe didn't really drink anymore by this point in his life, but the underlying issues were all still there. We were all used to that. But he thought Diane was looking at him like he was trying to steal her purse. She did think he was too emotionally dependent on the world; he let himself be constantly disappointed. Diane was indignant about him the way some people are pissed off about welfare.

And that wasn't about to get any better. Joe found out in the summer that he had a baby on the way, a little girl due in February. The mother was a woman he had known for several years, but he didn't want a relationship with her. It's a story as old as dirt, but Diane just could not believe any man could make that kind of mistake. Whenever Joe talked about his life, she regarded him with openmouthed astonishment. Maybe the rest of us had just stopped being astonished. I was pretty excited about the prospect of a cousin for Spenser, but I'm an optimistic person. When Joe and Ayron laughed about their group home jobs and griped about whether they should stay on, with the high staff burnout and all, Diane opined freely that Joe was going to have to "grow up" and get ready to take care of his child.

"Well, what else do you want me to do?" Joe said calmly, headed out the door for a cigarette. "I already work twenty-four hours a day." He hadn't quit the job or anything, he was just bitching about it.

"Dad just smiles and pretends nothing is happening," said Brett. "Ayron and I are trying to stay out of that whole discussion. We'll probably run into Walkerville later, just to get out of the cabin for an hour or so. When I'm here I'm just going to focus on being out in the blind. That's the only place that makes any sense."

~

By the light above the basement door we loaded our rifles, and then the light was out and we walked onto the camp. There was an old feeling that always returns. A feeling of answering a call. We smiled at one another in the darkness, then Brett went north with me at the two-track and Joe went south to Shouldabeen. We kicked through the dust of First Field, and Brett stopped to climb into the Taj, and I walked on alone under gunmetal clouds that warmed the air. The walking out is a prayer, an invocation: Let it all come.

I could see my breath, but the five A.M. darkness was not cold. All the way out to the blind I felt a presence, like turkeys were about to drop down out of the pines, but nothing showed. Or rather, everything showed. The forest thrust itself at me, demanding that I acknowledge what was there rather than what was missing. I felt foolish for creeping along, looking for what was hidden, when so much was reaching out, limbs and leaves slapping at my coat, cold sand under my feet, blue-white clouds pouring sideways through the night. I got in my box and settled into my plastic chair, listening to the faintest rustle of wind in the beech leaves, always the first to leaf and the last to drop. The edges of the visible forest crept toward me, closing in the space around me, and the parts of the forest I couldn't see receded from me, beyond the big lake, beyond the curve of the earth, in a never-ending night. The darkness was moving.

Spenser was still asleep in the bunk next to me when I got up, and Dad had volunteered to stay in with him. "We'll hunt from the cabin" was how he put it. That had never happened before; Dad had always been the first one up and out the door. But Dad had already hunted a month's worth of days that fall: he'd made an early trip to hunt mule deer out of the Box Y Ranch, a spectacular and remote camp on Wyoming's wild Greys River, and then taken Joe on a bowhunting trip for elk in Colorado ("We never even saw one elk," Joe said) to celebrate his master's degree. Joe, Brett, and he had fished hard for steelhead in the fall, too. I was happy they did those things, but I didn't really want to do them. I wanted to be on this sand farm, where my brothers sat and the thinking was loudest. This was the place that was enmeshed with my family.

What I felt was sand, tree, and cloud thinking.

I was overwhelmed by how much thinking was going on out there in the dark. The barred owls called out of the south twenty, a pair that had been there for years, with their gentle *Who? Who? Who cooks for you?* But underneath the owl call was a sensation. Silent life made itself felt from the deeper dark under the hemlocks, where the black muck at the roots of the trees seemed to suck up all the light. Underneath it all was a sense of active knowing: the uncountable life forms that made up the sandy woods were making demands on me, asking for my undivided attention. There was nothing to see except the outline of some trees in the purple predawn, but I wasn't just sensing, I was also being sensed. There was a reversal of the subject-object relationship. It became clear that the idea of subject and object work only if they are reversible. In the great dialectic between subject and object, each making the other in a flow of constant making and unmaking, everything that *is* must do both. The things out

202 The Deer Camp

there were regarding me from their own point of view. They had their own subjectivity.

We built these boxes in the woods that we called "blinds" or "hides," with the nominal goal of not being seen by the wildlife, and we painted our faces and spent ridiculous amounts on camo coats and veils and odor-free shampoo and scent-stopper underwear with charcoal filters that you activate by tumbling in the electric drier. But it was all really an inside joke and a scam, because everything in the forest clearly knew I was there, even if I didn't stink, which I did. How many leafy bushes do you know that smell like an electric drier? Every river otter and skunk cabbage and springtail in the dirt for miles around knew I was sitting there. Sitting in a blind is not hiding; it's just an agreement with everything around to present yourself in a nonthreatening form. It's a deal.

Every thing out there in the darkness had a stake in not only knowing the other but being known by the other. I thought of the old Greek idea, from the time of Aristotle, that any object seen by the eye must *ray out* some idea of itself, making itself visible. Things wanted to be known.

Even with my eyes closed, the woods around me was presenting. And not just to my eye and not just to me. The creatures that made up the woods and the swamps were presenting to one another. It wasn't about me; this was fundamental to how they survived.

The depth psychologist James Hillman wrote extensively about this presentation. In his essay "Anima Mundi: The Return of Soul to the World," he reasoned that a thing can be known, or have some being, only because it contained some *anima mundi*, or "world soul." This soul was a kind of animating agent or principle, created by the constant friction of relationships. Hillman proposed the existence of this soul or psyche, a Neoplatonic idea come to him by way of Plotinus and Ficino and then Jung, as an intentionality on the part of all things that exist. They *want* to be known. They ray out to the senses and to the imagination their desire to be known. What I love about Hillman's theory is that it assays to identify the building blocks of the imagination. If everything out there has its own subjectivity, its own piece of the language or raw stuff of the psyche, then that raw stuff lets it signal to the imagination of the other, via the senses and whatever other faculties we may have. All those subjectivities are flowing into one another, lighting up the imagination like electricity. Where they become known. Where they attain being.

Everything is part of this flow. If everything has psyche, and wants to be known, Hillman is proposing that everything has imagination. Not like a human imagination, probably, but some version. This is the radical project implied by the "return of soul to the world." He was attributing to the material world the agency and influence that had been stripped away by Abrahamic religion and human-centered culture. That agency is as old as the hills: long before organized religion we already had umpteen millions of years of history with trees and sky, and those things have a long history with us, too, and with each other.

Of the inner life of objects, Hillman wrote: "Its intentionality is substantive, given with its psychic reality, claiming but not requiring our witness. Each particular event, including individual humans with our invisible thoughts, feelings, and intentions, reveals a soul in its imaginative display. Our human subjectivity, too, appears in our display. Subjectivity here is freed from literalization in reflexive experience and its fictive subject, the ego. Instead, each object is a subject, and its self-reflection is its self-display, its radiance."

A soul in its imaginative display. Was this what I was sensing in the dark? Something was pouring into my imagination, and it seemed impossible that I was merely creating it. I felt things that I hadn't consciously sensed. Something was transmitted: a felt meaning. How was this communicated? Via the unconscious? Via senses of which I was unaware?

And what was the working distinction between human and other-than-human, or even living and nonliving things, when all have their own subjectivity, their own interiority?

In this woods, in this dark, I realized the sand under my feet was presenting just like the rasping turkeys who started crying from their tree in the purple quarter hour before sunrise. They both demanded my attention, and their own being. I saw the figure of the sand itself: orange, multitudinous, a kind of tissue made of an uncountable number of individual grains of silicate. A one made of many. That image sank into me and would grow stronger as the years passed.

The sand itself wanted to be known. It made requests or demands on my imagination.

I thought this display must be working on us when we worked on the land. The more we put our hands in it, sweat over it, bled into it, the more it entered our imaginations and took hold. No matter where I was in the world, working on journalism pieces, on a glacier, at the taco truck on Rose Avenue in Venice, I thought about what was happening at this deer camp. Some old part of our minds was responding to the display here. This imaginative display made us feel good, and everywhere I went I felt like the lines were open to this place.

When I came back to the cabin around ten A.M., Dad was sitting with Spenser at the kitchen table, reading *Fox in Socks*. Spenser was so absorbed by the book he hardly noticed me walk in; his eyes were locked on the pages and he insisted Grandpa keep reading. Dad loved the Dr. Seuss books and they had inspired our tendency to rhyme and pun. If I walked into the cabin and said, "I saw a lot in the dark," someone would respond, "It was not a lark!" and "Hark, hark, the howling park," and so on. That's how we talked when we wanted to be surprised by the imagination. A rhyme invited words in from somewhere other.

Grandpa Bruce was making the connection: "This is where foxes live," he said, pointing out the open window to beyond Cabin Field. "They live here, in the woods. In socks." Spenser's mouth hung open.

Joe bagged a decent six-point buck that morning, which seemed to be good preparation for a guy with a baby on the way.

≈

Hazel Jane was born in the spring with Joe's dimples and saved his life. We were worried about how he would react, if it would drive him this way or that, but he discovered, much to his delight, that he loved this little girl with all his oversized heart. He acknowledged to me and to Brett and especially Ayron that his beautiful dream of suicide was now impossible. Too much love. Mom was over the moon to have another grandchild to spoil, and Dad doted on Hazel like he doted on Spenser. Dad did not come to Spenser's baptism that spring, however, because Meg and I had him baptized at Saint Monica's and Dad was pretty sure that Catholics went to hell.

Cutting trees for habitat generally happens in the spring, to give the forest humus a chance to release suppressed trees and get them growing before the snow flies, but the 2002 season came and went and we didn't do any logging. I was burning through a lot of greenhouse-gas-causing jet fuel flying back and forth from L.A., but I got out there for farm work and spun around First Field on the John Deere with a T-shirt tied around my face, gagging on the fine gray dust and badger shit and blinking the deerflies out of my eyes. I think I was dragging the disc. I did figure eights around the field and a fine glacial powder crunched in my teeth.

Dad finally started listening to Brett about the need for more inputs: our fields had phosphorous off the scale and okay potassium but only traces of organic matter and nitrogen, so when they planted the next rotation of buckwheat, he went for the full recommended amount of fertilizer. And then Brett and the old man drove to the co-op in Fremont and bought a massive load of agricultural lime that came in a spreader wagon, but instead of pulling it with the tractor he dragged it twenty-two miles down the road with his new Eddie Bauer Explorer. It was so heavy that the truck smelled hot and the red warning light for the transmission was lit up all the way. I bought that truck from him a few years later and I guess it shouldn't have been a surprise that within a month I spent eight thousand dollars putting a new transmission in it.

The more Dad put into the place, the more he let it under his skin, the more it irritated him. Brett took the brunt of it, because he was our forester and he was preternaturally skilled with machines. He had always been the guy who fixed the outboard motor or the downrigger on the boat, who re-blued an old gun, who put a new guide on the salmon rod, who got Dad's Harley running so he could take it out for its annual trip into town and back. Because he was so good at these things and Dad was so relatively bad at them, and Dad wouldn't let him cut the trees, the two of them were always a few words away from a blowup.

Dad announced he was going to take the spreader off the tractor and put on the brush hog so he could clear a new spot for a food plot in the aspens to the southwest. As he went out the door Brett yelled, "You remember how to do it?" "Yes, yes," Dad said, slightly offended. Then: the tractor plop-plopping to life, ten to fifteen minutes of maneuvering, revving the engine, grunting, pounding on steel plate with a hammer, "God DAMN it! Fuck!" and he reappeared at the mudroom door with hands black with grease.

"Brett, can you take a look at this? I think it's broken."

"It's probably not broken. Are you pulling the collar back on the driveshaft? You gotta wiggle it off there."

"It's not coming off. It's bent or something."

Brett put his jeans and Red Wings on and tromped out there and checked the three-point connections to see if the spreader was twisted in the hitch. "These are hard to get on and off," he said, taking the drive-shaft in his hands.

"No, no, it doesn't matter what you do. It's broken."

"Are you going to let me fuckin' show you, or what? Look—"

"I know what to do but it doesn't work."

"Why is it always like this? Why can't you remember how it goes on? This is your tractor, and you were supposed to be a farmer. I can't always fucking do this stuff for you!" And then he popped the shaft off the power takeoff and pulled a couple of pins from the hitch and the spreader sat free on the pine needles.

"There," he said, wiping his hands. "You know how to put the mower on, right? And how to engage the PTO and all that? You know it won't work if you're not sitting on the seat." That was all stuff that Dad knew, of course.

"God, you can be a real prick sometimes, Brett."

"Oh, yeah? Well, you're an ass. You assume everything's broken, or a person you saw drink one beer must be a drunk, or the sand won't grow anything. Look at it! It fucking grew!"

There was a decent crop of buckwheat that year, a loose green grass about high enough to tickle a deer's knees. It never really headed out all the way, but it grew. The extra fertilizer and lime made a difference. Similarly, a deer plot mix of purple-top turnips, canola, Russian kale, chicory, and other brassicas and cold-season grasses had gone off like a half-dead bottle rocket in Cabin Field; it came up but never really popped. When you kicked through there you'd find little turnips the size of your big toe.

"Don't snap at me like that," said Dad, looking at him hard.

"I wish you believed in what we were doing here just a tiny little bit. Just enough to care. That would change everything," Brett said.

∾

I was on my own in Montana that summer, writing a piece on wildflower touring for *Travel & Leisure*. I stayed at the Ruby Springs Lodge and at the Old Hotel in Twin Bridges and fished the Beaverhead and the Ruby with a superlight, four-piece pack rod Brett had made me, which is still my favorite fly rod. The bottom was sand and the water in the Ruby was barely up to my knees and I caught trout. I sent a postcard to Dad telling him I was in the good water, just across the Tobacco Roots from the Madison and the Yellowstone, where all of us had fished on our RV vacation long ago.

A biologist named Catherine Cain drove me in her four-wheel-drive truck up into the Pioneer Mountains above the Big Hole River to a remote high meadow called Vipond Park. We topped the last of the dirt switchbacks and slowly rolled onto a wet plateau packed with blue camas and Lemhi beardtongue flowers, and I was stunned into silence. The blooms stretched away for miles, pulling all the indigo and pale violet out of the sky and spreading it on the earth. She stopped the truck and I just hung on the door, unable to talk. Native American tribes had fought wars over these edible camas bulbs, which were an important food source in winter, she noted. I nodded, scribbled in my notepad. But all I could think of was Dad, Brett, Joe, and Mom. They needed to see this. I needed to go get them and come right back here. Because this, *this* is what Mom and Dad had been good at. Because of them, I would stand in a river for no reason at all and let fish bump my ankles and fall in love with a mountaintop sea of flowers.

~

"If we really want the place to take off, we have to get the timber guys in here to get those trees off," said Brett. He and Ayron, Dad and Joe were circulating past the table in the cabin, which is where all the arguments started. Dad was showing them photos of the fishing trip he and Diane took to Alaska.

"Brett, I'm just not ready for that. We've done a lot, let's just focus on getting some grass and some turnips and chicory and stuff to come up," said Dad, making his tea. He drank Lipton and he would wrap the string around the tea bag where it sat in the head of the spoon and wring it out into his cup so he wouldn't leave drips anywhere.

"Look, all that is great, I'm so happy we got some buckwheat and turnips, but it's not the big move we need to make," argued Brett. "The big move is to take out those Scots pines and cut back the aspen. It's in our habitat document."

"If you take out those trees, nothing will grow back. That sand is poisoned."

"What do you mean, 'poisoned?'"

"Salted. Someone salted it. Burned up."

"Are we really having this same discussion again? The trees will grow. Aspens will sucker. The Scots pines will probably grow back. But a lot of other trees will see the opportunity and move in. Nederveld wrote it right here in the plan."

"Well the grass doesn't grow like it would normally. So maybe he's wrong."

"God *damn*, Dad," said Brett. "Why is it always one step forward and two back? The buckwheat came up." He got up and poured himself a highball glass of whiskey, then rolled a cigarette.

"You have to make little moves. Don't disturb too much," said Dad.

"Fuck! I'm so fucking frustrated!" Brett barked. "There's nothing wrong with the sand! It's totally fucking normal fucking sand. The red pines over our heads right now grew in that same sand and they are forty feet tall. Trees are going to grow."

"You just don't know that. You don't *know* it. You wreck this place and then we got the tractor and everything for nothing. Then we just have to sell it. And nobody will buy it because the trees are all wrecked."

Ayron saw the cords standing out on Brett's neck, and she stood up to get him out the door.

"Yes we do know!" shouted Brett. "We put in all this time and effort and you put in all this money because that's the best science available! That's the expert opinion! We emulate the disturbance and the forest grows back! Shit!"

"You just don't know."

"I fucking hate being here so much and I hate doing this with you!"

"Brett, I don't appreciate that kind of talk."

"Any other person in the world would see that logging as plain old common sense. Anybody but you. I just don't get it."

Ayron got Brett by the shoulders and turned him out the slider. She shut it behind them. They sat at the picnic table as he smoked. After a few minutes of talking, they both came back in and Brett patted Dad on the back.

"It's going to be okay," he said to Dad, already planning to call Nederveld privately and get bids on the logging. But he didn't say that.

"Okay, good," said Dad.

∾

"Your brother just puts his horns down," Dad said to me on the phone, upset.

"In this instance, he's right," I said.

"He's not right. I've been here for almost fifteen years. I know this place. Nothing will grow."

"So what? He's still right," I said. "He's right because it doesn't hurt you to go with the plan. Who cares if the shitty Scots pines don't grow back? Not even birds like them. Maybe there will only be a pile of sand there afterward; I say enjoy the beach. Is it worth losing Brett's involvement up there? I want him to be there. I come out there to see everybody in one place. So just rip the damn Band-Aid off."

"I wish he could just—"

"Just what? Be like you?" I cried.

"No, I don't—"

"He *is* like you. Congratulations. That makes it relatively easy to know how to get beyond this impasse: be *not* you. Cave. Let him run all over you. Let him put in a motocross track or a bullfrog ranch or put in a gladiola farm or be a chainsaw sculptor, hell, I don't know, who gives a shit? Just let him win. Be his biggest fan. That's what *my* Jesus would do."

"Heh. Yeah. Heh," Dad laughed and for once it wasn't nervous laughter. It was real. It was the sound of his ego deflating and coming out of his mouth in little chunks of breath.

"Joe wants to plant apples," he added.

"Good, so let's do that, too. See how easy? Put in a whole giant orchard. What don't deer like about apples?"

"They like 'em fine. I'm thinking about it, I'm thinking about it."

"What's there to think about? We are your sons. We want to do this stuff with you."

"I'm thinking about it."

Dad bowhunted the place all fall and he showed me the tracks of a good-sized buck coming off Mr. Carter's cornfield and right up the trail toward Desert Storm. The corn was down and the tracks were hard to miss: the big brute's weight split the two toes of the hoof far apart and the stretch between the tip of the toe and the dew claws behind was about as long as my hand. I spent a few mornings in that blind again before the season began, sitting in the dark for an hour or so before dawn. On both mornings, the buck arrived like clockwork just a few minutes before seven A.M. He trotted up the trail, keeping his heavy head down, moving fast, already in the rut. Whatever was happening with our camp, the wildlife was changing. I wasn't much of a mind to shoot this deer, but I did think about bringing home the venison for Meg and Spenser. Dad, on the other hand, was absolutely obsessed with this deer and that I should get it. He offered to stay in again with Spenser so I could be out there for Opening Day.

I went out early that morning and sat in darkness, letting the woods flood my thoughts. I had really grown to resent the name Desert Storm and was trying to think of a better one, something more personal. Joe reminded me that *Ritual de lo Habitual* came out the year Brett built this blind, 1990, when Joe was in the psych hospital, and I guessed we could have called it the Habitual or Three Days. But we needed some kind of new event, something to match the poetry or inherent violence of Desert Storm.

Poetics are a function of place. The beings and shapes in the darkness presented to my imagination and became embodied as felt meanings that I tried to turn into words. Those things out there, leaves, wind, projected their own mentation into me. As Merleau-Ponty had said: "It thinks itself within me." This echoed the speechless speech of Psalm 19. *Yet their measuring line goes out into all the earth.*

I wanted to say that big buck was thinking itself within me. The whole woods was forcing its way into my consciousness, the bent spikes of dry burdock, the volcanic eastern sky, the slowly fluttering beech leaves, the dark trees poured upside down out of the leaf litter and growing gray in the coming dawn. The deer was made of all that, was a walking version of it, and would emerge from it. At six fifty A.M. I looked at my watch and started peering intently down that shooting lane.

At that exact moment, a man in an orange camo jumpsuit stepped into the opening where the lane ended in Carter's field. He studied the sets of prints stomped into the ground there, then shucked off his heavy pack and proceeded to put up a tree stand in the tree directly over the trail, sawing and hacking off limbs and making an unholy racket as he did it.

I watched this for a moment and then reluctantly grasped I'd have to go over there, since he was on our property. There'd be no deer coming now, anyway. So I shouldered my rifle and walked down the shooting lane and tried to make a lot of noise, cracking limbs and scuffing the leaves so he'd notice me. He looked my way and kept on climbing as I approached, scowling at me, since I was ruining his hunt, and finally he barked, "What the hell's going on?"

"I'm going to have to ask you to get out of the tree," I said.

"What the fuck?" He was about fifteen years older than me, with a severe white brushcut and, as Captain Beefheart sang, particular about the point it made.

"That's my tree," I said. Indicating my blind up on the rise, I added, "And you're right in the middle of my shooting lane. It's not safe."

"Well, fuck this," he said, climbing down, and stood holding his bow as he whipped out a radio and growled into it. "Hey, this young man here says I can't hunt on this land."

"I'll be right there," said the voice on the radio.

We had a little argument while his pal made his way over. I was the automatic winner because my surname was on the deed, but that didn't mean he wasn't pissed off about it. He was armed to the teeth and so was I, and we both knew another guy was walking toward us also arrayed with various weapons. It was like meeting enemy soldiers in a Christmas armistice or something, except there was no hot tea or soccer so it wasn't as nice.

Turns out the guy who showed up lived right at the top of the hill, by the cemetery, and he didn't want any flap. He was downright neighborly, which I appreciated. So we directed his friend back to the swamp, where Mr. Carter's field bordered the USA, and the neighbor went back up by the road, well out of sight. And I went back to the blind and enjoyed the company of chickadees and crows for the next four hours.

When I told Dad about it at lunch, he was hot. I guess I should have recognized that his refusal to cut the trees was evidence of his absolute fealty to the place, but I was pleased that he would rush to my defense. I had almost decided not to tell him because when something went wrong in the past he automatically figured we were at fault. It was the first time I could ever remember him taking my side.

"Did the son of a bitch threaten you in any way? I'll call the sheriff and we'll have the asshole arrested!" he growled.

"No, no, we worked it out. It's fine. He went down the line, and the other guy's up by the road. They were both okay about it in the end."

"Did he leave his stuff in the tree?"

"No, I made him pull it down."

"But you didn't see that deer."

"Nope. Not after all his racket. He started putting his shit up in the tree right exactly at the time the deer usually came through. I'm sure that buck is long gone."

"Well, God *damn* it!" Dad hissed. "We're gonna go see Joe Carter."

He brooded at the kitchen table for a while and throttled his tea bag with the string and then got his winter clothes on and we drove over to see Mr. Carter, who insisted he had told these guys to stay out of our trees. Dad wasn't satisfied.

"You shouldn't have to deal with that," he said to me. "If you didn't know the guy was there you could have shot him or something, or he could have shot you."

That evening, Dad sat in Desert Storm instead of me, and he continued to sit there the next few days, staring intently at the property line like a dog with a rival. The guy didn't come back, but I don't know what Dad would have done if he had. Maybe went over there all juiced up on the Holy Spirit and got an arrow in his ass. Either way, we didn't change the name of the blind.

~

When the loggers finally rolled up in April 2003, with their humongous, big-wheeled feller bunchers and a low-boy carrying a chipper the size of a railroad caboose, neither Dad nor Brett were there. Dad had a lot of meetings that week for Delta Design and Brett was busy with a bronze pour that couldn't wait. The foundry was only him and a couple of other guys, so they couldn't really do a casting without him. Both Dad and Brett said they *wanted* to be there, but I think the truth was neither man could bear to watch. They both denied it. But Brett had been demanding this for fourteen years, and really beating his head against a brick wall for five, and if that wall was crumbling he was wary about what was beyond it.

Everything we were was in that sand. It didn't seem obvious until suddenly the trees were coming off. I had said to Dad that it didn't matter if this forestry gambit succeeded or not, but I knew it did. It was the entirety of our relationship in one gesture. Anger and blame and separation would grow out of that sand if nothing else did, and if Brett left, then Joe and I would probably fade away, too.

For years, we'd monitored the fertility of that sand, and suddenly it seemed suspect. We'd obsessed about the composition of the habitat down to its finest detail, down to the health of our one scraggly hawthorn tree and a single tupelo we'd watched for a decade back by Gonzo and our one big Juneberry tree and a few stunted hazelnuts, down to making spot estimates of the white oak acorn fall, down to recording the numbers of whitetails and turkeys that came by in the weeks before any season was open, down to taking pH samples of the raw sand and hoping for a change of even a couple of tenths of a point to the base. We kept going back to the sand, spreading it on a flat palm and looking for evidence of any new organic matter, any new worm castings or bugs, any new indicator that our beautiful new fields of grass were changing the soil, that boot-top alfalfa was imminent, that new clover would be fixing nitrogen like pulling lightning out of the rheumy clouds. Every day we hoped that prime habitat was just a season or two away and that the animals were poised at the property lines waiting to stampede for it. We kept track of the grosbeaks and pine warblers, anticipating a songbird tsunami once the new habitat took off. What would any of this mean if the whole forest simply failed?

Joe stayed at the cabin during the logging to make sure the men took only the trees within a cut area that the forester and Brett had marked with spray paint. The loggers worked mostly from the proposition that it was easier to ask for forgiveness than permission, and Joe ran from spot to spot waving them off trees we wanted to keep. I couldn't be there, either, as I was prepping the launch of a new weekly alternative newspaper called *Los Angeles CityBeat*. The job of safeguarding our deer camp fell completely to Joe.

Ayron had earned her MSW from Western the year before and had slid right into a great management job with another mental health provider, well paid, where she was overseeing patient clinical care. Joe felt like everybody else was too busy because they were doing better than he was. He'd already taken all the equity out of his house and used it to provide for his daughter. He didn't care for the mental health field, but he couldn't think of work that would be better. This logging business didn't look so bad. At least they got to work outdoors. The sand farm needed him at this moment, and that felt good.

Ayron thought it best that Brett had stayed away. "Too hot," she said. "It's just too loaded. If he and your dad had been there, Bruce would have been micromanaging everything. He'd have been stopping the guys every second and calling Nederveld to ask him whether to cut this tree or that one, when Nederveld was not the actual forester doing the job. He and Brett would have probably gotten into a fistfight or something.

"Who else would care so much about this?" she added. "Seriously: Can you believe this shit goes on in your family?"

Dad and Brett had put so much energy into this event, it was squeezing out the sides and running into other people's lives. Some of the effects were just plain spooky. For instance, the forester who ended up laying out the cut and bringing in the loggers was named Randy Kuipers, and his boys were named Bruce and Brett. They weren't directly related to us; they were just guys who worked with Nederveld and got the contract. So the resident Bruce and Brett stayed away while Randy and the Other Brett, who was still in high school, tore the hell out of the place. His little brother, Other Bruce, was too young at the time, but he did come out to the worksite. Do you see how every little world, every home, every work-site, is an irruption of the ecological unconscious?

The Other Kuipers were like the arrival of pure Id. They did what we couldn't. Their guys nuked the place. There is nothing even vaguely romantic about commercial forestry, nothing at all, even on the tiny, boutique-y scale of the seven or eight acres that they actually cut. They hauled ass around on hulking feller bunchers that ravaged the woods like a hatch of nightmare locusts, thirty-thousand-pound trac-tors each equipped with an all-in-one lumberjack arm that cozies up to an old yellow birch two feet in diameter and fifty feet tall, grabs it with horrible mandible-like pinchers, saws it off right at the ground, turns it horizontal and bucks it into sawmill-length sections or just carries it to the howling chipper, where it's stuffed in stump-first and fifty or one hundred years' worth of tree is reduced to sweet-smelling chips in seconds. With smaller trees, they "bunch" it with other trees they've already ampu-tated, continuing to grab and cut trees until they have a full bunch for the whirling chipper blades.

The fragrant softwood chips filled one trailer after another and were carried away by diesel-belching big rigs to be burned for electricity in a biomass plant over in McBain. Our climate change debt was going through the roof.

When the Other Kuipers were done, the place was shattered. The heavy tractor tires tore the surface of the sand like a winter beach that had been bulldozed into berms against heaving storm surge. The bumps and scars of the place were revealed like a newly bald head, the shaved-bare earth dotted with ground-level stumps like so many thousands of white dining sets had been pressed into the sand, from saucers to turkey platters. This style of whole-tree-into-the-chipper logging meant they left little slash on the ground. When they craned the chipper onto its trailer and departed, the place was tore up but fairly clean.

With one exception: per advice from Nederveld and orders from the Other Kuipers, the loggers cut a tiny hill of aspens just off the eastern end of Cabin Field, a little stand that swept down to a tiny 250-square-foot pond under tall cottonwoods, and they had left the slash on the ground for grouse cover. We were meant to leave it lay there. It's true that aspens will regenerate more quickly without the slash, as they are very shade intolerant, but it was left as an experiment, to see if this cover would eventually produce more birds. It would be hard to hunt for a couple of years, with thick slash tangling your legs, but then the rotting limbs would produce mushrooms and bugs and raspberry tangles and cover and everything grouse and woodcock like.

~

Dad had driven up to see the last day of the logging and take a few photos, but he didn't stay. A couple of weeks after the cut, when just enough of the psychic heat had radiated off into the cold spring nights, the resident Bruce and Brett walked the place with Joe to see the newly shaved face of reality. Dad was despondent beyond words. All he saw was ruin. He sagged here and there without saying much. He stopped often to lean against a remaining tree and heave heavy sighs. He'd found this place with his own brothers, who agreed with him that nothing should ever be touched, and now he'd gutted it. He was ashamed.

Brett, on the other hand, was thrilled by the new browse that was sure to come exploding out of the ground. He was bursting to talk about the years to come, but he tempered his enthusiasm in deference to Dad. They toured in relative silence until they reached that little hill covered in popple slash. Dad started picking up branches and dragging them into piles.

"We want to leave that, Dad," said Brett.

"We can't just leave branches laying all over the place," Dad said.

"No, that's the plan. Let it stand and decay. The grouse like it."

"We'll just make some piles. That will be better," Dad said, missing the point.

So Brett and Joe joined in to make him feel better. Cleaning up the woods. Then they moved on to other spots and it turned into back-breaking work and took most of the day, which eventually turned hottish.

"Dad, why are we doing this?" Brett said finally.

"We'll burn 'em," Dad said.

"We're not going to burn anything! Christ!" Brett barked.

"Rabbit piles, then," Dad said quietly.

Twelve
Does Sand Dream of Trees?

Dad and Diane were married in January 2004, in a simple ceremony in the Great Room of his house. The snow was banked up against the windows and flooded the room with a soft, flat light, through which bursts of sun slashed and beamed. Joe, Brett, and I were the only ones invited, other than the pastor from his church. We all showed up in nice suits, but as I walked up the stairs in Dad's house, the soles ripped off my only pair of hard black dress shoes. They were nice but the soles had rotted off. I probably had twenty pairs of new hunting boots and running shoes that cost thousands, but I didn't have dance shoes.

With the gospel Bill Gaither Trio on Dad's stereo, we weren't going to be dancing anyway. Plus, we didn't have dates. I don't know about Diane's sisters, but Ayron and Meg were pissed they weren't invited. They didn't really want to attend; they just wanted an invite. But Dad was one of Van Raalte's children: always separate. Always excluding. He said he didn't want the event to become a "circus."

"You wonder why I don't go there anymore?" said Meg. "I really don't need more of the hegemony. But I feel bad that Spenser missed out. Weddings are fun for kids."

We went to a restaurant after and Brett swung home and got Ayron. I wore my running shoes with my suit. In case I had to flee.

"Thanks for letting me come to the dinner, Bruce," Ayron said, smiling fiercely.

~

In the spring, I got to spend a night at the cabin. I was on a reporting trip for my book *Burning Rainbow Farm*, which brought me to Michigan every few months for a couple of years. I had skipped deer season the year before because of the logging and Spenser starting preschool and my new job as deputy editor at *Los Angeles CityBeat*, and I hadn't heard anything encouraging about the cutover fields. I knew there had been continued efforts to grow grass and deer plots, but no one seemed to talk about the trees and I just figured that the growth in the logged areas hadn't been that good.

I banged through the screen door of the cabin and into the mudroom with my bag, and before I could get a look at the early evening fields, Dad came in the slider. I took a deep breath. When I saw him, I realized that I had been expecting bad news about the Scots pines and aspens, that it had all gone to sand or produced a field of pure bull thistle or knapweed or something. I expected him to be a wreck.

"My boy!" Dad exclaimed. Then he wrapped me in a big hug.

"Hi Pop," I said, preparing for a brief embrace. But he wouldn't let go. We just stood there in a clench under the taxidermied head of Aunt Sally's old buck and he said, "I love you," and kissed the side of my face. The last time my father had kissed me was probably a quarter century earlier, when I was sixteen and he and I were both baptized before the congregation—which, for the record, had been Dad's third baptism, a sprinkle-dunk-sprinkle suite that had to look a little suspect on the big board where they keep track of that kind of thing. Dad had a lot of things to be happy about that spring, first and foremost his wedding to Diane, and maybe it made him a little gushy. She had also been coaching him on being less rigid and less controlling, because she knew like we did that it was crippling him. Dad's construction company, Delta Design, was at a real high point, too: only a few days before, he'd attended the ribbon-cutting on the 120,000-square-foot Kalamazoo Air Zoo, a giant aviation museum and the most high-profile public building he'd ever built.

But something else was happening. Dad's face was different, his shoulders, his posture. I'd never seen him so good in his own skin. It took me a minute. I kept thinking it was a matter of facial hair or a more fitted shirt or something but it eluded me.

"It's good to be here," I said.

"Oh, it is *so good* that you make the effort to get out here. It's so important to your brothers. And look at this place, it's just perfect."

All the blinds were up, the drapes pulled back, and the spring wind blew straight through the open windows to lift and drop the pull-cords against the wall over and over where they rattled like someone throwing dice on a table. The red oaks shook their catkins in the current and the tips of the pines glowed yellow-white as they heaved out their pollen cones and prepared to dust the swamps to the east. The coming twilight flowed cool and sweet all over the carpet.

It hit me then that Dad had allowed the gap between him and those fields to close. At least for this moment. The forest pushed itself up against him and he didn't grimace or constantly dust himself off or slam the windows shut. He was exposed, fully exposed, and he was turning his face into the breeze out of the southwest. He was letting it turn him. The pull-cords beat against the walls in a rhythm that mirrored the waves on the big lake pushed by this same wind. After a minute, he turned away from the windows to put water on for tea. Something in him had released.

"If you can stay another day, the steelhead are still running in the Manistee," he said. "Brett's got most of the early planting done."

I could see sky to the west where the five acres of Scots pines had been. The low-angle sun shot through it and flared on the windows. Dad held up one finger and then he pointed out the tiny kitchen window toward the east, and we both stopped to listen to a grouse drumming on the old drumming log on the edge of the big swamp.

When the thumping fluttered out, I said, "Let's go look at those cuts. Is anything coming up?"

"What?" said Dad, looking confused.

"The Scots pine cut. The aspen cuts. How's it looking?"

"Oh, it's great. There's a whole new forest there."

"WHAT? Why didn't anyone tell me?"

"Oh, yeah, it all came up."

"Well, aren't you overjoyed? You were so worried! Shit!"

"I was never worried," he said straight-faced. "Those cuts are going to fill in and be *fabulous*."

The way he said it, it sounded like false enthusiasm, like a form of denial. I didn't know how to take it. Dad was acting weird; he never said the word *fabulous*. He seemed a little unmoored. Maybe the logging had broken his mind. Maybe the spring, with the big building, the wedding, the new wing he'd put on his own house for Diane, had been too much for him. I tugged open the slider and we walked off the porch and started out there.

The old relief surged through the soles of my boots. Through the glare from the west, beyond the red pines, I could make out the shapes of Joe, Brett, and Ayron as they came out of the cutover fields. A lone bullfrog whomped from the ditch. Oak pollen rained past in a sideways current visible in the sun's hard glow, and cottonwood seeds floated on it like tiny puffs of breath. The radiance out there was choked with a passing traffic of insect, spore, and seed. When we met in the red pines, there were hugs all around, but I was madly distracted by what was going on ten yards away in that field.

Brett followed my gaze and said, "You better come out here and see."

We walked across the two-track and into the Scots pine cut and Dad and Ayron were laughing together as I stopped there with my mouth open. "It's comin' in pretty good," said Brett as he bent down to examine a sapling.

One- to two-foot-tall sapling trees stood thick like a field of grass, thousands and thousands of them, glowing incandescent green and yellow-white and magenta where they jutted up through the bracken fern and knapweed and foxtail. The new trees were backlit by the last of the spring sun and caught midleap as they busted out of the sandy earth. The dinner-plate-sized stumps were barely discernible, turned gray and brown by winter, buried under the flags of new saplings. Just about every inch of orange, pine-needled sand displayed new trees.

Tallest among them were the hand-sized, heart-shaped leaves of aspen saplings. But right alongside were new Scots pines and volunteer saplings of red and white oak, black cherry, beech, red pine, paper birch, red maple, sugar maple, yellow birch, a few white pines, even the odd Norway spruce that had migrated over from trees Vern had planted around First Field. We hadn't planted a thing. This was all the colonizing work of bird and wind and squirrel and root sucker, and the five acres were packed with new life.

Here was that sand I had watched in the darkness, expressing itself. Here were its thoughts, its urgency. We had interrupted the pine plantations for the first time in over fifty years, and the sand took advantage to press from its watery glacial heart exactly the trees that it wanted all along, the mix that was implied by plants and animals that made up the surrounding forest.

I didn't know what to say. It was stupefying.

"This is unbelievable," I said.

"Oh, it's *glorious*," said Dad. He bent down and ran his hands through the tops of the saplings like a farmer feeling heads of grain. "It's coming in better than I hoped."

"I didn't know you had done any hoping," Joe said to him.

"I told ya it would grow!" Brett said to Dad, half-mocking. "But you didn't believe me."

"Oh, come on," said Dad, smiling. "I wouldn't have gone ahead with the cut if I didn't believe something would come back."

"That is absolutely not true," said Brett. "You believed the exact opposite."

"Well, Brett, you're really doing it," Dad conceded. "It's your plan."

"All of us are doing it," Brett said.

"With a little organic matter, those fields will grow some grass, too," said Joe, pointing toward the expanse of First Field, where the winter rye had been turned under. Despite better nitrogen, it hadn't done very well. "We've just got to pile on the manure or something."

The conversation immediately turned to grass, and how to improve the crops growing in First Field and Cabin Field. Dad and Brett started listing out how much more lime we needed and varieties of grass to try, and decided they'd ask Joe Carter if he had a cultipacker we could buy so we didn't have to walk the seed in with tractor tires and feet. It was as if the forest coming up around our legs had never been in doubt and now we were just moving on to other matters. Everything had changed. The cut that we feared would end this project was just its beginning; now we had real work to do.

We stood out there luxuriating in the new field for a while and then we all walked back to the cabin and I had a beer. Joe indicated the vernal ditch just beyond the edge of Cabin Field, saying, "That's where we need to put in a small orchard. Get some apple trees."

"We need to try again with some of your berry bushes, too," said Dad. "It probably all needs fence so it doesn't get eaten up. The deer are going to be in here like stink."

The spring air was cool but the low-angle sun burned my face. As we talked, we watched the last of it slosh around in the descending purple and royal blue of the night sky and finally drop into Lake Michigan behind the trees. Brett drank coffee and Dad told us about the hunts he had planned for the fall in New Mexico and Arizona. "You guys have to buy those preference points so you can get out there," he said. Suddenly everyone hushed and heads whipped toward the Scots pine cut. Joe had his finger up, waiting, as we stared through the stand of red pines at the last bits of sunlight painting the tops of the trees, and the sound came again, a piercing buzz, a strange electric cry that was half birdcall and half joy buzzer: *Peeeeeeennnt!*

"A woodyfriller!" Ayron said. That was her word for woodcock.

Peeeeeeeennnt!

A woodcock was doing its mating dance in the Scots pine cut. A couple of us grabbed lawn chairs to sit on and we hustled right back out into the five-acre cut talking about Ayron's nickname for the bird. Making up names for the woodcock is practically a sport unto itself; this little brown handful of heartbeat is the most nicknamed game bird in the country, called the "timberdoodle," the "mudbat," the "nightpeck," the "snipe" or "brush snipe" (lots of *Scolopacidae* are called "snipe," but, to be clear, snipe is actually another species), the "night partridge," the "Labrador twister"; sometimes they're called a "bogbird" or "bogsucker" because of their feeding method, which is to plunge their long prehensile beak into the thick black humus at the swamp's edge and pop open their uniquely hinged jaw a bit to suck up a worm or a millipede. In some parts of North America, they're called by their French name, *la becasse*. Ayron called them "woodyfrillers."

We swished into the field and took up positions to watch the sky, but I could hardly take my eyes off the sand and trees. In the deepening purple twilight, the saplings there looked as dense and thick as calf-high rye. One mature black cherry left standing thirty-five feet tall at the southeast corner of the cut shuddered in the evening breeze and showered us with white flower petals.

I said to Dad, "Seriously, did you know it would come back like this?"

"Not quite like this," he said.

"Ah, you dumbasses, what else was going to happen?" said Brett. "This is how forests work."

"Well, hardly any grass has come up without mountains of fertilizer. I am totally freaking astonished," I said.

"HUSH!" said Ayron.

Joe added, "We're trying to hear the woody!"

Peeeeeeennnnt!

I tried to focus on the dance, idly letting the tips of the saplings poke into the palms of my hands. These trees changed everything. There are few moments in your life when you are overwhelmed with the realization that all time will be measured by that moment, before and after, and this was one; it was clear that we all knew it was a significant moment, that it was *the one* we had been waiting for, because Brett, Joe, Ayron, and I were all sneaking looks at one another. We were prepared to be wrong, but the fields all around us were singing Hallelujah.

This sand wasn't struggling; it wasn't infertile. It was delivering up a promethean eruption of life. It was in upheaval. The land opened itself and came forth with an outburst of cells it had held within it, latent, an entire new forest just waiting in the sand for the cosmic signal, for release into a watery sky. The forest was growing so fast that I felt the saplings beneath my chair would lift me into the last of the sun.

Dad was like a completely different person. He was beaming. He had kissed me and said "I love you." He had been happy in the past couple years when I'd turn up here with Spenser, but it always seemed to have a limit; he was happy to pull his grandson close but hold the forest off at arm's length. No more. That gap had collapsed. He luxuriated in the sweet forest air. He grinned from ear to ear and looked up into the sky like he was praying.

The mating dance, or "roding," of the woodcock is one of the most ostentatious and bizarre in the avian world, especially for such a tiny dancer. They're the James Brown of shorebirds, coming out in a cape and falling on their knees screaming, *Pleeeaze, baby!* First there was the long and patient series of buzzing calls, the *Peeeeent!* as the bird strutted around in a clearing in the sand, stiff-legged, announcing his performance. We heard it but we couldn't see him. Joe scanned with binoculars and couldn't find him in the saplings, even though he was probably only twenty yards away. This went on for several minutes; we had plenty of time to adjust our chairs and put on jackets and open beers. Then, by some mysterious signal, he burst upward into the air and flapped madly in small circles, maybe thirty or forty feet in diameter, spiraling upward about five or ten feet with each revolution, and then the song became a fast, staccato twittering; *Tweet-twit-twit-twit-twit.* This was actually the sound of the wind rushing over fast-beating outer wing feathers. The bird was about as big as a bat and hard to see in the deepening twilight, but once he broke out over the tops of the trees he was suddenly quite visible as a spiraling black shape twittering against the indigo sky.

The fast-tweeting spiral went up and up just about to the point where we lost sight of him in the night sky, and then he hesitated just a moment . . . *twit-twit* . . . *twit* . . . and began to tumble, like he'd been shot, like a leaf or a piece of paper sliding back and forth on the wind as he fell, all ruffled wings and ragdolling over and over and losing control, leaving no doubt *I would die for you, baby*, and all the while spilling out his actual mating song, a brilliant mockingbird-like run of tweets and wing squeaks that sound for all the world like a bird pouring his heart out.

And then he pulled himself together at the last second and landed lightly on the sand, resting for a spell under new leaves, craning his short neck to see if any females had stopped by. You felt like you could breathe then. We all waited five minutes, listening to peepers and bullfrogs on the swamp, and then *Peeeeeent!*

This went on for about twenty minutes and we didn't talk much. We just kept looking at Dad. By the time the woody gave up, night had fallen.

The bullfrogs increased in volume. Spring peepers shrilled and pulsed. The drumming grouse off in the swamp pounded his puffed-out breast atop his nooky log. Dad sat with a hugely satisfied smile on his face and his eyes closed for a long time, like he had fallen asleep in his lawn chair. He had white cherry blossoms in his hair.

Suddenly he opened his eyes and said, "Brett, we should go through this field and pull the red oak saplings and let the white oaks grow. The deer prefer the white oak acorns."

"You go right ahead and do that, Dad," Brett said.

"Don't you think that's a good idea? By next year they'll be too big to pull."

"Knock yourself out."

"The place really feels different," I said.

"It is different," said Brett. "We can see now that this place *wants* to change. It wants disturbance. It wants to grow a new forest. You just have to give it the right conditions."

We were different. I was acutely aware everyone had let their guards down, and even though it was not a feeling I could altogether trust, I thought if it could come once it could come again and stay. I had only been in camp an hour or two and I could feel it. Reassured by the land,

Dad suddenly regarded us as trustworthy. He could love us without having to suffer. He could be who he was, with all his failures and control worries exposed, without further injury or payback. He could let us want what we wanted. He seemed to be in a kind of ecstatic reverie, listening to the night that rushed in after the bird. We sat quietly in the dark on this fourteen-thousand-year-old heap of sand as the cool wind came up. I kicked a little at that sand with my heel and felt both in it and of it. All I could think was: *Thank you.*

~

The foresters had thinned out the strip plantations of tall red pines and Austrian pines that stood near Desert Storm, and Brett and Joe had decided that they would help grow more browse by putting some seedlings in there. So later in 2004, after I'd left, they picked up a thousand red pines and shoved them into the ground all over up there.

Later that year, we took a walk to check on the seedlings they'd planted, and discovered that there were about a bazillion foot-tall red pine saplings standing there like they were laughing. It was hard to distinguish the planted seedlings from the volunteers. The forest didn't need our help; the act of trimming the trees had caused them to reseed themselves.

"God, that was such a hard day of work," Joe said. "We planted one thousand trees in one day."

"Maybe we didn't need to do it," said Brett. "But maybe we did."

~

In *A Sand County Almanac*, Aldo Leopold marveled that, somehow, geese returning to Wisconsin from the subtropics predict with great accuracy when the ice is off the ponds back home. They don't return on the same day each year, but only when they are certain of the ice-out and their own safety from winter-sharpened fangs. The geese are too exhausted from the journey to turn around and go back south again if they're wrong. "His arrival carries the conviction of a prophet who has burned his bridges," Leopold wrote.

How do they know, across a thousand miles? Leopold, like Ralph Waldo Emerson, was satisfied to leave it a mystery, writing, "What a dull world if we knew all about geese!"

Oh, no, not dull at all. Joe and Brett and I wanted to know all about geese, and ponds, and the communication that flies between them. That mystery was everything.

Somehow, in the social cosmos, the goose turns to his comrades on a golf course in Florida and says, "Honk," which translates to: "There's open water on the ponds in Wisconsin." And off they go.

What are the signs? What information or substance or knowledge pings back and forth in the air? Is it in the air, or does it thrum through the earth, or suffuse the ecological unconscious and then pop into the goose's imagination, or what?

That mystery is everything because without it the real world fails. Geese die. People die, too. Year after year, this sandy deer camp had been calling to us. We couldn't run away to some other place in the world to find a new dad, any more than a goose could just fly south instead of north. This was the place. You have to defend a place to even know who you are. Staying put is the radical act.

Leopold's sand county shack was the mirror image of ours, lying directly west across Lake Michigan on a silica heap a couple of hundred miles away in Wisconsin. As he and his wife and five kids stuck thousands of pines into the sand in their own years-long restoration effort, he sketched in the members of what he called the "biotic community" and how they were implied in one another—how a goose thought itself into a pond and how the trails thought themselves into deer and how the glaciers thought themselves into the Wisconsin River and how, finally, the sand thought itself into a family. The point was to *pay attention* to the thinking of the place. His celebrated "land ethic" arose from these observations: "A thing is right when it tends to preserve the integrity, stability, and beauty of the biotic community. It is wrong when it tends otherwise." That is clearly about maintaining the communicative order. If you remove the wind, or a trace mineral from the earth, or a kind of pollen that flies, maybe you remove the exact thing the goose needs in order to talk to the pond.

We were lucky. The medium we needed in order to talk to one another lay everywhere under our camp. Waiting.

∿

A new affection flowed out of the sand and trees and grew thick among us, and my phone bills doubled and tripled. We called and planned and opined. We got downright blabby. The present and the future seemed to merge; the things we had been hoping to do on the deer camp were happening with such regularity that it felt like we were dreaming in real time. Those trees made Bruce a dad like he'd never even known he could be. The love had always been there, but he had never accepted us. The acceptance had been suppressed in the sand. Dad's new faith in that soil extended to us and grew and grew.

The farm work intensified, but the new focus was birds. For years, Joe, Brett, and Ayron had spent weekends scouting public land near the cabin looking for honey holes—swampy breaks in the forest where logging or blowdowns or high water had let the sun in and produced berry-laden thickets for grouse and woodcock. Now Dad was scouting birds, too, looking at maps, figuring out where the good places were, and he felt guilty that his dog Rose was getting too old and frail to hunt after all the years she'd been kept in her pen.

I was months into writing my book about Rainbow Farm when it became clear to me that the changes at our cabin were partly responsible for my interest in that story. The story was about two men, Tom and Rollie, who had been killed when they protested a marijuana bust on their campground and music venue, just southwest of Kalamazoo. It was a gorgeous stretch of swampy, roller-coaster hills in the midst of vast Michigan farm fields, and when I went out to see it for the first time, my feet craved it. Tom and Rollie and a whole crew of other people had done a ton of work to make that place their livelihood and a home for their son, Robert, and I know they felt their relatedness flow upward from that place. Its magnetism had pulled them together, just like what was happening on our place.

I talked to Mom and Dad about my Rainbow Farm research pretty much every day. The place was only twenty miles south of Dad's house and sometimes Mom and Dad even helped out, picking up a package or finding someone for me in the blue-collar towns of Vandalia and Cassopolis, Elkhart and South Bend. Tom and Rollie were gay and had been killed over a pot cultivation charge, so at first Dad was inclined to dismiss their deaths as some kind of justice. But the more he and I talked about the case, the more indignant he became. "It seems like they got a bad deal," he finally said to me, which was tantamount to a revolution.

∾

In August Mom was sitting on the beach in Amagansett, New York, as night fell, her face lit by the glowing coals of a fire. Meg's sister Jane had put on a family reunion that was the most elegant party any of us had ever been to before or since, with white tents on the beach luffing in the evening glass-off and lobster and drinks, even a bagpiper to lament the end of day. Tom and Spenser were at the water's edge, and we were wishing that Joe and Brett and Ayron had come.

"Oh, this isn't Brett's kind of thing," Dad said.

"Well, I just thought he would enjoy this," Mom said. "He's so happy. In his work, and in the stuff you guys are doing at the cabin. He's like a different person."

"He is in a good mood."

"What do you hunt up there, Bruce?" asked another guest.

"It's a deer camp," he said.

"And birds," Mom said. "Brett hunts birds there."

"Yes, birds," Dad said. He turned to the other guest to explain. "My son organized some logging on our camp to give us some better habitat for grouse and woodcock. They like it best when there are young trees and bushes. And it turns out that deer really like it, too."

"Our son Brett did that," Mom added. "He's not here."

"Oh, it's fabulous. Trees are coming in like crazy."

"It took some convincing," Mom said.

"When you start out, you just don't realize how all these things are connected," Dad said.

The land reaches up through us to express itself in the form of a person. On August 8, while we were in Amagansett, I wrote in my daybook a line from a Galway Kinnell poem, "The Last River": "What is it that can make a human face, bit of secret, lighted flesh, open the earth?"

≈

"You go out and sit in Buck One tomorrow," Dad said to me as we all walked together through the cuts. Whenever we arrived at the camp, the first thing we did was walk. Your feet couldn't stand it any other way.

"Really? But you always sit there."

"That's the best blind and I think you'll see more there. I'll hunt from the cabin with Spenser."

"We gotta rig up that easy chair the way Mr. Card had it," Brett said.

After Bernard built his log cabin, he would hunt out of it. He had a big overstuffed recliner that he had put up on a wooden platform about a foot high, so he could see over the window sills, and he'd throw open all the windows, no screens, and sit there in his winter gear with a rifle across his lap, sometimes with a fire going if it was really snowy. He'd also dug a little pond out front for waterfowl, and one year I came in and helped him pick up a deer he'd shot that had expired right on the ice.

"Nothing like finding that spent brass on the carpet," Joe said.

The new aspens in the cuts were four and five feet tall. Brett pointed to where he'd found a bunch of woodcock around a vernal depression in the cut, right on the border of the USA, which we started calling Woodcock Holler. There still wasn't enough grass on either field to call it grass. But Dad was bursting with plans.

"Hey, we've got a mule deer hunt out of the Box Y in Wyoming next fall, why don't you come? We'll hunt on horseback."

The old man devoted huge amounts of time to applying for hunts out West, so you knew any time he casually mentioned something like this he'd already put twenty or fifty hours into it, collecting preference points, poring over the maps of game management units, and then often driving across five states to visit those units so he knew precisely where he wanted to hunt and talking with outfitters who hunted them.

"You guys are going?" I said to Brett and Joe. We'd never said yes to a group trip like this before.

"Oh, yeah."

"Yep."

"Were you going without me?"

"If you didn't go. But now it sounds like you're going."

"Damn!"

"You've got a year to get ready. You have to be able to shoot five hundred yards," said Dad.

"Not a problem."

"Ha!"

"Not a problem."

Later, when we were working outside, I said, "I can't believe Dad brought up that hunt in Wyoming and everybody just said yes. That never happened before."

"For the last six or seven years I would do just about anything to be here *without* Dad," Brett told me. "Ayron and I would sneak up here without telling him, sometimes get some friends to come. I'd lie to him and tell him I was going somewhere else and just pray he wouldn't get suspicious and go to the cabin—and sometimes he would and he'd just turn up. But I craved being here without that tension. Now it's completely different."

"Now we call Bruce and ask him to come up," said Ayron.

"I check in to see if he can drop work, and he almost always does. Now I don't want to be here without him."

On Opening Morning, the dark was dense with presentation and I sat facing the new cut, which came to its easternmost point right at Buck One. Even in the dark it was easy to feel the open space to the west, and that wasn't the way I'd normally face but that's where all the action was. A tiny sliver of moon was going down and slender hoofs and porcupine paws and bird feet rustled the leaf litter. We'd always had a few deer but they were coming through nonstop, high stepping and single bounding through those young trees. They weren't feeding in there; they were busy gorging themselves on farm corn and sometimes the thin grass in Cabin Field, but they'd go back for those tender young trees when other food ran out in the winter. Just like me, they felt compelled to pay attention to the new clearing. It was the point of interest or novelty in this part of the swamp. Our ice age brains wanted to love it.

In the evening, I sat out in Desert Storm again so that Dad could sit in Buck One. He went out late in the afternoon and Spenser went, too. He was five.

"Spenser did great," said Dad when I came in after dark. Dad was beaming. "He sat there just as quiet as could be. It was hard for him to see out but I think he really watched." He turned to Spenser: "Hey Spense, did we see anything?"

"Yeah," he said. "Some tweety birds. And deer."

"No big bucks?"

"No, but that's okay. I don't really want to shoot anything."

~

Bruce showed us pictures of a gigantic mule deer he'd shot in Nevada earlier in the fall. He told me he'd killed something unusual but I had no idea. It was a wonder such an animal could even walk. When the guide put glasses on it, he said as calmly as he could, "Bruce, don't look at the horns. Don't even look." Lots of people will get buck fever and shoot the antlers off. Which I think is fine—the madness over antlers is just that: madness. I have hunted for meat all my life and the only reason I wanted to see bigger antlers on our place was to give evidence of improved nutrition. If we were really honest about meat hunting, we'd leave the antlers in the woods for the porcupines, though I honestly can't imagine anyone doing it. Maybe putting the antlers on the barn or on the wall is an important tribute to a creature that became a meal, that literally became my flesh. Those osteocytes sure meant something to Dad. He shot his muley at over three hundred yards and killed a Nevada record, still within the top ten largest mule deer ever shot there according to posted records, and as he went through the photos he clearly felt like he'd accomplished something. "That's a monster!" I said, and he laughed, "Yaasssss. YAASSSSSS!"

Dad was invited to put his story in *Huntin' Fool*, a magazine full of glossy photos of white people in ball caps posed with dead stuff, and he needed me to help him write it. I told him that sounded fun, and then we had an argument over how to talk about hunting in the press.

"You have to say 'harvest' now, instead of 'kill,'" Bruce said. "We *harvest* the deer."

"God, that's disgusting. It's like you just bought it at Meijers Thrifty Acres," I said.

"Well, that's kind of the point. We have to make it sound less bloody."

"Exactly. But it is bloody," I said. "Just like people buy chicken at Meijers and have no idea that it used to be a living bird, and that it died bloody. It's just PR horseshit. A lie that separates people from reality."

"Well, if we don't make it less bloody then your eco-radical friends are going to take away your right to hunt."

"No, the eco-radical people go the other way: They want to make sure people know it is bloody. Several of the ones I know are bowhunters, and they hunt for the same reasons we do: so we don't eat factory-farmed chickens and pigs and cows. Those animals suffer. The animals we kill don't suffer. They live wild lives and then we eat them. Like cavemen."

"I don't think that caveman part is going to go over very well."

"Cavemen never made a pig live in a cage."

$\approx$

In the spring, we were all sitting around the table drinking coffee and tea in the cabin before going out to plant Joe's apple orchard. The watery smell of aspens and relief was on us. A yellow-green cloud of pollen puffed out of the pines with every little knot of breeze. It was early. It was pretty rare for any of us to be in bed at dawn. When I was a kid, Dad used to come wake me by kicking the post of my bed, which I hated so much that I would wake up before he got there. Maybe he had done that to everyone. We all flew out of bed in the morning.

The cabin suddenly felt ancient or full of history, like the insides were covered in cave drawings. We were humbled by the new knowledge that had swarmed up into the place after the trees came up in the cuts. We could see that new forest through the red pines. It felt like it had come back after being far away.

Dad's story had come out in the April 2005 issue of *Huntin' Fool*, and the word *harvest* does not appear in it.

Joe drove the trailer down the two-track so we could off-load rolls of six-foot pig fence and studded steel T-posts along with the apple trees. Dad figured our orchard would be deer-proof if we went ten feet tall, which meant lapping the fence over itself two rows high. We estimated we'd be done with this job by noon, and then maybe we'd plant some clover in Cabin Field to get some nitrogen back in the soil. Every new plant we put into the ground seemed to beg another plant somewhere else. Maybe that was because we knew now that it was worth doing.

We kept looking over at the Scots pine cut, as though some part of ourselves remained there. The new selves, the ones we'd dared to hope for going on six years, were there. They'd shown themselves. I was sure now.

Brett had brush hogged the bawdy canary grass off this patch along the vernal ditch, and the mowing had laid bare the mucky black topsoil that outgassed rot and methane. We dug pits for the trees in the sour-smelling muck, struggling with cottonwood roots and carpet remnants and a World War II–era stove and other metal buried in what must have been somebody's household dump. Bruce stretched out about four hundred feet of hose from the house and began watering the trees as we started whanging the fence posts into the ground with a steel post driver—the kind that's a steel tube with one end welded shut and handles on both sides, and you sink the post by slamming this thing down over the end of the post with both hands. The steel-on-steel percussion will make you deaf real fast. We stopped and got earplugs. And then whanged and whanged. Got the sound muffs we wore for sighting in rifles and put those over the earplugs. Whanged some more.

We only put in six trees, but the post-setting went on all day. I tried to imagine fencing a forty-acre pasture and figured that would take us a year. Our shoulders ached. We kept deferring to Joe, who is much bigger and more powerful than any of us. We called him Hoss after the guy from *Bonanza*. "I'm powerful hungry, Pa," Joe said, quoting the actor Dan Blocker from the show. "I ain't had but two breakfasts this mornin'." Pretty soon it was late afternoon and our shadows draped long over the tall ditch grass.

Dad was pretty quiet as we stretched the fence around and circled in the apples. He was so protective of the trees, careful not to knock the little blossoms off. I kept catching him leaning on a shovel or a post and raising his closed eyes to the sun. The lower layer of fence stretched real nice, but then when we put up the second layer, with not much post to support it, it looked like hell, bent inward by its own weight. We built in a little door. Dad was a stickler for the aesthetics, but he didn't say much. He let it go.

"It'll keep the deer out tonight," said Joe, knowing Dad hated the way it bent.

"That will work just fine," Dad said, gathering up the tools. It was twilight.

We kicked back through the short vegetation of Cabin Field, and Joe said, "What's up, Pa? You seem real quiet today."

He smiled. "I wish it could be like this every day. It took so damn long to get here, to this point," he said. I thought he was going to cry.

"Tomorrow we'll disc this field," Brett said, deflecting any forthcoming expression of regret.

"Brett, you've really made this happen. It's incredible," Dad said. "Is there anything we can plant on the scale of a whole field that will attract grouse or woodcock?"

"We're doing it. They don't eat any of this deer mix stuff, at least not that I know of, but they will forage in clover or alfalfa or orchard grass and use it for cover, too, if we can get it to grow."

"If it doesn't kill us first," said Joe.

We walked a little bit.

"I'm thinking about retiring," said Dad. He was only sixty-one, but it wasn't the first time he'd mentioned it. "I'm tired and I've been working since I was a kid, since I weeded onions in the muck for ten cents an hour. I'm going to sell the business."

He knew none of us were interested in running Delta Design, but that fact fell among us like something wounded and hard to ignore.

"What would you do?" I said.

"Hunt. Travel with Diane. Mostly be here, probably. Look at this place, it's like a miracle."

Thirteen
Sends a Deer

This line of Paul Shepard's stays with me: "But the soil was the source of complex life long before men or agriculture first appeared. It is as fundamental to our well-being now as ever, though most of us never put our hands in it."

Shepard believed that contemporary human beings are sick because we no longer read the "divine language" of that soil, or the rest of nature. Our brains want to read it. They are evolved to converse with it. In his 1973 book, *The Tender Carnivore and the Sacred Game*, he points out that the human consciousness you and I enjoy now took shape hundreds of thousands of years ago in the Pleistocene, when we were hunters and gatherers. That's when the structure of our brains achieved its current form, and our brains have changed very little since then.

That ice age brain and that ice age consciousness evolved to communicate with the dirt, sky, swamps, bears, ticks, and all the other forms and creatures that co-evolved with us. Shepard felt that to be separated from that stratum of information is to be broken or insane. "If man's environmental crisis signifies a crippled state of consciousness as much as it does damaged habitat, then that is perhaps where we should begin," he wrote. "The secret lies in the darkness of the human cerebrum. But to see it we must turn our eyes toward the sidelong glimmer of a distant paradise that seems light-years away." Calling the savage world of the Pleistocene a "paradise" invited all manner of critique from folks who believe it is humanity's fate—or divine mission—to transcend this world, but that completely avoids his main point: your brain works better in the field.

The human brain is pliant and adaptable and maybe one day it will live in space, but its basic alphabet is terrestrial earth. We live on that earth and eat from it to survive, but at the same time contemporary culture forces us to devalue it and all its creatures—so we live in dissociation. We have to live in denial of our actual being. Torn by duality. Shepard digs deeper into this question in a later book, *Nature and Madness*, writing in the very first line: "My question is: Why do men persist in destroying their habitat?" His answer, in short, is that we're mad.

E. O. Wilson wrote, "The green prehuman earth is the mystery we were chosen to solve." Chosen, along with all the other life-forms that have survived with us. In *Nature and Madness*, Shepard probes for the source of our contemporary fury in the way we raise our children. Many people—like my father and mother, and my brothers and me—are allowed to solve the mystery of the green prehuman earth until a certain age, a time when we are required to "grow up" and become adults. At that point, we're often asked to relegate nature to a second-class status and acknowledge the "real world" of jobs, religion, technology, and social mores, and to build our adult relationships around those. Which is where our mental health starts to fail. Shepard wrote that the failure to base adult relationships on wind and tree and river prevents us from maturing. We're asked to separate ourselves from nature. Consequently, we lose the basic set of symbols and referents that had been connecting us to reality early in life. So we thrash about, trying to find a new set of ideas to make sense of the world, and often end up trapped in a culture of enraged adolescence, addicted to tribalism, war, extreme ideology and religion, porn, romanticism, and fantasy. Not a culture in crisis, but a culture *of* crisis.

As Shepard wrote: "The only society more fearful than one run by children, as in Golding's *Lord of the Flies*, might be one run by childish adults."

Chellis Glendinning, a clinical psychologist, points out that we've only been farmers and herders for about three hundred generations, or just 0.003 percent of the time we've been *Homo sapiens*. We've only been building the box of industrial or technological society for six or seven generations. The rest, 99.997 percent, of the time since we evolved as humans, we've been living by our wits as hunters and gatherers, hand to mouth, "a hundred thousand generations in synchronistic evolution with the natural world. We are creatures who grew from the Earth, who are physically and psychologically built to thrive in intimacy with the Earth."

You look at the night out there, you tell yourself you don't belong. But it is what made you.

My father became a mature adult when those trees came out of the ground. I know that's a lot to say. Before that spring, he had lived as what society called "a good man" for four decades. He ran a well-respected local business and made lots of money, he had kids, he was a church man, he was a pillar of Kalamazoo society. But he was also utterly childish: he kicked at the dirt and swore and called it "poisoned," and honestly believed that ordinary soil—the regular, trustworthy soil on which all life on earth depends—was prone to failure, and would certainly fail him. Was, in fact, out to get him. Mother Earth treated the farmer next door better than she treated him. Maybe this distrust of the feminine started with Henry's anxiety when Dad was just a kid: the soil on the farm could fail and the immutable principles of life simply turn against you. Grandpa taught him that the male sky god and the life after this one were better. But whether it started there or flowed out of Dad's lifelong distrust of women and was extended to the ground as the mother of us all, he blamed the earth for failing. For long and ugly years, he treated us like we were part of that failure, too: Brett's restoration efforts at the camp were futile, I was wasting everyone's time trying to stop environmental degradation, and Joe's troubles were proof that earthbound life was capricious and mean. Dad had pushed back against a Gaian conspiracy. He had come to believe the dirt was in conspiracy, which is as childish as it gets.

He couldn't even talk to us about his religious beliefs, or ask us about ours. Until the trees came, the subject had been too threatening. We always thought his church life was fake because he never mentioned his faith at home. He had never once sat with any of us to talk about our salvation. He only barked out little clues about Jesus when he was angry or challenged. Instead, he took us to that church building and hoped we got it. It was back to the river: *You just fish upstream until you find me at the hole with boulders as big as Volkswagen Beetles.*

Diane changed his relationship to women by telling him he was full of shit. Prior to meeting her, any desire for intimacy sent him out into the night looking for less demanding company, and any sharp words were more evidence that women were against him. But she had the right kind of authority, and experience, and facts. Dad trusted her.

Because of her and because of those trees, he began trusting life on earth. Maybe for the first time ever.

Joe, Brett, and I all desperately needed to witness this change. Not because Dad was an ass and we needed him to stop being an ass, though that was certainly true. But because we were like him. We were all living some version of the childish adult and were as lost as he was. We needed to see him mature so we knew the way. We saw him arrive at the cusp of a mature relatedness and watched it strengthen his faith, repair his relationships, and make him happier. Without that, we might not have had any chance of getting there ourselves.

I didn't go marching into the Kuipers Hunt Club with my books feathered with sticky notes to lay out this thesis to Dad. I was just glad he changed.

≈

"You never struggled with farm life like Dad did," I said to Mom.

"Well, no."

"Why not?"

"I guess because my dad, Grandpa Bub, loved farming."

"He had all his birds, his horse, his goats."

"Yeah. He had all this life. He surrounded himself with family and the farmworkers and animals and plants. Living things."

"You're not worried about what happens to life after you die?"

"My spirit goes to be with the Lord and this world goes back to dust."

"So the world carries on."

"The world carries on."

≈

Joe, Brett, Dad, and I were on the Greys River in Wyoming, looking for mule deer. We had the Wyoming Range to the east and the Salt River Mountains to the west and snow dumping out of the sky. No power lines. No phones. We'd been up since three A.M., and the snow poured past us as we clung to the horses in the cold, rifles in the scabbard, Orion so barbed-wire sharp it left black scratches in the sky as it sank over a ridge to the southwest. That morning we rode up a short box canyon and made a fire under some Douglas fir to wait and watch. Dad said we'd probably never see anything with a fire burning, but the young guide muttered without even looking at him, "That don't bother 'em."

Leopold wrote in *Round River*: "The deer hunter habitually watches the next bend; the duck hunter watches the skyline; the bird hunter watches the dog; the non-hunter does not watch." We were watching the side of a mountain in front of us like it was a drive-in movie: for a couple of hours, we listened to a young bull Shiras moose coming down the valley to confront us, grunting and huffing. We would never shoot a moose, as they are already rare enough and their populations are fragile, and we cheered out loud when this ungainly giant finally reached the valley floor and broke out of the trees, prancing into the meadow and pacing back and forth, snorting and mad-dogging us.

"It was worth the whole trip just to see that," said Dad, an inch of snow on his hood and flakes in his mustache.

The next morning we rode up a mountain in the Wyomings, getting colder and colder until long after daybreak, following some precarious knife-edge trails in the snow where one false step by our mounts would have meant a plunge of thousands of feet. We arrived at a high meadow park where the horses could stand in some trees that made a natural windbreak and we glassed the valleys all around. The trees where the horses were hitched smelled of puma piss and the horses stomped and complained, but our guides stayed close to them and made a small fire where we could eat lunch. A snow squall came through and we sat peering into the storm through our field glasses and right behind it came blazing sun, so hot it made our clothes steam, and we cut branches off the pines and laid them in the snow and pulled our hoods around our heads and went to sleep.

After a half hour I sat up and looked over at a guide named Okee peering intently through glasses at deer moving way across the valley, far out of range. Dad was lying next to me and Brett and Joe farther over, the four of us lined up and sunk a foot and a half in the snow as though the rifles across our chests were pressing us into the mountain. Dad had the most exquisite smile on his face. I had seen him so uptight and nervous in the company of guides in the past. But he wasn't chasing a trophy up here—we didn't bring home a single deer from this particular five-day hunt—and it was already a success: He had us all up on the hill, watching the deer, watching one another, watching the skies for the speechless speech.

Dad's face was sunburned but he was smiling the smile I'd seen him smile while the woodcock danced in the Scots pine cut. It had become his smile. It had followed us here.

"I could stay here forever," I said.

"We'd miss you at the cabin," he said, not opening his eyes.

~

Michigan was broken open and all kinds of information poured out of it. I began to wonder how much information is howling around us at all times that we just don't catch. Relatedness opened deep channels. Maybe there's no limit to what can travel over them.

A month before deer season 2006, I was fast asleep on the couch in my home in Los Angeles. I slept on the couch more and more, as Meg and I were fighting, and in the middle of the night I'd usually shuffle into the living room to close my eyes. It was a difficult time for us, and my dreams were full of fear and worry. But I was shocked one night when I sat bolt upright in the still darkness with a great in-whooshing of breath, a gasp, and said out loud, "Oh my gosh, Judy just died."

Judy Stevens was the mother of the big family that farmed two hundred acres of cherries and grapes and asparagus across the street from our house near Crooked Lake. I hadn't talked to her much, recently, but she had been on my mind. During the years in the 1970s that Dad didn't live with us, I'd go to the Stevens house every morning and sometimes eat breakfast there and ride with her oldest son, Matt, to school. Matt and I were still close. Judy developed Lou Gehrig's disease in her sixties and I had visited her while she was ill, but I hadn't had any news for months. I decided not to call Matt on that particular morning, either. What do you say—*Hey, I just had a dream that your mom died*? Instead, he called me from Michigan a few hours later.

"I just wanted to let you know that Mom died this morning," he said. "She always considered you one of her kids, and I thought I should call you."

"Well, I'll tell you something weird," I began. I explained the abrupt wake-up earlier that morning, which was about the time she had died.

"That is really weird," Matt said. We talked about it for a while and he decided, "Somehow it makes me feel good. You were connected."

Judy and I were friends at a time when I needed friends. Friends talk. Sometimes I think that the clock of her life was wedged into my mind when I was a child and just remained there, spinning down, so the whole thing was internal to me and didn't require any external input. But this would suppose I knew the hour of her death decades in advance. And that clocks of other dear family and friends might still be inside me, winding down, a clamorous crowd of clocks waiting to spit a deadly cuckoo, which seems borderline insane.

But let's be clear: I really did wake up at the moment of her death. Just like I really have a cabin and brothers and mosquito bites that itch. It was an actual event.

When I tell people this story, they say things like, "You were on her wavelength," or "Everything is connected." But here's what that means: somewhere 2,153 driving miles away, Judy's mind went supernova and I caught the edge of the spreading light. Once you start talking about this, you realize that every explanation or even metaphor includes the notion that *something moved*. Some information traveled. This begs two questions: what is it that moves and how does it move? How does this awareness instantly get across two thousand miles of prairie and Rocky Mountains and dangerous mall parking lots and into my head?

I'm going to make a wild guess and say this information moves through the ecological unconscious. It's a clunky term, but useful as a way to describe the vast flow of psychic experience that runs through all life. Even a purely psychic medium or layer of consciousness, however, is still a medium, a *stuff*, physical or not, a tissue of ideas trying to manifest before my mind's eye. And it may be that there is more than one. Maybe dreams have their own psychic channel. But the emotional shock of her death had to travel through some stratum of jellied cogitation or electron fog or force field or charged particles like solar wind or temporary mind-pipe to get from her to me.

Does that ecological unconscious have a basic alphabet, some kind of cardinal data set like ASCII code that all beings on earth can read— even rivers, rocks, and wind—thus giving rise to the invisible solicitations? An alphabet that constantly re-births Jung's archetypes? Or are those images themselves the alphabet? Is this what is "read" by the imagination to form images in dreams or even in active, wakeful imagining?

Is this what seeps into me from the dark shapes in the blind at night? Is this the bedrock of what we know as reality?

Sensory perception works differently than imagination, but I like Gregory Bateson's idea that our senses are designed to read "difference." His take on perception is that you see a kingbird on a pine branch and all along the edge of the bird you see the outline where the bird-ness is different than the pine-ness and the sky-ness. You see the difference between where one feather begins and another ends, where one pine seed in the cone stands out from the next. All these things are seeable because they're composed of billions of bits of difference. There are lots of problems with this, of course. Bateson was a cyberneticist and a systems theory guy, so it appealed to him to render every bit of info into a discrete particle. Which lends itself to determinism, and makes it hard for a dream to travel two thousand miles in an instant. But I like this idea of "difference," because it is never static. It suggests that the perceived thing, like the image in imagination, has to be constantly built and rebuilt, over and over every moment as those bits of difference change. The constant flow of change.

Judy was alive and then Judy was dead, and there was a massive amount of difference between those two moments. Like a shock wave.

Bateson certainly wasn't the only ecologist or early computer theorist to think about information traveling in unique pieces. Howard Odum, who along with his brother, Eugene Odum, wrote the first textbook for the field of ecology in 1953, *Fundamentals of Ecology*, and popularized Arthur Tansley's idea of an "ecosystem," was absolutely transported by the notion that every bit of difference or information could be considered a discrete bit of energy. He was a systems theory guy, too, and he designed his own circuitry drawings to represent energy flows of any size or complexity from single bits of carbohydrate entering, powering, and leaving a cell, to the energy budgets for entire forests or watersheds. He called this science "ecoenergetics" and figured it was theoretically possible to budget the energy flows of the entire planet.

The Odums figured that bits of thought or mentation could also be considered units of energy. After reading their books, it's hard not to think that information moves in particles like grains of sand. But that system gets messy when I think about Judy, or dreams in general. How does the particle move from her to me, across America, instantly? Even if we think of the "particle" as just a figurative idea, an abstraction, an image of a difference signaled to the imagination, it still has to move, through what would necessarily be a psychic rather than physical medium. What is that medium? All day I think about this. It carries real information, like the death of my friend, so the information is material as well as magical. As Aquinas noted, even God is restricted by the laws of nature. Einstein ran into this with his "spooky action at a distance," a communication between electrons that may be separated by vast distances and which (as of yet) has no Newtonian explanation. The idea that this unconscious is like a torrential flow of information and "thoughts" from anywhere and anything in the universe makes me ponder its role in the everyday lives of you and me and farm crops and oceans.

Maybe when Judy died there were billions of changes or warps in that flow that formed a disturbance that took her shape. Perhaps physical perception is inadequate to know what we need to know about the bazillion relationships required to live. Evidently there's no limit to the length of the circuits looping mind with mind; if they can stretch over two thousand miles, then they can probably jump any gap. Astronauts report they reach at least as far as the moon just fine: we still dream terrestrial dreams there and get intuitions about our loved ones back on earth.

Like geese, like trees, we are fluent in this language beyond perception. It is native to us. I might not know when the ice is off the lakes in Wisconsin, and maybe that is signaled by a change in the Gulf Stream or some other physical sign, but the most outrageous thing about my dream of Judy is that it's so ordinary. People have these kinds of dreams every day, these spooky experiences, and we call them premonitions, or intuition, or synchronicity. Other beings probably also have them: we know that dogs and rats dream like crazy. I am beginning to think now that these premonitions are just tiny coronal flares of news that break out of huge flows of difference and pop up into consciousness. Deep underneath what Jung called the "tyranny of words," this communication could be going on between everything, everywhere, all the time. *Day after day they pour forth speech; night after night they reveal knowledge.*

~

Dad retired and he was in the woods from September till Christmas. It was not unusual for him to be out eighty or ninety days in the fall, sitting in blinds and walking fields. The deer camp had made his life so good that he lived more and more of it out in the field. His sweet dog Rose died, but he and Diane got two new griffons, Libby and Greta; they were trained as hunting dogs but were allowed to live in the house.

"You would have loved this elk hunt in New Mexico," Dad started at lunchtime, sitting at the cabin's big table and voicing his reverence for his bowhunting guide, a Carlsbad fireman named Jason Lowe. "Jason and I were up on our spot on the mountain for three days and we didn't see or hear anything. Nothing at all. No scat, no bugling, nothing. We know the rut is on, and we always see elk like crazy there. This year, they've moved elsewhere.

"Finally, on the third day, we're coming down the mountain and we run into this kid who sometimes guides up there. He says he didn't see anything, but several days earlier he had seen some animals down this other road. He didn't tell us exactly where, but Jason had an idea.

"The next morning, we go down that road and we hike up to a ridge and look into the canyon and there are about six hundred elk there."

Dad stopped and his eyes got misty. "Six *hundred* elk. *At least.* I'm not exaggerating. They had all yarded up in one place—not because someone put them there, they have nothing but wild terrain to roam, but because that's where the rut took them. Jason turned to me and said, 'Bruce, let's just watch 'em for a while. You will never see this again in your lifetime.' And I knew that was true. So we decided not to kill any. There were big bulls in there. But we just sat there watching them, eating our lunch, drinking tea, marveling. Oh, boys, it was easily the most beautiful thing I have ever seen and I felt so privileged to be part of it."

"That's a beautiful story, Dad," I said. "I'm glad you told us."

"I get so close to them, now," he said. "Now that I know what I'm doing, a lot of times I'm just standing there about fifteen or twenty yards from a seven-hundred-pound bull. He probably knows I'm there, but I call him in and he comes anyway. Sometimes it's like that for days and days and you never have a shot, but that's okay. I just want to be that close."

∾

Joe quit his job running the group homes in order to go on the hunting trip to the Greys River in Wyoming, and after he got back to Michigan he basically collapsed. It was his last job in the mental health field. He spent some time staring at the night from the porch of his house and riding his mountain bike around and around Fort Custer over by Mom's place in Augusta, riding with his teeth gritted in rage, taking brutal falls, breaking one of his ankles again. He had developed a fixation with Hazel's mother that was unhealthy at best, and he was trying to keep his body in motion to avoid circling the drain. I never met Hazel's mom and Joe never told me much about her, but he did not want to make a family with her. Joe loved his daughter and he didn't want her to grow up in an unhappy marriage like the one he'd grown up in. He probably saved them all a lot of heartache, but the inevitable result was that they each raised Hazel separately. They didn't talk. Joe worried constantly about how to pay the child support and had to go to court several times to sort it all out, and on at least one occasion Dad had to go, too. Joe felt more and more isolated, and mountain biking was one way to get out of his head. He grabbed at every possible opportunity to get in a river. The people in the world had lost their last fine filigree of trustworthiness and life had been reduced to a series of financial transactions, so he returned to the nonhuman world that had kept him alive prior to his foray into being a professional.

"I just have nothing left," he told me. "I'm just wasted. The whole thing with the court and Hazel's mom has just fuckin' ruined me."

The place to talk about all this was at the cabin. In the past, Bruce had tried to make it a place where no such troubles were allowed, but as our relationships with one another got better and better it was only natural that it became the place where emotions would erupt because this was the place they *could* erupt, braided into the thick communication in the place.

"Joe, you've got to stop being such a baby," said Diane. She was always totally direct, which drove Joe crazy.

"And what more do you fuckin' expect me to do?" he growled. "Whatever I do, it's just not enough for you!"

"Now, Joe," said Dad, warning.

"Get another job. Pay the bills. People deal with this kind of situation all the time. Just make sure Hazel's okay," said Diane.

Joe went out the door and spent two hours breaking twigs and pulling knapweed. What other people saw as the human condition—working, paying the bills, having children, being responsible to a community—he saw as being trapped. He was fixated on getting out. He told me that he quit taking care of those people in the group homes because he felt like a liar. He was trying to make them feel better when he himself felt like shit. He never said anything about this when we were in Wyoming, because it wasn't the cabin and the channels weren't wide open there.

He went right back to work. He got a job working on metal roofs. It was a small company, a two-man operation, but they worked on structures from a gargantuan Whirlpool warehouse in Perris, California, to old and rare copper mansards and gutters around Kalamazoo. Sometimes they'd build the odd custom gate or security grate. He found some quiet there. Not too many people mess with you when you're up on the roof.

Metal was Dad's line of business, so our father felt good about that, but they didn't talk shop very much. Dad was the boss at his company and that was one place where he was very talkative and charismatic and smoothing everything for everyone; Joe, on the other hand, thought any boss he had was purposely designing their business to ruin his life. But this job was better than most he'd worked, and it allowed him to focus on protecting his relationship to Hazel. Joe had worked with Dad to get attorneys and such for sorting out his child support, and that actually brought them closer. They'd never get fully close until the relatedness could become mature—which, in Joe's case, meant that he needed to feel like his own man. But he was slogging his way down that road.

I don't think it was any coincidence that both Joe and Brett ended up working in metal. Dad approved of it. Brett and a partner bought the Alchemist Foundry, and Dad was very pleased to invest some money in that. One of their first commissions as a new company was a larger-than-life bronze sculpture of the Detroit Red Wings' Gordie Howe, which, in Michigan, might as well have been a sculpture of Jesus. That went up inside Joe Louis Arena and was the beginning of a good business making sculptures of sports figures. They continued to pour fine art pieces for other clients, but their sports statues are now all over the country, including the Luc Robitaille, Kareem Abdul-Jabbar, Jerry West, and Chick Hearn figures at the Staples Center in L.A.

Brett and Joe were close as ever, and they skated in an amateur adult hockey league in Kalamazoo. They were both on the same team for a while, where Brett, who was wiry from metal work but a little on the small side for hockey, would get checked too hard by someone on the other team and Joe would come off the bench smiling and fists a-flailing. It worked out good for everyone.

~

"Oh, did you hear about Joe getting hit by the tree?" said Ayron, her eyes shining, as we walked the property in summer. Stories about Dad had become funny instead of infuriating, and we loved telling them. Joe spent more time with him than anyone.

"What?" I said. "More injury?"

"Oh, it's a classic," said Joe. "I'm still having trouble walking."

"Where were you, out at Dad's?"

"No, up here, at the cabin. Dad's always had a tree stand at that crossing where the pond by Buck One drains into the swamp, but we put up a new one, and then he wanted to clear brush for sixty yards in every direction. You know half the time he shoots an hour after dark, and when you're shooting in the dark you don't want any trees in the way.

"Anyway, there was a pretty big blowdown red maple that was laying right up against a tree there. It had been broken off in a storm, but big, like about forty feet tall. So Dad says, 'Joe, let's push this tree off there. We can't just a leave a widowmaker hanging there; it'll probably fall on one of us one day.'"

"You can see your dad doing that, can't you? 'Oh, I know this is totally unsafe, but let's just do it,'" said Ayron.

"'C'mon, don't be a big pussy!' 'All right, Dad.' So I get over there and we start heaving on the thing and rockin' it and then it starts to go and so I turn to move away but you couldn't really see that the stump end was completely severed and free and it just popped up and caught me right in the back and flung me about twenty feet into the air. I'm not exaggerating. I went way the fuck up in the tree-stand tree and slammed into one of the steel climbers we had drilled into the trunk; it just about poked through the skin and right between my ribs. And then I fell to the ground and landed flat on my back. It knocked the wind out of me and I laid there choking, but I didn't even care about that because I was pretty positive I broke my back. I was absolutely terrified to move."

"Dad goes running over there, half pissed off," said Brett.

"He's standing over me, screaming, 'Oh, SON! SON! YOU GOTTA GET UP, SON!' There was no fuckin' reason in the world to get up. I needed to catch my breath and see if my back was broken."

"It's just that Dad is so anxious that he has to have a resolution instantly. Partly he's worried you're really hurt, partly he's worried that he caused it, and partly he's worried it will be expensive," said Brett.

"I lay there about two minutes unable to breathe, and finally I get a real breath and Dad's still screaming, 'GET UP, SON! GET UP! YOU GOTTA GET UP!' and I say, 'Gimme a second, my back is hurt.'

"'NO!,' he screams, "YOUR BACK IS FINE! YOU GOTTA WALK!' He's losing his mind, and I know I really shouldn't get up but he's freaking out, so I reach my hand up and he jerks me onto my feet. I swear to God, he could have paralyzed me right there.

"So he's yelling, 'GOOD! GOOD! NOW WALK!' and I've got my arm over his shoulder and he's practically carrying me back to the cabin. It was only about two hundred yards, but it took about a half hour, I was walking so slow. We get back there and I'm saying, 'Dad, I gotta go to the hospital, I need to get this checked out. It's serious.'

"'No, no, you just take a shower. That's what you need.' He actually would not let me go to the hospital. He said I could not go."

"A shower!" Ayron squealed, laughing. "Just like when you got stung by a bee and almost died!" Tears were coming out of her eyes.

"So I lay on the couch for a while, and I knew Dad would never take me to the hospital, so after a bit I said, 'Dad, I'm going to drive home. I don't feel good.'

"'What? No. *No*, son. C'mon, I'll help you get in that shower.' He literally will not let me get to a doctor."

"Bruce is a very clean person. You know he rolls the lint off his socks every morning?" said Ayron.

"What?" I said.

"It's true. Gets worse and worse every year."

"So I never do go to the hospital, but eventually I drove home. And the very next day, I was up on the roof again at work."

"But you did get clean, though. And that's what matters," said Brett, wiping away tears.

"So clean. How could anything be wrong if you're clean? 'Dad, my back is fucking broken.' 'Have a shower and a cinnamon bun from Rykse's. Oh, that shower is so good.' "

"*A shower!*" Ayron's laughter rang out under the trees by a food plot we called Bruce's. Now everything was different. It was just Dad being Dad.

Sometime after Joe resumed working, he got an MRI and confirmed that he had not only broken a rib but also broken his back. He never mentioned it to Dad.

We walked another hundred yards up the two-track, and Spenser pulled up short in front of a red oak sapling about eight feet tall.

"Oh, hello," he said, and leaned in.

Clinging to the branch was a young porcupette, maybe a couple of weeks old, and it looked at Spenser without fear. The two of them were nose to nose. Spenser was smiling. The porcupette's quills didn't stick out every which way like an adult, but shone black and slick as though they had been combed back. It started to mew like a kitten. The babies don't ordinarily stray far from their mothers, so she had to be right there somewhere. We'd never seen one so far from the porcupine tree before.

"I think it likes you, Spense," I said.

"Baby Wendell," said Spenser.

~

In the fall of 2009, I was feeling pretty ragged. Meg and I had really struggled to find a relationship between us, but it wasn't working, and we split up. It wasn't anybody's fault, but for eleven years we had talked and talked and talked, and it always seemed we weren't talking about the right things. Or not in the right way. Or not long enough, or too long. We argued and even had horrible fights, but mostly it was just talking every night from midnight to two or three A.M. And then I would end up on the couch. I wrote two good books during these years, and Meg had made brilliant artworks, including a show inspired by her mother's death that produced one of my favorite pieces she's ever made, a yellow papier-mâché donkey with a plunger for one front leg, appropriately titled *Yellow Donkey*. I couldn't even look at it without sobbing. I guess it had come to represent our relationship, too. Both of us were so madly in love with our beautiful son, and I told myself I'd never leave that house, so I slept on the couch year after year.

But one morning in June I got up and realized I was living like my mother had, day and night on the couch, and that I couldn't live like that anymore. I didn't want Spenser to grow up watching us fight and me sleeping on the couch. So I announced that, in a few days, I would go. That day came and Spenser was outside on his swing in the big ash tree in the front yard, and I told Spenser to come inside because I had to tell him something. He came in with his chin on his chest and wouldn't look at me. Meg encouraged him to give me a hug and Spenser climbed into my lap. He was nine years old and I held him and wept and assured him it would be okay. He just shook his head and said, "No, no, no, no." There was no worse feeling in the world. It was the worst day of my life. As I walked out to my car with a bag in my hand, my knees were shaking. I just wanted to die.

I found a tiny apartment down the street from our house, and on the nights Spense was with me he slept on the couch. He felt a little better once he found that I wasn't moving far away. I saw him and Meg every day. I was working at the *Los Angeles Times* but I was flat broke. We had been spending as much time at the camp as we could, and it was the one place I could be assured of sanity. Spenser looked forward to seeing Grandpa Bruce and Joe and Brett and Ayron because he could feel I was empty. I was hollowed out like the old porcupine tree.

I called Mom to talk to her one day in October. She asked how I was doing. I was going out on dates, but I didn't feel that good. I felt like a failure. It was hard to accept that Meg and I couldn't make it work. I was looking forward to going to the cabin, and we talked about that.

"Well, there is something good happening. Something good besides the cabin," Mom said.

"What's that?" I said.

"Joe is getting married," she said.

"To Hazel's mom?" I was surprised by that.

"No, no. That would be a little bit weird, as they hardly know each other," she said. "No, Joe met a woman from Sturgis, her name is Becky, and they've been spending a lot of time together over the last few months. They met through mutual friends, I guess. She's very nice. She's very **soft-spoken and** has a big smile, and they both said they realized pretty quick that they were meant for each other. Joe just called me a little while ago and said they were going to get married."

"Holy crap!" I said. I didn't recall Joe ever mentioning a new girl-friend. I worried suddenly that I had been so down about my own home life and things with Meg that I had simply failed to hear it when he told me. "When is this going to happen?"

"Well, uh, tomorrow. At Sturgis City Hall."

There was no way I was going to get there for a wedding the next day. I had to go to work at the *Times* and I had no money for a plane ticket, anyway.

"Oh, that's fine, honey. Joe and Becky say they don't want anyone there," Mom said. "They just want to have a small private ceremony."

"Well, are you going to go?"

"Well, sure, Tom and I will go. And your father and Diane, prob-ably. I mean, we all want to be there. I wouldn't miss his wedding!"

Poor Mom had never been able to put on a wedding. I had been engaged for a while, but none of us had ever been married. She'd come to graduations and to Spenser's baptism and probably Hazel's, but other than that she'd never had any of the big ceremonies that normally mark your kids' lives.

"Damn, I wish I could be there. Will that be okay for you, being there with Dad and Diane?"

"Oh, sure. We see them all the time, for the boys' birthdays and stuff. Your dad gets along good with Tom, and Diane and I are totally fine to sit and chat."

"But what about you and Dad?"

"Oh, we've been fine for a long time. But things are definitely better in the last few years. Maybe because he got married, but also lots of things have changed for you boys since you've all been going to the cabin. Brett talks about it all the time, how much Bruce has changed. I don't know the details, exactly, but I'm so glad. Because you were all frustrated for so long. It certainly makes things better for me. He and I are more like friends now."

∽

I was glad when hunting season came again and I could feel that sand under my feet. Just after light on the second day of the gun season, I was wet up to my knees and sloshing out of the sucking blackwater of the swamp. The snow boots I wore in the blind, Dad's old size twelve Sorels, were full to the top with skunky ice water and leaves but I didn't mind. My heart was pounding and my mouth was full of news as I made my way back to the cabin. *Skorsh. Skorsh.* With every step, water squeezed out of the top of the boots as I kicked through the oaks alongside the swamp, and I stopped when I noticed for the first time that the understory was full of young white pines, knee- to head-high, in every direction. They had been seeded by the small copse of white pines James Askins had planted, but suddenly they were erupting through like adult teeth. They must have been suppressed and came up when the other forest had come up in the cuts five years earlier. In the summer, when the oak, beech, and maple were in full leaf, I just hadn't seen them.

I sloshed down a trail of soft pine needles and through the chest-high canary grass in the vernal ditch, and when I stepped into Cabin Field I spooked about sixteen wild turkeys out there, maybe half of the resident flock, and they flattened out like prehistoric roadrunners, bending horizontally from beak to tail, and scurried toward the west. I don't know if they ate anything we'd planted in the field, but they liked scratching there. The fields were starting to bloom. Two years earlier, Dad and Joe had hand-pitched trailers full of cow manure onto the fields. They had spent two days hauling manure from a dairy farm in Walkerville on the trailer we used to pull the tractor, pitching by hand until they about wore out their welcome and themselves. But it had helped with the organic matter. The deer had kicked at the purple-top turnips and gnawed the puna chicory and kale and canola right down to the dirt. Ravens and starlings followed behind the turkeys, a train of gleaners hoping for uprooted treats.

Joe already had a five-point buck hanging from the buck pole.

The dogs barked from inside the sliding-glass door. Brett and Ayron had not only brought their new griffon, named Dorothy after our other grandma, but brought their white Lhasa apso, Jimmy, too, with all his ruction. The dogs slept right in the bed with Brett and Ayron. Spenser and I loved it, and even more shocking, Dad loved it.

"Oh, I was on the couch and that little Jimmy just jumped right up there and snuggled in next to me and we had a nap," Dad said. "He sure is a cute little bugger."

When I heard Dad say this, I thought there was nothing more the world could show me by way of surprise. But, of course, the world was just getting started.

I sat on the edge of the weathered porch and dumped the water out of my boots in the cold sun. I sniffed at my one spent seven-millimeter shell—one of the smells I love most in the world, the metallic odor of heated brass against the mix of burnt nitroglycerine, sawdust, and graphite that constitutes modern gunpowder. I'm not a gun freak and I only have the one rifle, the same Ruger Dad bought me when I was fourteen, and it was a running joke that I was still using the same two boxes of Federal brand ammo that we'd bought at Meijer's for my first trip to Card's in 1976, more than thirty years before. I used one shell a year to sight in the gun, and one to kill some food. But a lot of years I just didn't shoot anything.

"Was that you shooting, or the neighbor?" Dad said, walking up to the slider. He had stayed in with Spenser to hunt from the cabin and he missed the fact that I was huffing at a spent rifle cartridge. "I thought I heard Randy shoot."

"No, that was me," I said, playing it down. I tried to pass off my shivering as if I were simply cold. I had spent years and years just watching and listening, trying to comprehend the voices that carried over the water. But Spenser was ten, and I wanted him to see the old contract fulfilled: to make a habitat for the deer, to celebrate its wild life, to kill it and enjoy it as venison stew. My dream was that he'd never eat supermarket meat again. I wanted to validate all of Brett's effort with his schooling and forestry on this place. The other creatures in the forest saw me as a predator, and in this instance I wanted to be one.

"You got one?" Dad looked at me kind of stunned, openmouthed.

"Yeah, I just came in to have a cup of tea."

"Little one," said Dad, responding to my false calm.

"Pretty good," I said.

"Go *on*," he said, face breaking into a smile. "How good?"

"Well, it seemed pretty heavy. Get your boots on."

I had been watching a couple does in the dark, listening to them chew the thick orchard grass about eighty yards from Buck One. Their jaws moved back and forth in the binoculars and I didn't even have my rifle in my hand when the biggest buck deer I'd ever seen in Michigan stepped out of the trees. *Well, shit.* I was so used to watching the darkness for everything but deer I was caught flat-footed. He was looking right at me and I moved with the deliberation of a sloth as I set the binoculars down in the dirt at my feet without moving my head, picked up the rifle, and worked it up to my shoulder. It took a geologic epoch and the instant the scope got to my eye I pulled the trigger.

The deer pronged straight up into the air, put his head down and lunged in huge leaps into the swamp, smashing into trees, and fell over dead midstride. After the shot, he had lived about five or six seconds.

I racked in another shell and waited a few minutes as the silence began to roar. If there is such a thing as superpresentation, it was happening then. The entire mucky forest turned to face me, with the brightness turned way up. Every black root of hemlock, wobbling brown leaf of beech, chickadee and titmouse, gray tuft of morning cloud lit by new sun, every shining bit of swamp ice screamed, *Here! Here I am!* I had to clamp my mouth shut to keep it all from pouring right down my throat.

I sloshed out knee-deep into the swamp and hauled the buck out onto the frosted leaves. It was heavy for a Michigan deer, maybe 180 pounds, plus it was wet. The heaviness felt good. I counted the tines by force of habit; it was an eight-point. As I dragged it, a smaller buck came out of the trees on the ridge, eyes wide like a horse in a fire, and started charging me with his horns down. He snorted and stomped and thrust at me like a fencer, trying to get me to let go of his comrade. Oh God! Their social lives are at least as complicated as ours! I kept heaving, but I have to admit I shed a few tears over that. Brave little buck, risking its life. I made no move to shoot it, of course, one deer is more than enough, but I had to stomp my feet and wave my arms. "Go on! Get out of here!" I yelled, choking on tears, and finally it wheeled and fled in huge leaps over the ridge.

It took me a minute to get over that. I knelt in the leaves, smelling the rich, wet-dog odor of swamped buck, running my cold hands over its beautifully efficient short hair. "Thank you, deer," I said. "Thank you for the food. And thank you for giving me a family."

I meant it. Deer were the reason we had this place and this place was the reason we were all still together. I probably wouldn't even have known my Dad or my brothers as adults if it weren't for these deer.

I thought of the native tales of bear and deer that Gary Snyder had written about in *The Practice of the Wild*: the Ainu indigenous people of Japan held that the bear, the most human-friendly of animal spirits, would send a deer to the human village to see if their songs were any good and if their food was nice and if they danced and made a worthy party. If the deer spirit came back and said the people were good singers and the feast was righteous, then bear would send more deer their way. Bear and deer cared about culture. I hoped we measured up. Dad and Diane were unlikely to appreciate me blasting the music of Hüsker Dü or even Steve Earle, so it's not like we did a lot of dancing to celebrate our deer. But I did recite the occasional verse and we had learned how to make a very fine dish of grouse and woodcock and one of Mom's peppery venison stews, and all those things were gorgeous.

In the cabin, I made my tea and one for Dad, too, then I rooted around in the cupboards for some cornmeal. Ottawa and Potawatomi hunters would put some cornmeal on the deer's muzzle for sustenance in the world beyond. All I could find was popcorn, but that would do.

We all walked back out to the swamp and Dad was walking fast, eager to see. Spenser looked at his grandpa and laughed, running along in his snow boots and ski coat, holding the Daisy Red Ryder BB gun that Dad had bought him a couple of years before. He knew something important was happening.

"Nice eight-point," Brett said as he knelt down next to the buck and put his hands on it instinctively, saying to the deer, "Thank you, brother. Thank you for growing here and coming to live with us."

"Eight," Dad said, reaching out to shake my mucky hand. "Well, that's a dandy."

"That's the biggest one we've ever had around here," said Joe. "By far."

Dad was very competitive about weights and antlers, and I could see this was a significant event for him. We were seeing bigger deer on our camp. An eight-point buck is very average for North America, in general, and they certainly get much bigger. The hunting magazines routinely feature genetically modified monsters grown on high-fence operations with bizarre atypical racks of twenty or more tines. But the deer on our place had always been smaller than this one. For me and especially for Brett and Joe, it was a validation of all the field work: we all figured that better nutrition was growing bigger and healthier deer.

Spenser put his hands on the deer and was quiet. I sprinkled some popcorn on his muzzle. I thought of the bear spirit: See, we are trying to make the party as good as we can!

I lavished the buck with praise and thanks and did it out loud so that Spenser and the whole woods could hear that the killing was done right.

As Brett and Joe helped me wrestle the buck onto a cart to roll it back to the cabin, Brett was clearly thrilled. Dad was really happy, too. He was not impressed by many things, but this made a difference to him. He loved North American wildlife more than almost anything on earth and had spent a lot of his life watching these woods. Seeing this buck, he was like an old farmer gazing at the prize bull at a farm sale, happy just to know it exists.

"That poacher must not be hunting on here anymore," Dad said. "He's been shooting all these deer for years."

"Well, it could be about the poacher," Brett said. "But there's also the chance that this extra nutrition is changing the herd."

We stopped again in Cabin Field to examine the turnips and purple kale, talking about the work we had done that helped grow this big whitetail.

I field dressed the deer, and Spenser put his hands in the warm steam that escaped from the body cavity. He wrinkled his nose at the smell of sour corn and gas from its stomach and the hot iron of the blood.

"What do you think?" I said, up to my elbows in sticky gore.

"This isn't my favorite part," said Spense.

"Nope, it's nobody's favorite part, buddy," I said. "But this is what we have to do if we're going to eat."

~

Joe was the best I'd ever seen him during this hunt. I hadn't realized how much I had simply assumed he'd feel like shit forever. He was happy. As we hung my deer next to his, he lavished it with the hose like he loved my deer more than any deer before or since. He and Becky had been married by the mayor of Sturgis, Michigan, who was one of Becky's childhood friends, and even though they didn't want anyone there, Dad, Diane, Mom, Tom, Brett, Ayron, Hazel, Becky's parents, and a couple of Becky's best friends flooded into City Hall at the appointed hour. I forgot to bring them a wedding present. I was the worst brother ever. My life had come apart and I just didn't have it together until I got to the cabin, when the world started to take shape again.

Becky was there at deer camp, a new bride wearing a giant smile and one of Joe's old hunting shirts, tall, brunette, a little intimidated, and staying out of the kitchen and out of the traffic. She laughed a lot and joined in the card games at the table at night. Joe was grinning like a man who'd snuck out of perdition. He cooked, which he hardly ever did, and he was good at it. He looked at his smokes like somebody'd filled them with ambrosia. He stood with his arm around his wife like an ordinary human being.

I had a lot of room inside for good feeling, so I borrowed some of Joe's. Joe had always been the kind of guy to give it freely. I told him and Becky how happy I was for them, but it felt like the words came up from the bottom of a cold cave. I'm not sure they heard them. I was not an ordinary human being. I felt like I might just go flying off into space if it weren't for the gravity of this camp.

The next morning, Dad and Brett and Ayron went out and I stayed in with Spenser, and when Dad came in for lunch he went to his truck and came in with his compound hunting bow. He brought it out on the porch in the cold sun. He had sat for hundreds of hours with this bow, but he had a new one and he didn't use it anymore.

"You take this one," he said to me. "If you're going to kill deer, you should learn this way. It's more intimate. You like to be close to the animals, to know them, and that's what bowhunting is like. I think you'll like it better."

The draw on this bow was set at fifty-five pounds and I clicked the release into the loop on the drawstring and pointed it toward the clouds and tried to draw it but couldn't.

"What? Come ON!" laughed Dad. His new bow was a Matthews set at sixty-five pounds, and he pulled it like drawing a piece of spaghetti out of a pot. I pulled and pulled, and he about pissed himself laughing. My arms shook. Finally I got it back after about a dozen tries.

"Damn!" I hissed, arms trembling wildly as I held it. Even after the cam released, it was wobbling all over the place.

"You'll get used to it," he chuckled. "This way you can come out earlier in the season and go up in a tree before dawn and watch the dark and bowhunt for a while and then go after birds in the afternoon. Do all the things you like to do in one trip."

Fourteen
Trails End Motel

Jeannette Armstrong, a Native American educator in British Columbia, wrote in a wonderful essay that the Okanagan word for the human body and its senses translates as "land-dreaming capacity." I read this and cheered and it stayed with me forever. She didn't mean dreaming like a story that is born in your mind and seems isolated to your private thoughts. She meant the kind of dream that interprets information flowing in from elsewhere, like my dream about Judy Stevens. Your body is how the land thinks itself into you, and vice versa.

I didn't want to turn Spenser into a hunter. He could be whatever he wanted to be. I just wanted to open this capacity as wide as a dream would go.

With some practice, I found I could pull Dad's old bow, and so I began to shoot it. And once I started shooting it, all I wanted to do was shoot it. I became that weirdo hunting guy at the outdoor archery range, and I started taking Spenser, too.

We went to the range at Rancho Park in West Los Angeles, a big public park and golf course across from the Fox lot where they were busy separating people from the earth. I'd be in a line of fifteen shooters under the big eucalyptus trees and the shooters would all have sweet recurve bows, and there'd be a couple of Olympic-style folks with complex stabilizers and incredible accuracy and then at least one trad guy shooting a superheavy seventy-pound recurve with no sights and a leather quiver strapped to his back, *Assassin's Creed*–style. At the end of the line there'd be me with a whole lot of camo. The bow was camo, I wore camo, it had sights and stabilizers and dampeners and looked like a whole lot of machinery and when I'd release my arrow it would be buried in the wall before most of the others' had even left their bow. The geezers playing pétanque on the sand court next door regarded me with concern. Guys wanted to talk tech with me and asked what kinds of limbs I had on there and how I had the lighted pin sights set and how the draw was regulated and so on and I'd tell the truth and say, "I don't really know. I just pull it back and let it fly." It was deadly accurate and to me that meant that Dad was deadly accurate.

On January 3, 2010, I went to the range with Spenser and my new girlfriend. The fact that my relationship with Meg had fallen apart left me wondering just how these things were supposed to work, but my girlfriend and I were having fun. She and Spenser had both already taken the bow-safety class with the well-known rangemaster Oliver Saunders, who had taught thousands of people how to handle a bow and not shoot anyone or themselves. We were all shooting and I was channeling Dad and it was a gorgeous warm blowy Sunday about eighty degrees Fahrenheit and the Maxima Hunter carbon-fiber arrows Dad had given me were singing true. With every shot I was in a tree at the cabin. I heard my phone buzzing in my bow case.

At last there was a break and I looked at the phone, and there were messages from Brett and from Joe so I wandered off into the grass and grabbed a eucalyptus cap to sniff as the phone rang and Brett picked up.

"How you doin'?!" I sang. "I'm on the range shooting Dad's bow."

"Oh God. Did you talk to Joe?"

"No, why, what's up?"

"Uh, I don't know how to say it so I'll just say it: Dad went out hunting earlier today up by St. Helen and they think he had a massive heart attack and . . . well, somewhere out there he passed away. Our dad is dead."

I stood there smiling. That just didn't make any sense. Dad was six foot three and kind of a beanpole, probably 180 pounds, in pretty good shape, and made a practice of walking his two dogs, Libby and Greta, an average of two or three miles a day for exercise. He climbed up and down trees like a monkey. He climbed up and down mountains in New Mexico with elk quarters strapped to his back. He never drank, took no medications, quit smoking around the time I was born, still did everything like pitch manure by hand. Hard Way Productions.

He wasn't the fat, red-faced guy who gets an infarction dragging a deer out of the woods.

"What?" I said.

"Dad is dead."

I crumpled to the grass and laid there under a giant spreading coral tree. "No, no, no," I said, sort of arguing with Brett. The tree was all watery and tottered around in the air. "But I'm here shooting his bow."

"Yeah. I love you. I need you to come home now. I need my big brother to come home."

I had a blurry conversation with Mom full of wailing. She and Dad had been divorced for twenty-two years, and yet she choked out, "*But he was my childhood sweetheart!*" I'd never thought of him being anyone's childhood anything.

My girlfriend saw my face was wet and laid down against me in the grass and Spenser crawled right on top of me with his head on my chest. When I was off the phone I told him what had happened and he looked stricken: "Grandma????!!"

"No," I smiled. "Grandpa Bruce."

Spense gave me a big hug, clearly relieved. It was cruel but real. "At least he died doing something he loved," he said. How did he even know that phrase? When had he ever heard it?

The massive coral tree spreading over this part of the park had spent a century accreting wood. As I lay under it I realized through tears that it would die, it must die, for life to work. The soil under our heads was made of it and also of the billions of plants and animals and people that came before it, and the lava flows and ocean sediments and tectonic collisions before that, and the stars that had come apart and salted us with their ragged flotsam. But if the coral tree died *right then*, and threw its enormous weight on me, I'd be crushed. In a quiet panic, I struggled up and moved away with my child in my arms. These land-dreaming capacities were going to live.

I was not ready for Bruce to cease being Dad and resume being stardust. We had worked so damn hard.

I packed up the bow in its case, his bow, suddenly an object that belonged to no one, and eucalyptus leaves were jabbering in my face in a strange tongue. Every person seemed to have a hard outline that I couldn't penetrate and the bark chips on the ground were spreading wider and wider like I might fall through. The chain-link fence around the old range was sharp and hard to navigate and outside it were all these miles of grass and weirdly tropical clouds that flew defiant and aloof. The pétanque balls flew toward my face and cracked loud enough to break bone. A dog tied to the big coral tree barked at me with a blunt sound like a hammer banging on a trash can lid. I stood and looked at it for a moment and flinched at each bang.

The coral tree heaved and lashed as we climbed into the truck and I quickly pulled away. Spenser was talking but I couldn't hear what he was saying. The asphalt juddered loudly under the tires all the way home and drowned out the words. The world was so raw.

I dropped Spenser at Meg's, at the house where six months earlier we had lived together. She held me and said, "You know, I talked to Bruce a week ago and he wished me Merry Christmas and we talked about church traditions and he said he regretted now that he hadn't come to Spenser's baptism. He just couldn't accept that we'd baptized him in a Catholic church, but now he realized that was wrong. He said, 'I know now there are a lot of ways to worship.'"

"Thank you for telling me that," I said.

"I'll always be grateful for him sharing the woods with Spenser," she said.

Outside, the trees writhed against a pale blue sky. Ravens talked from the roof of my apartment, making low comb calls. I expected everything to fly apart before my eyes. I couldn't believe it when the door did not come off in my hand when I opened it.

~

So much depends on one person. In the airport I wondered at this. All these faces. Each one remakes the world.

We had made a family with Dad at the deer camp. We only became a family when we included trees and sandhill cranes and sand as true relations. This field-family was held together by affection and humility. Affection was the bond and humility was the solvent that made it work. It is the only thing that will ever make it work, anywhere.

When I was shooting with the archery nerds at Rancho Park, I felt secure wearing my ridiculous camo and shooting his ridiculous camo bow because there was at least one place on planet Earth where my land-dreaming capacity was fully grounded, where my identity was backstopped by dirt. From there, that grounding had spread. From the ground at the deer camp we had grown a strong surety of belonging, and from there it had flowed out to the entirety of the material world as all one fabric.

But that was a relatedness that had only bloomed when Dad finally accepted us the way we were. I don't know another piece of dirt where this would have happened. Joe, Brett, and I had been on separate paths. But the fact is that it could have been anyplace we put our hands in the dirt together. Dad had presented that piece of dirt to us in a gesture that was bigger than his ideology or his fear. He was locked away in a closed community that utterly rejected us, that demanded dualism to work, that was built on a dirt that didn't talk, a dirt you could be *in* but not *of*, and he reached out to us anyway. Love drove him to open himself in humility.

The relatedness we had found was not a static field but a product, remade over and over every instant. With his death, some piece of it had stopped being made. It had come to a grinding halt. Some amount of belonging had been stripped out of the world. And now what? The ultimate test of a mature relatedness, I figured, was whether it could survive death.

The next day, a Monday, five of us left Kalamazoo to drive to St. Helen and get Dad's effects. It was me, Brett, Ayron, Joe, and Becky. Becky had only joined our family a little more than two months earlier and I was so glad she was there. I made little effort to conceal what had pretty quickly become a mad crusade on my part to collect up the pieces of Dad's life and use them to restore the community to full functioning. I thought if I could get all the parts we could pat them into place in the common ground and *voilà*, a new way of being. No one else mentioned this. It was my role, to gather up everything Dad was and re-present it to everyone as a new community. I was the oldest. Not only that, I was a reporter, so I started reporting.

I was prepping to face Harold Searles's question of "what is one's position about this great portion of one's total environment." In my grief I couldn't see my behavior as grief. I called the guide who had been hunting with Dad and asked him to meet us at a restaurant so he could tell us what he knew. I called the guy at the cheap-ass motel where Dad had been staying, which was, incredibly, named the Trails End Motel, and asked if he would talk to us. I called the police. I called the morgue. Everybody humored me.

Dad had gone on a bobcat hunt, which he'd never done before. Joe, Brett, and I did not shoot predators. I had talked to Dad a lot about the role of predators in helping maintain deer and bird numbers, and Brett probably had, too. If a predator moved into a territory, that meant there was sufficient game to support it, and if you shot it, then another one would just take its place. But if you let it live, the prey species would generally increase to balance the numbers again, and then you got to live with a beautiful wolf or puma or bear. Dad had once shot a black bear and regretted it, and the mangy old fur was hanging on the wall downstairs at the cabin. But he was conflicted, because on the farm they had always shot predators. He had us gut our deer on Cabin Field so it would attract a coyote for him to shoot and then he never did shoot one. There was no reason to shoot a coyote or a bobcat except as a trophy, and that was weak. But on an ice-cold day in January, he went after bobcat with a young guy named Hoot Massey. Massey was only in his early twenties and was too upset about the whole thing to talk to anyone, so his dad and partner, Bill Massey, showed up at the Hen House Restaurant in his place.

"He's pretty tore up over it," Massey said of his son. "I'll try to help you with anything I know."

It was about five degrees Fahrenheit on the Sunday morning they set out in the guide's pickup and headed out of town into a flat and cold boreal forest of thin jack pines and birch and aspen stuck in the frozen sand. St. Helen is an unincorporated area between Houghton Lake and Rose City, where we used to hunt with Bernie Card, and it's in that strange heat sink in the center-north of the state that just holds cold. There was no wind. The guide let the dogs out and they bounded off through about eight inches of snow, flushing crows and jays as they went. Massey had found a cat in the area recently, so he wasn't much surprised when they got on a trail right away. Dad had his stainless steel Savage .22-250 and they walked off through the shallow snow following the howling and yapping of the hounds.

The walking was relatively easy and the clouds overhead were a susurrating dark gray, threatening more snow, and Dad and the guide were chatting away. They got a couple of hundred yards off the dirt fire road when the hounds started to bay: they had a cat in a hole.

"My boy told Bruce to 'Come on up here,'" said Bill, "and they'd been talking the whole time they were walking, maybe they'd been out there a half hour or an hour. He started messing around by that hole and your dad was standing behind him and suddenly he just stopped talking. My son heard a little sound like a grunt and he looked back and your dad was facedown in the snow. He had fallen right on his gun and it didn't go off or anything. He just lay there. He never said any kind of cry like 'Help me,' or anything. He never said a word.

"My boy went over there and tried to revive him but he was just gone. He got on the radio to me right away and said there was a problem and I got the paramedics out there and they got there pretty fast, too, but he was gone long before they ever got there."

We were all crying again by that point. Massey seemed embarrassed.

"I'm so sorry," he said. "It really is a hell of a deal."

~

We all agreed we needed to see the actual spot for ourselves, so we piled out east of town and made a few false starts down the unmarked fire roads that looped into the jack pines but finally found the right road. We stopped at a spot where the snow had been stomped down and a sled track led out into the bush. They'd used a sled to drag him out through the snow, one track in and one track back. We didn't really have winter gear on but we felt compelled and we followed the tracks in our running shoes and no gloves and no hats. We high-stepped through biting cold, maybe ten degrees Fahrenheit, the blued sheets of cloud barely moving and a stillness in the birches, flapping our arms and rubbing our hands to stay warm.

A couple of crows followed us through some red pines and then set themselves up in a copse of paper birches ahead of us and watched us as we came to a spot almost directly beneath them where the sled tracks ended. A gentle trickle of water leaked from a horseshoe beaver dam woven into the trees and topped with a dusting of snow. The clouds were a low lid from horizon to horizon. There were a lot of boot prints there and a hole with dog tracks all around it where the cat had gone to ground. I imagined the cat must have been in there the whole time they worked on Dad, and then in the deep quiet afterward, after the dogs, after everything, it slunk away, like a guest who'd mistakenly attended the wrong funeral. The crows were about a foot above our heads and said nothing. The place was gripped by a great stillness.

"Of course, it's like Bruce to die in the most beautiful place in the world," said Ayron.

"I was thinking the same thing," Joe said.

Brett and Joe and I huddled together and I said, "This is the place where our daddy died." We put our heads together and stood there for a while, silently. When I looked up, the crows had bent down like I was going to throw them a piece of cheese.

"I just can't believe I'm not going to talk to him now. I keep thinking he's going to come walking out of those trees," said Joe.

"But I am so happy we did the hard work that we did and that there was no unfinished business with Dad," I said. "There wasn't anything left unsaid, right? We were good."

"We had come to a good place," said Brett. "But it's so odd that he's just gone without a word. It makes it hard to believe."

Dad had grown so gabby in the last few years, it was not like him. He'd want to explain. He'd want to apologize. He'd want to make a plan. Dying had been a long way off. Up until that moment. Maybe even right through it. Sometimes a heart attack hits so hard it knocks the subject instantly unconscious, which is what seems to have happened here. On his death certificate, where it says "Approximate Interval Between Onset and Death," the medical examiner wrote: "Seconds." Maybe he never even had to think that terrible thought, but only saw it in the rearview, on his way to wherever he was headed. Whatever was the case, part of him had remained and was still implied in this place. He wasn't looking down from heaven or any of that horseshit; he was simply still there as a member of the biotic community. Something remained. I was completely, utterly relieved to find out those infinite connections can't be undone overnight. The relatedness remained. The whole place hummed with him and he'd only been here once, just like us as we danced around in our cold wet shoes. If that was true here, it had to be true at the cabin, too.

"We love you, Dad," Brett said to the trees.

～

Dad always traveled like he was on safari with a tribe of bearers so we knew he'd have a lot of gear. He never took planes because how can you fly with stacks of guns and hundreds of rounds of ammo and twenty or thirty changes of clothes and books and boxes of food and bags of calls and range finders and whatnot and ten different pairs of boots? I wish I were exaggerating. We went to the weather-beaten blue pole building that was the Richfield Township Police Station and I signed for his .22-250 and two shotguns, which had been impounded, and the bag that had been in the guide's truck, which was full of ammo and lunch and cash. The officers said they were real sorry and shook our hands.

At the Trails End, Bruce's cavernous Denali SUV was the only vehicle in the lot, parked in the snow right in front of his room. It was a snow-mobiler joint, and the guy at the counter didn't have much to say other than that he sure was sorry. We paid Dad's bill and the guy let us into the room. Dad was a frugal traveler, to be sure, but when he traveled alone he'd always find the absolute cheapest room he could stand and the forty-dollar-room at the Trails End was no exception. The bed was ancient and musty and the paneling half a century old, the sink iron-stained and the bathroom mirror darked with missing silver.

His box of breakfast fixings was still on the table, his cereal bowl unwashed, and his Bible still open. It was open to Matthew 13, the Parable of the Sower. You can't make this up.

> That same day Jesus went out of the house and sat by the lake. ²Such large crowds gathered around him that he got into a boat and sat in it, while all the people stood on the shore. ³Then he told them many things in parables, saying: "A farmer went out to sow his seed. ⁴As he was scattering the seed, some fell along the path, and the birds came and ate it up. ⁵Some fell on rocky places, where it did not have much soil. It sprang up quickly, because the soil was shallow. ⁶But when the sun came up, the plants were scorched, and they withered because they had no root. ⁷Other seed fell among thorns, which grew up and choked the plants. ⁸Still other seed fell on good soil, where it produced a crop—a hundred, sixty or thirty times what was sown. ⁹Whoever has ears, let them hear.

What had he considered us, in the end? Were we good soil? The few words he had scattered on us from his Bible study hadn't led us to the church, but they weren't ignored, either. We listened. We let the words in. In his last few years, he and I could talk about spiritual questions in a very matter-of-fact way, such as the mechanics of how the sand farm itself might be part of our psychic life, or how it was necessary that the son of God be an earthling, born of a woman. He had grown beyond the nervous laughter that marked his early life. He was no longer threatened or angry about challenges to his own views, and that was true maturity on his part, because his church still told him in no uncertain terms that it was his fault if we were not saved. That meant something to him and he struggled with it.

I know he struggled because he and I talked about it. He had not given up on us. Our experience at the Kuipers Hunt Club had filled him with hope. If our collective faith in the desiccated, sandy soil of that farm had been rewarded by an abundance of trees and, eventually, rich grass, then that begged a question about what was truly "good soil." We had led Dad to a love that flourished far outside the parameters set by his church, and it was real. It raised no end of possibilities.

I drove the Denali home, a gargantuan truck that Dad had bought because it could hold an enormous amount of stuff, and I drove home alone because Brett and Ayron and Joe and Becky needed to smoke. They needed to smoke like I needed to record all Dad's idiosyncrasies. On the way home I decided to catalog everything that was in the truck as part of my mad inspiration to collect every piece of data that we might need to put our deer camp community back together.

Diane understood what was happening, I guess, or else just looked the other way, but I sat on the floor of the garage and then in the basement for two days, cataloging. I went through every item he'd taken on his last hunt, including the trash bag of stuff they had cut off his body, and entirely filled a yellow pad with a list, and I write small, that I titled "What My Dad Was Carrying, Jan 3, 2010." Cabela's could publish those pages as Gear Freak of the Year. The list totaled some 579 items from guns to clothing separated into bags tagged with duct tape and Sharpied "scent-free" and "cold weather camo" to cameras to enough knives to outfit a platoon of Army Rangers to food to cleaning supplies to maps and media. There was no junk or trash in the car because he couldn't abide that. This count did not include multiples of any one thing such as briefs (counted as 3 styles Ex Officio, 2 each) or bottles of water (Ice Mountain, 23) or shells (Hornady .22-250 Remington 55 gr. Vmax, box of 20, among dozens of others), which, even if you counted the packs of Tic Tacs or GUM Soft-Picks as being one item, would put the total number of items in the many thousands. All jammed into his truck. I recorded make and model and size and color or camo pattern, and sometimes condition, such as vomit-covered (heart attack). I counted the change in the cupholder ($4) and in his bags ($1.36) and paper money ($765) and chronicled his somewhat surprising collection of books on tape, which included Jimmy Carter's *Sources of Strength* and *Half Broke Horses* by Jeannette Walls and Billy Graham's *Just as I Am*, and little sticky notes from Dad to Diane and back again saying "I love you" with a smiley face and "I love you, too."

I didn't feel as good as I had hoped when I was done. I said good-bye to Diane. I am sure I hadn't been much comfort to her. I went out to the car and sobbed.

When I had to return a shirt to Cabela's later that month and informed the customer service agent that Bruce was deceased, there was a pause on the other end of the line and she said, "Bruce Kuipers? Oh my, he was a *very* good customer."

But after I'd written it all down, it was clear that none of that stuff was Dad's life. It was just the wagonloads of shit he pulled along with him. It was relatedness that gave him life. He lived that parable from Matthew; it was about him. It described what kind of soil he had been—once extraordinarily hard soil where nothing grew, and then softer and richer and so much more complex and fertile. The more complexity and kinship he accepted, the more fatherly he had become, and more of a man. He had started participating in the communicative order, became permeable to message, available for intersubjectivity, available for love. He was good soil. In the end, what mattered more than anything else was that he had cultivated a new and wide-open imagination and let the world in.

Whoever has ears, let them hear.

~

At the funeral service, Vern told me that Dad had showed him pictures of the deer I had shot that fall and he said, "You guys are growing some big deer up there now. Sally and I walked in there last fall and looked at the place, it's absolutely amazing. It's so grown-in."

"Those trees you planted got it started," I said.

"Those trees are probably one of the best things I've done in my life," he replied.

Dad had shockingly few work friends, considering he built a big swath of southwest Michigan's industrial infrastructure, but his buddy Stan Whitaker was there and I told Stan the story about what happened to Dad out in the woods, how he went without a word. Stan listened and he said, "How did he get so lucky? Huh?"

Joe spoke, and I read the obit I'd written for the *Kalamazoo Gazette*, and Jack wrote something nice about losing his big brother, but he found it too hard to read so his son, Chris, read it for him. Diane was not one to talk much about her emotional life, but at the viewing she stood with the three of us and put her hand on Bruce's chest and said, "Good-bye my prince. He was my prince."

A couple of days later, I was sitting at Brett and Ayron's kitchen table at night, sharing some whiskey. I didn't even care about the smoking anymore. I half wanted to smoke, myself.

"I feel okay now," I said. "I want to grieve and count all the shit in Dad's house and write everything down but when I really think of this I'm okay with it. If he were to walk in right now, I wouldn't say, 'Oh, thank God, because there was something I really meant to say to you and never did.' There wasn't any unfinished business."

"You said that the other day and Brett and I have talked about it," Ayron said. "You guys are so damn lucky your dad made himself available to talk it all out."

"I talked to Dad on the phone at least every other day and I knew every detail of his life. I couldn't possibly have absorbed any more," I said.

"I know, Ayron and I talked about that, too," said Brett. "There wasn't anything I wish I would have said to him, because I'd said it all. I just wanted more of it."

"Well, you created this whole new dad. That was all you, man," I said. "You demanded that dad and you got it. And we are all a hell of a lot healthier because of it."

"It was like ramming my head against a brick wall for fuckin' years. All those shitty years. And then when it got good, it got really good. But I feel like we just got there. I wanted another twenty-five years of it, at least."

He drank his whiskey. "But for five years I had the dad I always wanted."

~

Joe didn't quite find the peace that Brett and I did. He agreed that there wasn't unfinished business, but he took the death hard. So maybe there was. He stopped sleeping. The injustice that attended him had always been embodied by someone close—Dad, Hazel's mom, Diane, ex-girlfriends, various colleagues at work, bosses—but after the funeral, the source of his irritation or disquiet seemed to lodge within himself. He'd staved it off for decades and then it took up residence, seemingly for good. He sat in a chair at his house and watched TV all night while his new bride lay in bed. I could call him at midnight from L.A. and he'd pick up, three A.M. in Michigan, and mumble, "Whazzup."

Joe spent more time with Dad than any of us from the mid-'90s up to 2004, and I hadn't noticed that that had changed after things started to get good. But Joe said it did. He said that after Dad got married in 2004, Joe saw him less and less. Except when we were all at the cabin. When we were all in the middle of our big family throw-downs at the deer camp, Joe mostly lay on the couch or chimed in from the porch because there was peace in that place and he didn't feel like he had to assert himself. He let Brett and I do the talking. But he really hadn't had a satisfying talk with Bruce in years. Or maybe ever.

"[Dad] was torn, because he was happy doing his thing with [Diane]," Joe said. "It became less and less over those years, that I saw them or talked to them at all."

I said, "For me and for Brett, life at the cabin was just like this massive relief, like Dad letting go of his control issues. You could have a beer, and you could sit outside, and you could plant things. You could do stuff outdoors besides hunt, you know?"

"Yeah, well, for sure. That was all so much better. He was so happy. The changes there made him happy, and not just there but everywhere," said Joe.

But he felt judged when he was with Dad and Diane, like they regarded him as a fix-it project. Dad wanted to see Hazel on the weekends that Joe had her, but Joe would avoid going over there if he could because this meant submitting to the project, and he didn't want fixing. He wanted the kind of relating he got at the cabin.

"And all of that kind of boils down to my shit, and how just pointless and useless and more fucked-up than anybody else I felt. Especially in their eyes, so I never wanted to go feel that."

We all noticed that Dad had changed his ideas about the past and what it meant. These changes were on full display at his house. He had put a new wing on the house for Diane so that, as a cancer survivor, she didn't have to go up and down the spiral staircase, and part of the new hallway was a brag wall where they had put up their Air Force photos side by side. I reminded Dad he had told me on a long drive to Rose City that I was absolutely forbidden from ever joining the military, but he brushed that off. "Ha ha! I don't think I ever said that."

One other historical revision is that they started critiquing how Mom had raised us. You know, during the years that Bruce was off having sex with other women. Joe got an earful of that a couple of times and didn't care for it, because the implication was that Joe's troubles were partly Mom's fault, and Joe didn't believe that.

Joe was kind of lurching around on a hair trigger and since he was staying up all night and getting more and more frustrated at home, his one refuge was the cabin. Brett and Ayron proposed they all go up for Fourth of July the year Dad died, and when Joe mentioned that to Mom, she hinted she'd like to be there and he said, "Yeah, you guys should come!" But Joe hadn't understood that Brett and Ayron had invited their friends and intended it to be a party weekend, the kind of thing they never could have done when Bruce was alive because he had never dropped the "no friends" rule, and when they told Joe about this, he just collapsed. "I'm sorry I messed up the fucking schedule!" he screamed at Ayron over the phone, and when Brett called to see what was going on, Joe just said, "I quit. The cabin's yours." And that was it. Joe gathered all his stuff from the cabin and left. It all happened in the space of a few hours.

I didn't think this split would last, but I got more concerned as the days passed. I didn't want to be at the cabin without Joe, so I tried to reassure everyone the feeling would knit itself back together. A few months later, Brett and I ended up cutting Joe a check for his interest in the cabin, and he bought himself a different one, a good-sized house near Frederic on a private piece of the Manistee River. That deeply tannic water under his dock was so cold and so full of the soft language of big brown trout it was hypnotizing. His neighbor was a lovely English fly fisherman who made beautiful cane fly rods, and Joe became fast friends with him and his wife. The Manistee was where Joe had always wanted to be, where Dad had first acknowledged that he was a real person.

The new place helped and the crisis passed. By the following summer, Joe was helping with the planting at the Hunt Club again. He had ceded his room to Spenser, but he took one in the basement. A bunch of his stuff reappeared. That relatedness was sticky. Then we had two cabins, one for hunting and one for fishing.

And Joe had two porches to sit on all night.

~

Not everybody has a ninety-five-acre camp where they can make habitat changes and try to change the world or their own heads, and maybe we broke our backs doing physical labor there precisely because we felt privileged to have it. We were Bruce's sons. He absolutely craved hard physical labor, and after he died it seemed we only worked harder. Nobody told us to do it; we just have a thousand experiments we want try, to see if they make more or healthier wildlife.

Dad had finally put in a wood stove, so in the steamy summers there were wet cords of wood to cut, haul, split, and stack, mostly windthrow oak and yellow birch and some hard maple. We put a new metal roof on the cabin, and when we did we replaced the old sun-scorched deck that overlooked Cabin Field with a huge sitting porch the full width of the building, with a peaked roof that opened up the space and broadcasts your vision outward into the green. It became the center of all our activity there. No matter how many people or dogs or cats are there, or what the day's task, we would all end up in chairs with tea and coffee gazing out on the fields from that porch.

Then we put in a pole barn and built equipment racks in it. The deck and siding needed regular restaining. The pipes froze and split twice in the basement. There were three water crossings on our two-tracks that needed regular rebuilding, and each time you pulled those old culverts out you knew you were in for a day of muck up to your knees and potentially getting the tractor stuck. The tractor and its equipment required maintenance. We built platform beds for the bedrooms. We felled and milled the lumber for tables and a new entry deck with an Alaskan sawmill, which allows you to cut straight timber with a chainsaw. We cut back some falling-down wild apples and pears that may be over a hundred years old.

In 2016 I married a wonderful woman named Lauri, a musician who built edible gardens for a living, and my two new stepsons, Milo and Gus, were anxious to see this mysterious deer hunting camp. On our first trip there, we spent two days cleaning roots out of the septic tank, which Lauri said was the most glamorous vacation she'd probably ever had and then laughed and laughed. Thank God she laughed.

But mostly what we did at the cabin was plant. We fenced in a heel-in garden against the marauding deer, and as Brett and I drove the dirt roads to get hardware or liquor we skidded to a halt at thickets of four-foot-tall gray dogwoods or wild honeysuckle or white spruce or highbush cranberry or Juneberry or highbush blueberry or hazelnut standing in the soggy ditch. Brett spotted this stuff like some kind of botanical detective. He should have a TV show. We kept shovels and plastic bags in the car just for the occasion. If they're on the public right-of-way they're going to get mowed by the county anyway, so we leapt out, dug up twenty or so, keeping the rootballs intact, roared off to the store to get whiskey and, you know, replacement chimney pipe parts or deck screws or whatever, and then carefully set the shrubs and trees in the garden for a couple of years to get as big as possible before we transplanted them into thickets we'd created out on the property. The bigger they were, the harder to handle, but the better chance they had of surviving cervid nibbling.

We once found a dense thicket of small hawthorns, a thorny, scraggly wild tree that makes beautiful bright red berries that grouse love and people can eat, too. (I don't: the seeds contain cyanide, which seems a bad risk for such a bitter berry.) They were already fourish feet tall when we dug them out of the ditch, so we loaded them onto a plastic sled six or eight at a time, dragged them out into the woods and meticulously made new thickets with our shirts torn and hands bleeding. Unlike the six hundred bushes planted in 2001, the new transplants mostly survived. Now we know you just have to transplant them when they're as big as you can handle. We have learned a little.

After a decade of planting First Field and tilling it under, twice yearly over and over, we finally hit on the right solution and planted those five sunburnt acres to native tall-grass prairie. Brett and Ayron hand-harvested switchgrass seed from a wild field and we supplemented it with Indian grass and big bluestem and cultipacked that into the gray-orange soil. The first year we got the tallest crabgrass you've ever seen in your life, up to my belly button, but that was hammered down by the snow and the next spring came a righteous prairie. This gorgeous expanse of chest-high prairie grass immediately became a bedding spot for summer fawns and a giant feeder for birds. Similarly, Cabin Field developed thick orchard grass, then Italian rye, then a mix of those two and alfalfa and clover. It would have made Dad cry just to see it.

The sand became more and more like loam every day, and the more we learned, the more we needed to put our hands in it. We've never had a single day at the cabin where we don't have a to-do list as long as your arm; it would be intolerable if we did. That sand was like a sacred river: we stood in it and we were renewed every day, and its needs were a big part of what we needed from one another.

~

A November came and I was sitting in Buck One, feeling a rimy frozen darkness move against my face. I'd been out for maybe an hour, but there was still a half hour before first light. Frost shimmered off the tufted, foot-tall orchard grass that had taken Cabin Field, the air pooling over the vernal ditch at about twenty degrees Fahrenheit. Tiny feet crunched in the frosted leaves outside my metal box. Squirrels, maybe. Mice. I focused like I always did on the feel of the sand under my boots. Images seemed to pour up out of that sand into my head—images of the sand itself seen from about four feet down, rusty yellow and wet and shot through with sticky fungal filaments; or the inside of Wendell's hollow tree; or the trails through Mr. Carter's middle fields from the viewpoint of a coyote on the trot; or empty, matted beds in the grass on the spruce island in the bog. Places I'd never seen but which seemed to force their way into my head.

The year Dad died, the poet W. S. Merwin told me in an interview that "the imagination *is* nature." There is no separation and there never has been any separation, he continued, letting that sink in. It sank in. Of course that was right. Perhaps the imagination was the basic organ of being and was in every rock, raindrop, and Ovambo tribesman. I became fascinated with the poetics of the imagination, the mechanics of it, how all the thinking outside my body became the thoughts in my own head. The imaginative displays described by James Hillman, moving through the senses, moving through an unconscious, flowed back and forth through me like water. Amid a boil of images were real facts, like the fact that the geese were on a golf course down south or the fact that the prophet Samuel was available for a chat.

A thick, irrepressible flow of subjective material poured through my body, wild, loose, and demanding attention, coronal eruptions of a great subjectival field, perhaps. Our imaginations can not only read that flow but must contribute to it constantly, dumping our psychic stuff into it. You are out there. You are knowable. The stuff in your head matters not just to yourself but to everything. Merleau-Ponty called this our "interinvolvement"—the thickness of communication by which everything reifies its being by displaying its own psyche and validating that of its neighbor.

And sometimes nature turns the imagination inside out and hangs meat on it. I was in the blind, feeling the bottoms of my feet, when the hairs on the back of my neck suddenly stood on end. I had my eyes closed, fielding images from within, when I felt eyes on me. Speaking of the subject-object reversal. I was wearing thick, cold-weather camo and I felt heat surge upward as my face flushed with adrenaline, choking off my breath. My heart lurched sideways and began pounding. I didn't hear anything and when I opened my eyes I couldn't see anything, either. When I tried to quiet my breathing, I heard only my heart squeaking in my ears. I couldn't smell anything. But I knew.

Something was watching the back of my hooded head.

Sitting in the woods in Michigan had always been a fairly tame experience, but the place was changing. This same year, Nancy had been nearly face-to-face with a puma on the Manistee River. The DNR didn't acknowledge that there were puma in the Lower Peninsula, or wolves, either, but Joe had also found wolf prints clear as day in the sand on a gas pipeline right-of-way along that river. Mr. Carter had been seeing a black bear around his house, and we had what we thought were fishers, a mean-ass weasel that is kind of like a small wolverine. We were growing a lot of prey, so who knew what was out there?

I held my breath and whatever it was that was watching me took a step and crunched. It felt me stop breathing and it knew. It felt its own arrival in consciousness. It was very silent. Then it took a few huffy breaths and

CHUUUUUUUUUU!

I flinched and smelled the sour corn breath then. It was a big deer and it had to be real close. Considering that it was the rut, I thought it might be the big boss we'd seen running around, a very healthy eight-point probably three and a half years old and goofy with hormones, leaping around and racing back and forth in Cabin Field. I slowly hunched my shoulders, hoping he wasn't aiming to stick an antler through my neck. We had been watching him and now he was watching me. Even if he couldn't see my face inside this hood he could see at least the outline of my head and smell that I was a human, with my stink of soap and fear and fried eggs. But the rut made him more brave than smart. I was in his woods with the does he was jealously guarding and I had become part of his problem. He took two steps toward me, crunching in the stiff oak leaves, snapping twigs, then stomped the ground a few times and hauled huge amounts of air through his flaring wet nose.

He stomped, wanting me to move, to declare myself. I took tiny sips of air.

When I refused to budge, he stuck his antlers into a couple of beech and aspen saplings and thrashed them, then stood, wheezing. I felt his fierce breathing. I heard him lick his snout inches away.

CHUUUUUUUUUUUU!

He blew his musty disgust and rage all over the back of my neck. He was so close I could feel it hit: he snotted me. For weeks we had examined his scrapes where he kicked the leaves back and pissed on the thin black humus and reached up to mash the glands on his brow tines against an overhanging tree branch; we felt high up where he used the outer tines of his antlers to tear the bark off both sides of a ten-inch-diameter pine at what would be about face height on me. I had imagined him and he had probably looked warily at the cabin and imagined me. Maybe we had imagined each other into a kind of contact.

Crazy then with curiosity, he moved along the south side of the blind as softly as wind. I have had lots of fawns do this, stick their heads right into the blind in order to see me, but never a mature deer. I think he was trying to see my face, and when I saw the curve of polished bone enter my peripheral vision, maybe two feet from my head, I cut my eyes to the right to see him better and for a brief moment that was us, eye to eye— like seeing into the center of a black hole, where all the light is held—and then the old fear and he exploded into the underbrush.

His hoofs sounded like pile drivers as he tore off, thrashing the saplings and hitting a small tree headfirst with a horrible thud, shaking it all the way up in the lower canopy. His white flag flashed as he ran with his head down into the hemlocks and then wild splashing through about twenty yards of blackwater swamp and up onto the slight ridge to the southeast. I never even had my gun in my hands. He raced around up there on the high ground for about ten minutes, snorting and stomping at me from the darkness.

As he ran off, he left behind a little piece of the real quarry: the claims we make on one another.

~

Spenser announced one day when he was fifteen that he wanted to go work at the cabin for an entire month after school let out. He's a Venice kid and an on- and offline gamer, and this declaration meant leaving behind his computer and school friends and his mother, Meg, for relentless clouds of deerflies and farm work and the painful absence of Grandpa Bruce. It was the first time I had any indication there would be another generation at the deer camp. There were only Spenser and Hazel, after all. But I guess he'd been hearing the speechless speech.

When I asked him why he wanted to go, he said, "I want to see Dexter catch grasshoppers. And see the beaver dam. And paint the porch."

Brett and Ayron had a fat gray tabby named Dexter that hunted grasshoppers. Dexter stalked the 'hoppers in the foxtail grass, coiling beneath them and leaping high to snatch them midlaunch. He mostly missed, but when he didn't, he chewed them with his head turned sideways like they tasted bad.

Spenser understood that we watched the fields for stories and visitations. He had encountered baby Wendell. Over the years we had found horses dragging tires, cows that had pushed down their fences, herons and cranes and vultures and bald eagles and badgers standing defiant in the fields. My friend John had watched a pair of river otters galumphing through the hemlocks. We'd freaked out over the bizarre quavering shrieks of long-eared owls in the night. My stepson Milo had poked me on his first day in the blind and whispered, "There's a dog-wolf thing." And it was: a coy-dog or coy-wolf or some such combo, longhaired and following a group of does until it saw us, then it stood behind a tree and peered at us with one eye like a wolf will, melting into the forest as though it had never existed. I couldn't identify it, and that kind of mystery is why we watch.

While Spenser and Ayron stained the porch, Brett and I worked along the ditch on the edge of Cabin Field, planting some viburnum that people call highbush cranberry. We had the bucket loader on the tractor and we were peeling back some of the dense canary grass when we hit a pile of buried granite boulders. Nice round boulders, rolled by the action of glacier and pushed into the ditch by who knows which farmer when they cleared this field. Brett got under one with the loader and I helped heave it into the bucket.

"Let's set it in the island for Dad," Brett yelled above the plop and throcket of the idling tractor.

The island was a thirty-foot-by-twenty-foot set of trees in the middle of Cabin Field, with two black cherry, a pin oak, and a white pine, all about twenty to thirty feet tall. It was a shady spot for Dad that we could see easily from the porch. The rock was good-sized, maybe a hundred pounds, and Brett jumped down while we set it in place. Then we both walked up to the cabin to see how it looked from a distance and without a word Brett got back on the tractor and we were back in the ditch getting another stone.

It was early in the morning, the orchard grass still heavy with dew, and we went on collecting and placing rocks till lunchtime without talking much at all. The tractor roared and a monument built itself, and finally, about two dozen or so large stones later, we capped it. We were both sweaty and filthy with black muck and our fingers were cut.

"Snakes will live in there," I said.

"Ooh, Dad would hate that," Brett laughed. "He couldn't stand a snake."

Spenser ended up painting the porch and the downstairs entry door and the Adirondack chairs and footrests, and probably some other things I didn't know about. He cleared red maples that had crowded the cabin and dragged them into rabbit piles. He oversaw the construction of a treehouse in a huge white oak at the edge of Cabin Field, and cleared and modified the motorcycle trails. He spread fertilizer. He hiked miles along the bog and walked the old M&O railroad beds in the USA across the road to study the beavers. He ate like a trucker, as Dad would say. He worked.

Spenser had his little dog, Jenkins, with him. A couple of weeks in, I asked Spenser if he missed anyone, and he said, "Mom, I guess."

"Would you do this next year?" I asked, expecting a no.

"Well," he said. "We could stay the whole summer and my friends could take turns coming to see me."

~

In 2013 I had traded some correspondence with Wendell Berry as I started this book. I had read several of his, starting with *The Unsettling of America*, and I felt he might respond to someone engaged in the kind of restorative farming he prescribed. I needed to send my measuring line out into the world to test the possibilities of this relatedness I had found. If this sand farm had given me a family, what else was in it? What was the value of this work to the human community? How were we supposed to respond to enormous crises like the chemical farming that went on around us, and climate change and species extinction?

"The problems *are* big, they are even big emergencies," Berry wrote to me, "but they can't be solved by big solutions. What our understanding of nature tells us is that the big problems can be solved only by small solutions, unrelentingly practical, that will be made by individuals in relation to small parcels of land farmed or forested or mined, in their home watersheds."

The humility in this answer opened worlds. What our understanding of nature tells us is that even big geophysical events like global warming emerge from tiny actions in a place, or a billion places, and the remedy is also in those places. Not everyone will have an old sand farm, of course, or a forest or a mine. Once again, Brett and Joe and I knew how incredibly fortunate we were to have a piece of dirt that we could work, and we were determined to do things with it that were good for the entire community. But anybody can do this, and must do it, whether or not they have any land of their own. Every single thing you buy and use all day long comes from some piece of ground. Our lives come from the dirt in someone's home watershed, and you should know about it. *Small solutions, unrelentingly practical.*

It turns out it's not so hard to grow a ruffed grouse. Mostly you create great habitat and the birds do the rest. It's probably the same for a rhinoceros or a polar bear, though I've never grown those. Every animal or plant that grows is a loud and charismatic voice in the community, but more than anything it's an interpreter of the habitat. It's the habitat that talks to your imagination. It's the sentience of rabbit and stone and wind that makes your mind, and without them you would be mindless. It's the habitat that speaks when you hear voices at night. Whatever you think God is, it expresses its many-ness as habitat. Want to get your head right? Work on the habitat.

Doing that can mean growing a garden. Or buying organic produce from a farmer who does. Or adopting a beach for cleanups with the kids. Or planting trees on your block.

Mom and Tom got the message and started planting deer plots on the land behind their house. They don't hunt there. They just want to care for the wildlife.

Doing that work alone only slows your progress. It's best done as a function of community. Berry writes voluminously about this in his essays about American farm life: those small solutions, unrelentingly practical, need to be shared and allowed to form the roots of a human culture. Work on the habitat *with other people*. Curmudgeonly nature writers like Thoreau and John Muir so often leave that part out, and the environmental heroes and adventure sports figures we all fawn over so often present their finest moments on the mountain or in the surf as so many solo breakthroughs in narcissistic self-fulfillment. We need to expand that engagement with nature to include all our human relations. All of our backbreaking labors on the deer camp wouldn't have had the same effect on my psyche, or on the mental health of my entire family, or on the well-being of the critters or of the camp itself if any one of us had been there all on our lonesome, celebrating our own, siloed relationships with the land. To produce *love*, we had to do this with Dad.

Andy Fisher told me there was more to this: without our family dynamic, our work on the deer camp would lose its enormous power to change global culture. Fisher is an ecopsychologist and therapist in private practice in Ontario, the author of the book *Radical Ecopsychology*, and I studied with him for a few intense months. He saw a bigger picture beyond my deer camp tale. My family story was one of ecopsychological healing, in that Dad really saw Joe and Brett and me for the first time and accepted us when he accepted the trustworthiness and agency of that lowly sand. Which allowed us all to thrive. Once Dad saw that the dirt wasn't going to let him down, he thought we were okay, too, and the better it got, the better we got.

The development of that ecological self, however, is also a path toward saving the planet. In the second sentence of his book, Fisher writes: "Ecopsychologists argue that genuine sanity is grounded in the reality of the natural world; that the ecological crisis signifies a pathological break from this reality; and that the route out of our crisis must therefore involve, among other things, a psychological reconciliation with the living earth."

That reconciliation requires a different culture, one in which we recognize both the material and psychic agency of the planet we live on. As Shepard had implied, Man must stop destroying his habitat. Fisher finds this a fundamentally radical project that needs a "psychologically based ecological politics." This kind of overtly political thrust is much too forward for many in the psychology community, but hopefully it will catch on. "To ultimately overcome dualism we must become different people, must overcome the mode of existence in which our dualistic thought is rooted, and for this our repressing and fragmenting society must itself fundamentally change."

Those politics have to develop from relationships, and those relationships have to include the other-than-human world. It's a world-sized project, but as Berry indicated, it starts small. It might not be a political revolution. It might be therapy. Fisher leads couples therapy as part of a practice that includes his wife, Jill, and when they get in a bad space, they take the session outdoors.

"We did it just the other day," he said. "We were out walking and Jill spots a feather. And suddenly we're good! I think it's a bald eagle, because we've got a bald eagle around here, and I'm wondering about these lines on the feather, they're called 'stress bars,' but they're also called 'hunger traces.' So this is sort of our Story of the Day. I'm thinking about this suffering eagle, it's really moving me, and suddenly we're in this space that is so rich and alive. We rely on that now: any time we're in a bad place, we just say, 'Okay, we're heading out!' "

∾

November came again and Cabin Field was all torn up and planted to alfalfa that had been stilled by the cold just as it started to erupt between the volunteer orchard and rye grass. The leaves were off the trees. Brett and I had moved the Desert Storm blind, pulled it out into an open patch of grass we'd created, and renamed it Eagle—partly because we saw bald eagles all the time that we hailed as visitations from Dad, and partly after the band Eagles of Death Metal, who survived an armed attack at the Bataclan in Paris only days before. Mom and Tom were hunting the deer opener with us at the cabin for the very first time. Tom had hunted regularly in the U.P. many years before, and he seemed very pleased to take it up again with us. The deer camp had called to him and he wanted to do the work. We were clearing shooting lanes over by Eagle the day before Opening Day and Joe, Brett, Ayron, Tom, and I suddenly pulled up short when we realized *there were white pines everywhere.*

I mean everywhere: every ten or twenty feet in every direction was a white pine ten feet tall in the understory. When we finished our work, we got Mom from the cabin and we walked around: the whites were ten feet tall in the vernal muck, blasting out of the swamp's edge, nosing even into the mature popple of the south twenty, racing up above the beech and black cherry in the natural regrowth of what had been the Scots pine plantation, appearing in the shade of the red pines and the big beeches to the west, volunteering in the sand rimming First Field. I had noticed them coming up a couple of years back, especially around the small grove planted by Askins, but suddenly they'd all heaved upward several feet and launched themselves into serious competition for a place in the canopy all over the ninety-five acres. They were spreading into the USA and over onto Carter's place, and Randy's, and all the camps around us as far as we could tell.

All around Buck One they were taller than elsewhere, fifteen to twenty feet tall and poking up through gaps in the red and white oaks. I had to trim the lower limbs in order to shoot through them. For about 140 years they didn't grow on our place, but they'd evidently heard the call.

Why did they wait so long? What brought them out? The appearance of these white pines correlates precisely with when we logged off the Scots pines and aspens twelve years earlier and created a rough disturbance for the benefit of game birds. But they had popped up even a quarter mile away from where we'd done any cutting or planting. They'd sprung from the ground at the approximate moment when we got our dad back. So was this a people dream, or a tree dream? Or did those dreams get tangled? It didn't feel like we could take even the tiniest bit of credit, but it was happening right then, and fast.

We had spent countless hours talking about how the place must have looked and felt in big trees, when Carpenter first homesteaded the place;

here came the prospect that maybe Spenser and Hazel would see it one day with their own eyes.

Dad probably would have been bummed out about this, as white pine lands aren't prime habitat for deer. Whitetails prefer the disclimactic white oak, the disturbed field of new aspen, the open grassland.

But we'd learned to respect the dream, to pay attention to the original instructions. The armature for our restored family was there in the sand; we had every reason to trust whatever new family ecosystem might lie implicit in a tall-tree forest. It's an adventure we had not foreseen, but it was one we were not going to resist.

And so we had ever-more reason to sit out and watch the fields at night.

The next morning, an hour before dawn, we stood outside in our thick, cold-weather gear and loaded our rifles by the light over the freshly painted downstairs door. There was the click-clack of shells racked in and we paused and smiled at one another. Mom was going out with Tom, and they were both beaming under their heavy winter clothes. Then the light was out and Brett and Ayron went north to their new Taj and the rest of us went south, Mom and Tom to Eagle, Joe to Shouldabeen, and me to Gonzo. The trees were hushed as the stars raked the frost out of the crowns and scattered it on the sand. We walked out into the darkness on our farm in Michigan, where we raise trees and grass and a love you can feel in your feet.

Acknowledgments

This story would have never been told without the devotion of my beloved wife, Lauri, who grows food and community and changes the world every day, who guides our boys with wisdom, and who read these pages for five years until a book emerged. My eternal gratitude to my mother, Nancy, and to my brothers, Brett and Joe, and to Ayron and Becky and my stepdad, Tom, for allowing me to stir up all the old hurt and for believing both the land and our family were worth restoring; to Jack and Jane and Vern and Sally and all my cousins for establishing the Hunt Club and filling it with stories; to Uncles Ron and Mike, Great-Uncle George and Great-Aunt Frieda, and to Diane Hamilton, Scott Stephens, Meg Cranston, and Anne Lehman for some history; and to the extended Kuipers and Nienhuis clans for making us who we are. Thank you to Spenser, Milo, and Gus, and to Hazel, who have filled me with hope that the next generation will care about the habitat. And to all my Mattawan schoolmates, especially Matt and Joann, Bruce, Mickey, Andrew, Kelly, Troy, Jeff, and Tim for a lifetime of love.

I owe an enormous debt of gratitude to my agent, Bonnie Nadell, for seeing a book where others didn't, and to everyone at Hill Nadell, especially Austen Rachlis, and to Sloan Harris for early efforts at shaping this idea. Bear hugs to my editor, Anton Mueller, for believing in this idea, and to Barbara Darko, Morgan Jones, and everyone at Bloomsbury for making it happen. Heartfelt thanks to Andrew Gumbel, Karl Taro Greenfeld, and Andew Blechman for reading drafts and versions, and to

Michael Wiegers, Doug Aitken, Dan Gerber, and Jim Harrison for pondering big questions about poetry, trout, and our place in the universe.

Deepest thanks to Wendell and Tanya Berry, and Mary Berry at the Berry Center, for hosting a Kentucky research visit for what was then a very different book, and to the incomparable W. S. Merwin for telling me in Maui, "The imagination *is* nature," which changed everything. A deep and humble bow to Andy Fisher for his indispensable tutoring in ecopsychology, and also to Robert Greenway, Betsy Perluss, Deb Piranian, Linda Buzzell, and Patricia Hasbach. A tip of the hat to the MSU Forestry Department, including David Rothstein, Rich Kobe, Larry Leefers, and Don Dickman, and to Tom Nederveld, Randy Kuipers, and John Barnes Logging for habitat work, and to our neighbors Joe and Marilyn Carter and Andy Sneller. Many thanks to Loretta Harjes, Bill Askins, Iran Huizenga, and Bill Dukes for the history of our property. And to Eric Nyquist for visuals.

I think every day of my father, Bruce, who took us to rivers and camps. He is alive in his family and in every grouse and deer and in the fields themselves.

A Note on the Author

Dean Kuipers has studied and written about environmental politics and the human–nature relationship for decades. He is the author of *Burning Rainbow Farm* and *Operation Bite Back*, as well as several books on art and culture, including *I Am A Bullet* with the fine artist Doug Aitken. His work has appeared in the *Los Angeles Times*, *Outside*, the *Atlantic*, *Men's Journal*, *Rolling Stone*, and *Playboy*. He lives in Los Angeles.